The Horn of Africa as Common Homeland

The State and Self-Determination in the
Era of Heightened Globalization

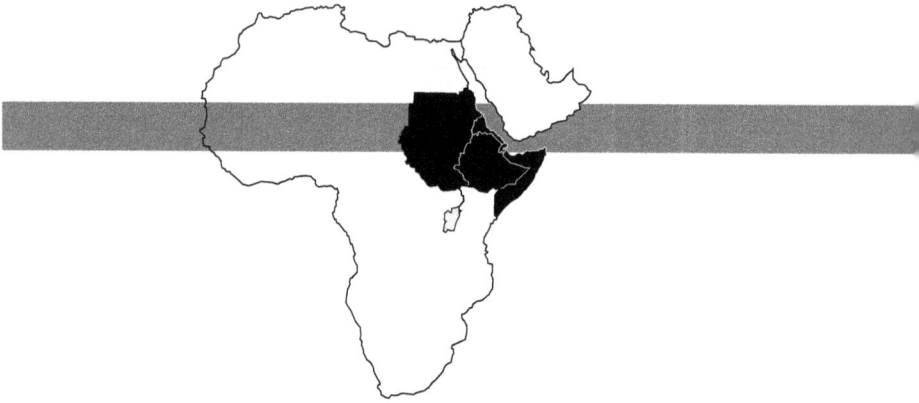

The Horn of Africa as Common Homeland

The State and Self-Determination in the
Era of Heightened Globalization

Leenco Lata

Wilfrid Laurier University Press

WLU

We acknowledge the financial support of the Government of Canada through the Book Publishing Industry Development Program for our publishing activities. We acknowledge the Government of Ontario through the Ontario Media Development Corporation's Ontario Book Initiative.

ONTARIO ARTS COUNCIL
CONSEIL DES ARTS DE L'ONTARIO

Library and Archives Canada Cataloguing in Publication

Lata, Leenco
    The Horn of Africa as common homeland: the state and self-determination in the era of heightened globalization / Leenco Lata.

    1. Self-determination, National—Africa, Northeast. 2. Africa, Northeast—Politics and government—1974- I. Title.

Includes bibliographical references and index.
ISBN 978-0-88920-456-0

DT367.8.L38 2004   963.07'2   C2004-905083-4

© 2004 Wilfrid Laurier University Press
Waterloo, Ontario, Canada
www.wlupress.wlu.ca
This printing 2010

Cover photograph: Mogadishu, Somalia. Gunman on guard outside the offices of a new radio station, Horn Afrik, to protect it from looting bandits or militiamen from rival clans. A sign on the wall asks that visitors leave their weapons outside the compound. Photo © Sven Torfinn/Panos Pictures.

Cover design by Leslie Macredie; text design by P.J. Woodland.

Every reasonable effort has been made to acquire permission for copyright material used in this text, and to acknowledge all such indebtedness accurately. Any errors and omissions called to the publisher's attention will be corrected in future printings.

∞
Printed in Canada

Dedicated to Gunnar Hasselblatt
for his solidarity and generosity at
a time when the struggle of the
Oromo people had very few friends.

Table of Contents

IT IS IMPOSSIBLE TO MENTION all the people and institutions that assisted me while I was undertaking the study that led to this work. I would like to let all those whom I do not mention here know of my deep sense of gratitude. If this work contributes minimally to the promotion of justice, peace, and democracy in the Horn of Africa, I hope that will serve as their reward. Nancy and Ernie Regehr deserve a special mention because their friendship and generous donation of their time were decisive in enabling me to complete this book. Dr. Siegfried Pausewang read an early rough draft of this book and gave me valuable comments and advice. I am grateful for his encouragement. I am similarly grateful to Dr. Asafa Jalata, who gave me valuable feedback after reading an early draft. However, all the shortcomings of the work and the views it reflects are solely mine.

I would also like to thank Anna and Tony Luengo for their friendship and encouragement. Their assistance was critical in enabling me to find an appropriate publisher. I would like to express my gratitude to Dr. Brian Henderson and other staff members of Wilfrid Laurier University Press for guiding me through the process that led to the publication of this book. I admire the patience of Charles Anthony Stuart who did so much in making this writing more comprehensible. I am very grateful to him for his superb editorial work. To my soulmate, Martha Kuwe Kumsa, I say once again say thank you for serving as the sole source of my refuge and intellectual motivation.

ORIGIN OF THIS STUDY

THIS WORK ORIGINATED FROM READINGS I undertook merely to satisfy my curiosity and clarify my thoughts. The search for clarification was prompted by two events that occurred in the course of my participation in the Oromo people's struggle for national self-determination. These were the end of the Cold War and my exposure to the interrelatedness of conflicts in the Horn of Africa. Let me explain why both experiences impelled me to seek improved clarity of thought.

First, I participated in the formation of the Oromo Liberation Front (OLF) and in framing its agenda for self-determination in the early 1970s when socialism was the most fashionable political ideology in the Horn region. Consequently, the Oromo struggle for self-determination was conceptualized as part of a worldwide process of ending both class and national oppression within the wider goal of bringing about a totally new world order. Despite the rising implausibility that I would witness the dawning of this new world order during my lifetime, its long-range feasibility remained comfortably possible until the momentous year of 1989. The initial rumblings of 1989 eventually resulted in the collapse of the Iron Curtain that stood between the "pioneers" of the promising "future" world order and their opponents, thus bringing the Cold War to an end and with it the political bearings that we as activists were accustomed to. Not only the neat left/right configuration of world political division but also the conception of movements as either forward or backward oriented went up in smoke. Furthermore, all such struggles for self-determination thereafter risked losing whatever universalist content they had had until then, at least theoretically. When the Cold War was unravelling I had no time to dwell on this emerging difficulty as I was busy reacting to one of its local repercussions: the overthrow of the

1

Soviet-backed Ethiopian regime commonly known as the Derg. I could hence afford the time to reflect on and read about political developments emerging in the post-Cold War period only after my colleagues graciously demobilized me in late 1993.

Let me now touch upon the second reason why I started the readings that eventually led to this work. During my participation in the Oromo struggle, particularly from 1978 to 1991, I stayed for varying periods of time in Djibouti, Somalia, and Sudan. During this period I was able to interact with these countries' common folk as well as their leaders, which enabled me to observe first-hand their similarities and differences. Much more importantly, I started to realize how quickly political developments reverberated throughout the Horn region. The Oromo people's struggle for national self-determination in particular had the peculiar misfortune of being negatively influenced by developments in Somalia and the Sudan. First, Oromia (the Oromo-settled areas of Ethiopia) stretches from edges of the Ogaden lowlands in the east to Ethiopia's border with Sudan. The first complication that the Oromo struggle faced was the redefinition of the area targeted for annexation to realize Greater Somalia. Mohammed Siad Barre's regime staked claim not only to the Ogaden but also to the Oromo-inhabited areas east of the Great Rift Valley, which constitutes almost half of the Oromo country. The rancour that inevitably ensued from this overlapping territorial claim had damaging consequences for both Somalia and the OLF. The Siad regime's ill-advised policy turned potential allies into enemies, thus prompting the OLF to resist the annexation of eastern Oromia. The perhaps understandable aspiration of gathering all Somali speakers into one state could have probably succeeded in the absence of this complication. When this aspiration, which once constituted the pillar of Somali national consensus and cohesion, started dimming, however, the course that led to the currently reigning chaos was set. At the same time, the same complication severely stymied the growth of the OLF. The fact that more members of its leadership were killed by Siad-backed fronts than by the Ethiopian Derg regime attests to the seriousness of the damage incurred by the OLF as the result of this unfortunate complication.

The second complication that interfered with the struggle of the Oromo for self-determination actually resulted from the steps the OLF took to avoid this initial one. Aiming to establish itself in areas free of conflicting territorial claims, the OLF launched a new area of operations in the districts bordering the Sudan in 1981. Despite the usual problems involved in initiating guerrilla activities, the OLF's new area of operations slowly expanded until 1984, when a new complication emerged. The Sudan Peoples Liberation Army (SPLA), evidently tasked by its host with the mission of expelling the OLF from its base area, started encroaching on OLF operational areas in the summer of that year. Conflict inevitably erupted and lasted until 1990 when the SPLA was driven out of the general area in an operation that the OLF conducted jointly with the Eritrean Peoples Liberation Front (EPLF).

I recall the above incidents not to revive the old practice of exchanging accusations but to explain why my colleagues and I started entertaining the resolution of the Oromo quest for self-determination within a regional approach. Some of us started questioning the plausibility of realizing islands of democracy and prosperity in such a closely integrated region. This evolving tendency was driven primarily by our intuitive observations of the interconnections between struggles for justice and democracy throughout the entire region. I was in a position to review the literature with the purpose of assessing the plausibility of this impression only after I was relieved of my responsibilities as member of the OLF leadership in 1993. Hence, the reading that I initially undertook was intended to answer two questions that have been bothering me since the late 1980s. First, what are the dominant features of the post-Cold War political developments that have implications for framing persisting struggles for self-determination? Second, does the resonance of political developments in the Horn that we witnessed first-hand have any historical depth, and if so, how does this reality impact on the various quests for self-determination?

PART 1: SELF-DETERMINATION IN HISTORY

Part 1 of this work attempts to sketch the development of the thinking that served as self-determination's rationale at various stages since the late eighteenth century. First we have to mention the elements that continue to crop up when articulating self-determination at these diverse historical junctures by citing some definitions. Cobban (1969: 39) defines self-determination in very broad terms as a "theory about the relationship that should prevail between the *nation* and the *state*" (italics added). Seeking such an explicit relationship between nation and state is commonly said to have occurred during the French Revolution, as the following assertion shows: "The history of self-determination is bound up with the history of the doctrine of popular *sovereignty* proclaimed by the

French revolution: government should be based on the will of the *people*, not on that of the monarch, and people not content with the government of the country to which they belong should be able to secede and organize themselves as they wish. This meant that the *territorial* element in a political unit lost its feudal predominance in favour of the personal element: people were not to be any more a mere appurtenance of the land" (Sureda 1973: 17; italics added). As can be seen from the previous citations, formulating some kind of correspondence between the *state*, the *nation*, the *territory*, the *people*, and the location of ultimate political authority, *sovereignty*, constitutes the foundational precept of self-determination. Assessing whether this neat correspondence has ever been achieved or is even achievable is the question being investigated in this work. I will commence this investigation by first looking briefly at just what happened during the French Revolution, which is commonly designated as the origin of self-determination. That revolution did not, of course, erupt *ex nihilo* but was the culmination of developments that were gathering momentum in the preceding centuries.

Since the late fifteenth century, the states and societies of Western Europe had been experiencing the steady expansion of their intellectual horizon commensurate with their ever-rising exposure to other continents and societies. By the time the non-aristocratic sector of French society rose up by proclaiming the slogan "Liberty, Equality, Fraternity" in 1789, France and other European states on the Atlantic seaboard were busy subduing, pillaging, and enslaving other societies of the world. The irony of proclaiming these idealistic principles while engaging in such iniquities is aptly put by the French historian, Jean Jaures: "The slave-trade and slavery were the economic basis of the French Revolution. The fortunes created at Bordeaux, at Nantes, by slave-trade, gave the bourgeoisie that pride which needed liberty and contributed to human emancipation" (qtd. in James 1973: 47). Furthermore, the capitalist economic system on which the European nation-state's liberal democracy rests would not have prospered in the absence of the slave trade, according to Pomeranz (1999: 74–88).

The economic basis of the nation-state thus rested on its ability to act in an iniquitous manner at the global level to access resources. Even the ideas that enabled European elites to much more clearly envision the nation-state were influenced by their exposure to the rest of the globe. As Benedict Anderson (1983: 66–69) argues, the dream of a nation "as linked to a private-property language" partly originated from the contraction of European *time* and *space* between the fourteenth and nineteenth centuries, European nationalism attaining its apogee by the latter date. He discusses how the shrinkage of *space* resulting from territorial discovery and of *time* from the discovery of ancient literature contributed to the levelling of the status of languages. This in turn fuelled vernacularization, which operated alongside the new attitude that assigned a language to a particular society to shape the environment in which the Nation and nationalism were conceived. Hence, both the economic foundations and the intellectual ambiance that brought forth the nation-state were the result of ever increasing globalization. Seeking particularization (distinctiveness) and universalization (local and global homogeneity) at the same time figured in conceptualizing the nation from the very outset.

The inherent contradiction of advocating liberty while preserving privileges in a new form came into the fore in a dramatic manner during the French Revolution, as sketched in chapter 1. The Revolutionaries easily achieved unanimity on the need to excise the aristocracy from French society to herald the birth of the *nation*. Who should thereafter embody the *nation* and capture the *sovereignty* snatched from the sovereign, however, proved much more contentious. It was the struggle over arrogating such a status to one's social group that fomented the most turbulent occurrences of the Revolution. Contests involving actors divided according to class, race, and gender were crystallized to an unprecedented extent, subsequently influencing the class-based theory of Marxism. Bringing all the adjacent areas inhabited by French-speakers (members of the *nation*) into the *territory* of France was conducted relatively fairly and democratically. On the other hand, the right of non-French speakers to depart from France evidently could not be countenanced. Hence, some social sectors found themselves residing on French *territory* but outside the *nation*. Others could belong to the *nation* on the basis of culture and language but were excluded from the genuinely empowered category of citizen due to race, class, or gender. Despite these incongruities, the notion of the nation was introduced to Europe in a powerful way during the Revolution and the subsequent Napoleonic period. After Napoleon was finally subdued, European monarchs and their representatives assembled in Vienna to chart a more peaceful order for themselves. They blamed the mayhem that Europe endured between the early 1790s and 1815 on the notion of popular sovereignty and thus agreed to proscribe Republicanism. At the same time, however, they began conceding the idea of *nation* and the previously non-existent thinking that some form of association should bind together the ruled and the ruler. The result was the spread of the idea of the *nation* now without the accompanying principle of *popular sovereignty*. The attempt to coerce all the inhabitants of sprawling empires into the national mould was ultimately responded to by the contrary demand of subordinate groups to realize their *nation-states*, resulting in the breakup of some of Europe's oldest states at the end of the First World War. Chapter 1 ends by briefly summarizing the inconsistencies that attended the explicit application of the principle of self-determination at the end of that war.

Chapter 2 deals with the peculiar way in which self-determination was implemented in Africa after the Second World War. During the First World War only the "mature civilized" nations of Europe were deemed qualified to enjoy the right to self-determination. After the Second World War, on the other hand, the right to self-determination was banished from the European arena and was reduced strictly to the process by which European overseas "dependencies" could achieve independence. The term "self-determination" was in fact used quite sparingly, preference being given to "decolonization." This chapter will also summarize the implications of decolonization for post-colonial African states' assumption of the status of *nation*. The practice in the Horn of Africa, which departed from the rest of Africa and paved the way for internal demands for self-determination, will also be discussed.

Despite gathering momentum since the era of European exploration, globalization entered a new heightened phase after the end of the Cold War. Looking at how this new stage of globalization impacted on the nature and function of the *state* is the subject of chapter 3. Whatever modification the nation-state is being forced to adopt to deal with globalization's pressures has clear implications for the mission of self-determination in the contemporary period. Montserrat Guibernau (2001: 244–48) identifies three different theoretical approaches concerning globalization's implications for the nation-state. They are represented by:

1. the hyperglobalists, who believe the nation-state has become a nostalgic fiction due to the borderless nature of the contemporary global economy;
2. the skeptics, who subscribe to the contrary conviction that the nation-state's central role in regulating cross-border economic activities is actually increasing; and
3. the transformationists, who hold the middle-ground position of admitting the nation-state's continued power while arguing that it is conceding aspects of its traditional functions.

This third group points out that nation-states are finding it necessary to restructure and reconstitute themselves to better respond to the undeniably more complex process of governance in an increasingly interdependent world. The conclusion Guibernau reaches by drawing on the third thesis sounds plausible to me. She writes:

> Globalization by strengthening some of the nation-state's classical functions and limiting and radically transforming others has prompted the emergence of the post-traditional nation-state defined by a type of sovereignty which manifests itself in its power to:
> a) decide upon the creation, functioning and financing of supranational political institutions;
> b) devolve power and provide legitimacy to regional institutions created within its territory;
> c) act as constitutional arbitrator and regulator of law and order within society; and
> d) govern public life and the relationship between plural groups coexisting within its territorial boundaries. (Guibernau 2001: 257)

It is this post-traditionalist version of *state* that is being explored in chapter 3. The various elements that achieve correspondence to supposedly bring forth the nation-state, (i.e., *people, nation, state, territory,* and *sovereignty*) are disassembled and examined to see how they are yielding to pressures arising from heightened globalization. Exploring current abstractions about appropriate state types elsewhere is one thing; envisioning the kind suitable for the realities of the Horn is another matter altogether. Externally inspired social and political blueprints have been avidly embraced and forced down the throat of the societies of the Horn during the last three to four decades with disastrous consequences. However, leaving the articulation of social and political structures to the concerned societies' knee-jerk reactions or traditions alone could also wreak havoc. A dialogue between contemporary abstractions and the lived experiences of grassroots communities is perhaps the best way to proceed. Because of my conviction of the appropriateness of such an approach, I will eschew drawing up a menu for political and social change. However, I will draw on grassroots innovations and try to relate them to the new thinking influenced by abstractive analyses.

One development that accompanied the end of the Cold War was the return of the quest for self-determination to Europe. And the broad outlines of the emerging features of the contemporary state discussed in chapter 3 had to be taken into account when conceptualizing self-determination. Hence, chapter 4 attempts to bring together the findings of chapter 3 and the emerging visions regarding self-determination's contemporary mission. Here again, the various processes and principles that go into re-articulating self-determination are disassembled and examined separately. Chapter 4 brings to an end the attempt to track the history of self-determination and the phases that it passed through to arrive at its contemporary mission.

PART II: A HISTORY OF CONFLICTS IN THE HORN

Part II of this work deals with the history of state-formation, nation-building, and the conflicts attending both processes in the Horn of Africa. The Horn of Africa as used in this writing refers to the area encompassing the Sudan, Eritrea, Ethiopia, Djibouti, and Somalia. The Horn of Africa stands apart from the rest of the continent in being the only region where states, not just regimes, are facing challenges. As Crawford Young (1991a: 44) rightly observes, "The self-determination versus territorial integrity conundrum is intense *only* in the Horn of Africa" (italics added). As this study shows, the Horn states took some policy decisions peculiar to the region which made this widespread invocation inevitable.

This study attempts to investigate the plausibility of adopting a regionalized approach in resolving ongoing struggles for self-determination in the Horn of Africa. The conclusions drawn in chapter 4 by themselves would have motivated exploring the feasibility of such an approach. There are additional factors that seem to render this evaluation even more imperative. First of all, the Horn entities came into existence as bridgeheads of grand imperial ambitions to control the area between the Chad border in the west, the Equatorial Lakes in the south, and the Red Sea and the Indian Ocean in the east. Foreign powers such as Egypt, Britain, France, and Italy coveted the whole or parts of this area. Mahdist Sudan also had ambitions to conquer large swathes of this zone. Meanwhile, two forces from within Christian Abyssinia got locked in fierce rivalry with each other while aspiring to conquer most of the same area. The most unscrupulously unprincipled of them succeeded in realizing the Ethiopian Empire. The processes that hence led (1) to this Empire's international recognition; (2) to the creation of the Anglo-Egyptian Condominium in the Sudan; (3) to the creation of British Somaliland; (4) to the emergence of the French colony of Djibouti; and (5) to the birth of Italian Somaliland and Italy's other colony of Eritrea proceeded in a highly interactive manner. How the birth of these entities came about is summarized in chapter 5.

The second reason for evaluating a regional approach to the resolution of struggles for self-determination in the Horn of Africa concerns the fact that each Horn entity has at some stage claimed, or at least coveted, parts of the other or its entirety. These claims and counterclaims are catalogued in chapter 6. Ironically, the rationale on which these conflicting claims rested routinely instigated fissiparous tendencies from within each claimant. The experiences of Ethiopia, Eritrea, and Somalia best exemplify this irony. These entities, while facing each other over issues of irredentism and counter-irredentism, were simultaneously experiencing internal pressures for at least decentralization if not full-fledged balkanization.

The whole affair was kicked off by the Ethiopian Empire staking claim to Eritrea and Somalia as the Italians were being expelled from the area in 1940. These objects of the Empire's irredentist agenda soon countered by airing their own counter-irredentist claims on their kinfolk inhabiting Ethiopia's adjacent provinces. The actors involved in this affair cited common historical, cultural, linguistic, and religious attributes to press their claims. The attributes invoked by one sector of both Eritrea and Somalia to unite with their kinfolk in the Empire, however, tended to exacerbate the alienation of other sectors, partly accounting for their demand for decentralization or even federalization. The Empire too, while aspiring to extend its borders to the Red Sea and the Indian Ocean, was facing the resistance of peoples determined to throw off its imperial yoke, such as the Oromos, Sidamas, Wallayitas, and other southern societies. The historical and religious attributes cited to carry out Ethiopia's successful annexation of Eritrea actually further exacerbated these communities' alienation, giving additional impetus particularly to Oromo resistance (Lata 1999: 163-70). Meanwhile, sectors of Eritrean society repelled by the same attributes became the first to take up arms to reverse the annexation. These were joined in due course by the frustrated elements of Eritrean society that were initially attracted by these attributes. An alliance was forged between the Oromos and Eritreans when their struggles started assuming improved coherence in the early 1960s, and it has survived even after Eritrea's independence.

The fate of the Sudan and its territorial definition remained susceptible to change well into the early 1950s. The British continued to toy with the possibility of detaching its southern third and to either attach it to their other possessions in East Africa or to guide it to independence as a separate entity. This remained a distinct possibility well into the late

1940s. At the same time, the Sudan's reversion to unilateral Egyptian control also remained a distinct possibility. Only an unexpected development connected with the Nasserite revolution of 1952 actually ended this possibility. The elaboration of the persisting tentative nature of the entities of the Horn of Africa is the topic of chapter 6.

Chapter 7 introduces the peculiar challenges the Horn states faced in implementing their distinct nation-building exercises. The bulk of the chapter, however, deals with the peculiar challenges connected with projecting the Ethiopian Empire as an ancient *nation* and *state*. How nation-building failed to erase hierarchization but instead actually entrenched it in areas incorporated by conquest and introduced it to areas constituting part of the conquering society is discussed here. The ensuing struggles within struggles and diffusion of ideas and organizational techniques from neighbouring countries are also dealt with. Chapter 7 concludes with a discussion of the developments that led to Eritrea's separation and to the reconfiguration of the rump state to address other outstanding quests for self-determination.

Chapter 8 deals with the Sudan's nation-building exercise. How the Sudan plunged into internal strife almost simultaneously with its ascension to independence is briefly discussed. Conflict erupted first in the south due to the southerners' understandable impression that the northern elite were interested only in stepping into the shoes of the departing British. The southerners subsequently tabled demands ranging from secession, to attaining regional autonomy, and to merely rearticulating Sudan's national identity. The southerners were ultimately joined by other marginalized sectors of the north in demanding self-determination. All along, the political actors who exchanged positions as rulers and internal opposition approached these other struggles in a very unprincipled manner, making it difficult to identify who was championing the forging of what kind of Sudanese state. In the case of the Sudan, too, struggles within struggles will be discussed to demonstrate how conflicts within elites, between elites, and at the regional level easily connect.

Chapter 9 discusses Somalia's peculiar aspiration to achieve congruity between *nation* and *state* by annexing large parts of adjacent countries, particularly eastern Ethiopia. Also discussed is the internal implication of even the merger of the former British and Italian Somalilands immediately after independence. The ease with which Somali politics could go from fragmentation to complete unity had already surfaced during civilian parliamentary contests. That the opposite could happen was thereby signalled, but nobody took heed. In the meantime, annexing the homelands of the Ogadenis and eastern Oromos remained a cementing factor that concealed the potential of fragmentation.

Various recommendations offered by scholars on how to resolve conflicts in the Horn are assembled in chapter 10. What is most remarkable is the fact that most of these recommendations tally quite closely with the kind of state developed in chapter 3 and self-determination as articulated in chapter 4. This work brings together these disparate suggestions and fits them into a more coherent vision of the contemporary state and the commensurate interpretation of self-determination. However, it departs from most previous studies in two particular respects. First, the dichotomy between the liberal class-neutral state and the class-based Marxist version is avoided. Instead, Gramsci's alternative hegemonic state in which the rulers at least partially reciprocate the allegiance and acquiescence of the societies they rule is invoked as the starting point for a more promising future. I thus concur with A.I. Samatar that perhaps this state variety could be more suitable for the Horn. Second, the kind of democracy suitable for enhancing the political participation of grassroots societies is adopted from feminist theory of democracy.

In the conclusion I will try to bring together the findings of both Part I and II. I avoid setting down recipes for social and political change but instead lay down some issues that need to be debated to further investigate how the problems of the Horn societies could be ameliorated.

WHERE TO LOOK FOR NEW IDEAS

The most troubling aspect of the post-Cold War period is the total silence regarding the next phase in the development of human society and political order. Never since the Enlightenment have intellectuals and political activists displayed such complacence towards existing local and global political structures. Never has so much pessimism prevailed to stifle the human imagination regarding a better tomorrow. The manner by which the Cold War came to an end obviously clouded the vision of that idyllic conflict-free future anticipated by Marxist theory. Despite criticizing Fukuyama's assertion that the end of history has dawned, thinkers and activists appear to tacitly concur with him that the liberal democratic state does not need any improvement. This presumption has very depressing implications for Third World activists, for they cannot imagine how liberal democratic structures and practices can take root in their countries in the absence of the requisite material basis. Human beings, however, need to dream of a future that contrasts with the sordid here and now even if they have to project it to the afterlife.

I am bringing up the above because I was at a loss where to look for ideas about the next phase in the development of political structures. The mainstream literature was not helpful as it simply elaborates or flourishes the virtues of the political thinking that supposedly came victoriously out of the Cold War. The history of the nation-state and self-determination that I read to write chapters 1 and 2 indicated the direction that I should focus on. Despite its relative success in the industrialized sectors of the globe, the liberal democratic state has tended to leave some social sectors within the *nation* but outside the genuinely empowered category of citizen. Women who belong to the state's *national* core seem to fall into this category. In addition, still others find themselves within the state but outside the *nation*. This predicament applies to nations without states. It is these kinds of social sectors that have vested interests in looking forward to and imagining a better tomorrow. And it is to the writings of these social sectors that I turned for new ideas. Writings about nations without states in the wealthy West, despite attempting to seek ways of stemming the exclusion of their subjects on the basis of culture and language, seem fixated on the liberal version of democracy. I appreciate how these thinkers are toying with the structures with the aim of reducing or ending the exclusion of culturally and linguistically distinct societies. Their continued glorification of liberal democracy, however, forced me to turn to feminist writing for new ideas. And that is how I came across the work Iris Marion Young. So this work draws on the writing of advocates of the rights of nations without states and feminist theory on democracy.

The section dealing with state-formation and nation-building in the Horn of Africa resulted from a straightforward reading of existing literature. What I perhaps did differently was to read the histories of the various entities together and not separately as is more common. I do not claim to be completely dispassionate, particularly concerning the history of the Ethiopian Empire. Regardless, I deliberately drew mostly on materials written by scholars known more for their positive disposition towards the Empire than to the contrary. This, I hope, more than compensates for possible biases resulting from any hangover of my past involvement in political activism. Finally, have I answered the two questions that drove me to undertake this work? I leave that for the reader to find out.

PART I

Self-Determination in History

INTRODUCTION

ALTHOUGH IT CAME INTO GREATER INTERNATIONAL prominence only at the end of the First World War, the principle of *self-determination* can be traced back to the Enlightenment belief that only the people have the *right to dispose of themselves*. Following from this belief emerged the notion that the *self* has the right to *determine its own political system and affiliation*, freely and without any constraints. It is this legal and political concept that supposedly "propelled the populace to the highest level of authority as the repository of sovereignty" (Grovogui 1996: 80). When the awkward phrase "to dispose of themselves" was further simplified by mid-nineteenth-century radical German philosophers as *selbst-bestim-mungsrecht* (Umozurike 1972: 3), the term "self-determination" was born.

The intellectual environment in which the principle of self-determination was incubated and ultimately blossomed was one possessed of the conviction that human groups have the power as well as the right to constitute their own state to serve some clearly defined earthly functions. The previous belief that the source of all laws was divine, "according to which all political authority and legitimacy ultimately belongs to God, as expressed by his representatives, the king and the church" (Baycroft 1998: 5), was thereby rendered not only obsolete but also illegitimate. As put by another authority, "Before the eighteenth century, the right to rule was legitimated by appealing to God's will, royal blood or superior physical strength and these reasons were premised upon the belief that legitimacy came from above, rather than from the ruled" (Guibernau 1996: 52). Debunking this established tradition and replacing it with natural law, which asserted that "sovereignty is not supra-natural but belongs to the people" (Guibernau 1996: 52), became the major intellectual legacy of the Enlightenment. Jean-Jacques Rousseau stands out for pioneering this concept in his theory of the Social Contract, which elaborated how the people could exercise their sovereign rights. He articulated the procedure according to which "certain groups form nations which choose their rulers from among themselves" (Baycroft 1998: 5). He premised the legitimacy of all laws on the concerned individuals' right to participate directly in their enactment. An intellectual ambience saturated with these beliefs was what ignited the first dramatic revolution in Europe, the French Revolution. Matching *people, nation, sovereignty, territory,* and *state* could retrospectively be identified as the project on which the Revolutionaries almost inadvertently stumbled.

THE LEGACY OF THE FRENCH REVOLUTION

Five Components of the New Order

The process of articulating a definite relationship and correspondence between the categories *people, nation, sovereignty, territory,* and *state,* though gathering momentum during the previous centuries, assumed unprecedented power and ubiquity only after the dramatic experiences of the French Revolution. The Revolutionaries' Declaration of the Rights of Man and Citizen, stipulating that "all sovereignty lies fundamentally with the nation; no body, no individual can exercise authority which does not expressly emanate from it" (Baycroft 1998: 10), emphatically established the source of legitimate sovereign power. This spelled the death sentence of the theory of the Divine Right of Kings, dominant until then, on the grave of which the "Divine Right of the People" (Cobban 1969: 40) was to be erected thereafter. The *people* category was not only transformed from subject to sovereign but also became the repository of "supreme authority, the single active principle in the state" (Baycroft 1998: 10). Furthermore, the *people* henceforth ceased to be treated as an atomic dust of individuals but took shape and form, and "became a *whole,* was called the *Nation,* endowed with sovereignty and identified with the state" (Cobban 1969: 40; italics in original). Similarly, the relation of people to territory underwent an equally drastic transformation with the people's treatment as "a mere appurtenance of the land" coming to an end (Sureda 1973: 17). Instead, the people/nation became not only the legitimate owners of the territory they inhabit but also its most defining element. Thereafter a relationship of mutual contingency came to exist between the fate of a particular territory and of the people who inhabit it. The overall implication of this new conceptual revolution is truly remarkable. It meant that the *people* coalesced to constitute the *nation* by assuming *sovereign* authority over the *state* whose power over a clearly defined *territory* is presumed unchallenged and unchallengeable from within as well as from outside the concerned geographical space.

What followed the introduction of this clear and intimate correspondence between the above five components of the emerging political order was also truly remarkable. Perhaps the most profound implication is the presumption that all the inhabitants of the state territory were to henceforth constitute a single community. As Anthony D. Smith (1999: 32) so cogently puts, the ideal of "one people, one state" was on the rise thereafter, ultimately rendering obsolete the previous order of "one sovereign" ruling over disparate peoples. Conceptualizing the single community that controls its territorially defined state was based on yet another critical presumption—that the political community should coincide with the cultural-cum-linguistic community. The positive and negative implications of this premise came to the fore dramatically then and continue to surface any time self-determination is invoked today. The most ironic implication of conceptualizing the single state-controlling community was the simultaneous process of inclusion and exclusion that it set in motion. Let us first look at those social sectors that the French Revolutionaries excluded from sharing in the sovereignty wrested from the absolute monarch.

Acts of Exclusion and Ranking

The exclusion of the nobility was in fact perceived as mandatory for the nation to come into existence. The nation's emergence required the noblemen's excision from French society because the nobility, denounced as a burden for the nation, could not be part of it (Sewell 1994: 58). Its members were actually considered "no less enemies of the common order than are the English of the French in times of war" (Sewell 1994: 59). The term "secession" was in fact first employed in reference to this social surgery of removing the nobility from French society (Sewell 1994: 59). The territorial version of secession ensued soon after from another act of exclusion. This was the exclusion of the non-white residents of San Domingo, as evidenced by Revolutionary France's refusal to extend to them the Rights of Man and Citizen. The spectacular revolution that this refusal set off ultimately resulted in the birth of the second independent state in the Western Hemisphere, Haiti. How this came about, accompanied with the racial cleansing of the oppressive white minority, is eloquently elaborated by C.L.R. James (1973).

Women constituted another social category whose exclusion from the empowered political community was taken for granted. Women's revolutionary fervour, instead of being welcomed, evidently terrified their male counterparts. Only a few days after women marched on Versailles on 5–6 October 1789 to bring the royal family back to Paris as virtual prisoners, the Constituent Assembly outlawed all "unofficial" demonstrations on pain of death. During the following weeks, the revolutionary government continued to strike at the women's movement, "which received scant support from the male chauvinist sansculottes" (Lewis 1993: 46), who were normally renowned for defending the right to insurrection. By the end of October 1789, the government could close all clubs set up by women without facing any resistance from the sansculottes and their allies. The fear of female involvement in the Revolution continued to rise as concluded by one authority: "There can be absolutely no doubt that, by 1795, men had become thoroughly frightened concerning the potential for a women's revolution within the Revolution. After 1795, women were not even admitted, unaccompanied, into the spectators' gallery of its national assemblies" (Lewis 1993: 89). Women were thus knocked out of the race for sharing the sovereignty that was snatched from the king.

All non-white males were excluded from the empowered political community, despite being supposedly free men and even, in some cases, wealthy, as were all women even if they were white, wealthy, erudite, and revolutionary. The exclusion of these social categories had one inevitable implication. Only the white male revolutionary population remained in the race to epitomize the nation and thus assume sovereign power, which led to the fragmentation of this social sector into various antagonistic factions. The most radical position was championed by the social sector known as the sans-culottes. The sans-culotte, described as "an estate of poverty, those who lived 'an economy of makeshifts'" (Lewis 1993: 17–18), and the propertied bourgeois class constituted the opposite poles of the political spectrum that was then crystallizing. The latter propertied class ranged from those who espoused merely reforming the monarchy to the Jacobin and Girondin revolutionary factions, who advocated radical republicanism. The various branches of this class, however, were united in the fact that they had evidently "acquired the philosophical certainty and the political power that they, not the nobility, not the less affluent craftsman or peasant, and certainly not the propertyless and labouring poor, were now the natural leaders of society—*la nation c'est nous*, as they might have put it" (Lewis 1993: 15).

Each sector of the white male population that claimed to best epitomize the nation and to thus assume sovereignty discredited its opponents by designating them as members of one type of aristocracy or another. In the process, the term "aristocracy" was defined differently to suit the agenda of the various contestants. The reformist constitutional monarchists wished to reduce the meaning of "aristocracy" to those "who had privileges that separated them from the common people and the common law." The more radical Girondin and Jacobin revolutionary factions, however, preferred to expand the definition of "aristocracy" so that it would embrace all "those who opposed the Revolution, or who opposed the radicalization of the Revolution," which could apply to the constitutional monarchists. The propertyless sans-culotte, in an apparent attempt to discredit as many of the above as possible, labelled as "aristocrats" all wealthy persons "who lived better than they and cared more about their gold than about the republic; or the haughty, who put on airs, wore breeches instead of the baggy trousers of the common people, wore powdered wigs, or *spoke in a 'distinguished' fashion"* (Sewell 1996: 303; italics added). The reference to distinguished speech is significant for it shows how even members of a single cultural and linguistic community could be differentiated into sub-cultural categories simply by their manner of speech. The greater alienation of those falling outside the cultural and speech community appears self-evident.

Despite the insurrectionary activism of the propertyless revolutionary radicals, one critical criterion was eventually adopted to systematically narrow political participation. Property ownership, as reflected by the payment of taxes, became the criterion for categorizing citizens as either *active* or *passive* types. This becomes apparent from the Constituent Assembly's declaration, according to which "although all men were equal (women, of course, were still outside the political pale), men who owned property (active citizens) were more equal than those who did not (passive citizens). It was eventually decided that to qualify as a voter one had to pay the equivalent in direct taxes of three days' work; this group of around 4 million, would then choose electors (around 50,000 in number) who qualified by paying the equivalent of ten days' work. To qualify as a deputy, one had to be very rich indeed, paying over 50 *livres per annum* in taxation" (Lewis 1993: 31; italics in original). Thus only 14 percent could qualify as voters and a very minuscule 0.18 percent as electors. Property ownership was thus used to pick the politically empowered portion by systematically grading even those who belonged to the nation on the basis of gender, race, and speech. A revolution that was instigated by the distaste for hereditary privilege ended up merely shifting the criteria for privileged status. Universal male suffrage did temporarily result from the mobilization that preceded the election of the National Convention on 20 September 1790 (Lewis 1993: 37). However, the number of the electorate actually fell to less than forty thousand (Lewis 1993: 50) in the subsequent counter-revolutionary swing. The restoration of universal male suffrage would be postponed for a long time and the recognition of the same rights for women would remain unthinkable until after the First World War.

Acts of Voluntary Inclusion

The complete exclusion of some social sectors and the partial exclusion of others were among the results of the attempt to achieve congruence between the political and cultural-cum-linguistic communities. On the other hand, the same factors rationalized the admission into the emerging French nation of culturally and linguistically allied communities until then residing outside France. In such cases, the peoples' right to self-disposal was upheld and the concerned peoples' treatment as "mere appurtenances of territory" was practically negated. This was attested to by the admission into France (and the French nation) of societies evidently subscribing to French identity along with the territories they inhabited. Plebiscites, adopted as the mechanism for determining these people's right of self-disposal, were conducted with relative fairness. The Assembly's decree "that before annexation a formal expression of the will of the people should be obtained by holding of plebiscites... were conducted on the whole with remarkable impartiality" (Cobban 1969: 41) when Avignon and Venaissin united with France in 1791 and Savoy and Nice the following year.

Respecting the peoples' right of self-disposal was, however, apparently unpalatable if it implied loss of territory and population. Some communities thus found themselves territorially within France but culturally and linguistically outside the French nation. We have records of at least one such alienated community fighting not only on the side of "its own nobility" but also of a foreign power. The Catalans of the Pyrenees fought in support of their royalist overlords as well as of Spain (McPhee 1993). The dispute could have been settled simply by allowing Catalan secession from France and union with Spain. The principle that the people's allegiance is a factor in determining the allocation of territory to one state or another was tacitly violated in this case. This principle was later on deliberately subordinated to the "idea that France was endowed with 'natural frontiers' (the Alps, the Mediterranean, the Pyrenees, the Atlantic, the Channel, and the Rhine)" thereby rationalizing the annexation of the "entire West Bank of the Rhine with its vast German and Flemish speaking population" (Sewell 1996: 311). While pursuing these contradictory policies in Europe, France was stepping up the conquest, subjugation, colonization, and pillaging of non-European societies. Meanwhile, the eagerness to export the revolution to the rest of Europe, particularly after December 1792, led to the imposition of "revolutionary governments" on other European societies, which rendered liberation and domination indistinct.

Politicization of Language and Culture

The novel attempt to conceptualize an empowered political community generated another chain of repercussions. The politicization of language resulted (intentionally or inadvertently) from the employment of a particular language as *the* medium for politicizing and mobilizing society. Language's politicization in turn drew culture into the realm of politics to a previously unknown extent. The explosive growth in pamphleteering and other forms of publications attests to increased reliance on the emerging standard French. No less than 767 pamphlets were disseminated between 8 May and 25 September 1788 just as the revolutionary fever was being felt. The period between 25 September 1788 and the end of the year witnessed the release of an additional 752 pamphlets. This growth of pamphleteering "was only a prelude to the 2,639 titles that appeared during the election of the deputies to the Estates-General in the first four months of 1789" (Lewis 1993: 23). The daily average for the number of pamphlets released in the first period comes to 5.5 and in the second to 7.7, reaching an astounding 22 during the first four months of 1789. A similar expansion in printing and publishing was witnessed during this period. There were 36 printer/publishers and 194 publisher/booksellers in Paris in 1789. A decade later, "the number of printing and publishing outlets had tripled" (Lewis 1993: 99).

Language policy in the pre-revolutionary period was driven merely by the need to pass the rulers' decrees on to their subjects, which included translation of relevant edicts into the various languages and patois. This came to an end after 1792 when the new policy of "one people, one nation, one language" (Guibernau 1996: 70) was embraced. At the time, no fewer than six million speakers of the Basque, Flemish, Celtic, and German languages were living in France's various departments. The role of culture in state and politics naturally experienced an accompanying

change. "[W]hereas before the French Revolution there had been no necessary connection between the state as a political unit and the nation as
a cultural one, the combination of these two elements in a single conception was the significant fact in the phase that now opened in the history
of the nation state" (Cobban 1969: 35).

The political order that was then taking shape was evidently obsessed
with achieving identities: the "one people, one state" notion operated
alongside the search of convergence between "one people, one nation, and
one language." The aspiration of forging a single entity out of "the state
as political unit," the cultural nation, and the linguistic community had
important implications. Some societies found themselves within the
French state but outside the nation. Even those persons who could fit
into the "nation" due to their cultural and language attributes were
denied admission into the political community due to their gender, race,
or class. This ranking of France's inhabitants was unfolding at a time
when Europeans were increasingly seeing themselves as the superior
race. What this implied concerning French attitudes towards non-white
humanity is self-evident. Ascendant racism ultimately rebounded even
into France, prompting the denigration of non-French speakers as inferior beings. France and other "dominant nation-building states" thereafter
started taking "their white subordinates to be of a different and inferior
race" (Feigenbaum 1997: 61). The English took to openly denigrating the
Irish as "white chimpanzees," no different from the equally denigrated
blacks. Similarly, the French started referring to the Bretons as savages
and "the Redskins of Fenimore Cooper" well into the 1840s. Keeping
the boundary between differences of race and nation distinct was proving difficult.

Spread of Revolution, Nationalism, and Republicanism

The influence of revolutionary and Napoleonic France irreversibly
changed European political thinking, radically changing the political
landscape of not only the Continent but of the whole world. The concepts
of revolution, nationalism, and republicanism reverberated from its epi-
centre in France to periodically rock the rest of Europe in the decades
after Napoleon's defeat at Waterloo. In the words of A.D. Smith (1991:
138), "The reverberations of the French Revolution in the hinterlands of
the Habsburg, Ottoman and even Romanov empires were felt well into
the twentieth century." One of the immediate impacts of this reverber-
ation had to do with the language policies of the dynastic rulers who
were restored after Napoleon's defeat. They were compelled to respond

to the rising "hostile popular linguistic-nationalisms" of their disparate subject communities by imposing one particular language as the official one (Anderson 1983: 45). The result was the introduction of Anglicization in Britain and British-ruled parts of the globe, the intensification of Germanization in the Habsburg-ruled expanses of Europe, and the adoption of Turkification and Russification by the sprawling Ottoman and Russian empires, respectively. This was coupled with the growing imperative of dynastic rulers' pretension that an identification exists between themselves and the disparate peoples inhabiting their sprawling empires. Hence, under the impact of "the rapidly rising prestige all over Europe of the national idea, there was a discernible tendency among the Euro-Mediterranean monarchies to sidle towards a beckoning national identification. Romanovs discovered they were Great Russians, Hanoverians that they were English, Hohenzollerns that they were Germans—and with rather more difficulty their cousins turned Rumanian, Greek, and so forth" (Anderson 1983: 82). The resulting "inner incompatibility of empire and nation" gave rise to the conceptualization of nation and empire as the mutual nemeses of each other. While this process simmered, ultimately resulting in the demise of the Habsburg and Ottoman empires and the reconfiguration of the Russian Empire at the end of the First World War by the explicit invocation of self-determination, new entities were making their appearances on the European continent.

Greece became the first post-Napoleonic independent state when religious sentiments motivated European powers to back Greek rising against their Ottoman Moslem overlords in 1829. Two years later, the Austrian Netherlands seceded from Holland to found the new independent state of Belgium. In both cases, a monarch was conscripted from some European royal family to serve as the embodiment of the new states' sovereignty. Separating state sovereignty and republicanism and by extension the notion of popular sovereignty, however, could not stem the rising rejection of domination by forces deemed alien. Hence, the manifestation of nationalism in this form continued to spread from Greece northwards into Ottoman-ruled Balkans and from the west eastward into Austrian-dominated central Europe.

Meanwhile, all who aspired to realize their national states were operating in an atmosphere in which republicanism remained officially stigmatized. The experience of Italy and Germany graphically depicts the consequences of making a distinction between seeking a nation-state and popular sovereignty. Nothing casts this in bolder relief than Giuseppe Garibaldi's admonition: "We should be ready *to accept a rigorous dicta-*

torship from Piedmont as a means of emancipating ourselves from foreign domination" (Smith 1969: 30; italics added). It was a similar attempt to circumvent republicanism's stigma that contributed to the failure of the popularly led unification of Germany in 1848. Hence, when the creation of a united Germany came about in 1870 it "was not a matter of German people coming together and uniting by consent" (Chapman 1998: 88). Rather, the new German state "was in practice an enlarged Prussia, just as Italy was an expanded Piedmont" (Chapman 1998: 90). The manner by which these two states came into existence created a number of anomalies. First, although they were inspired by the rejection of domination, they ended up qualifying this rejection by hinting at the tolerance of domination by a power considered "one's own." Second, the resulting new states were based on at least the acquiescence of the populace if not outright consent. These two states went on to play important roles in the First World War and to influence the distortion of self-determination's practical application at the conclusion of the war. To this story we now turn our attention.

UNRAVELLING EMPIRES IN EUROPE

Self-Determination's Ascendance to Greater Prominence

The principle of self-determination became much more explicitly defined and attained unprecedented international prominence at the end of the First World War. The factors that accorded it an even greater universal relevance and immediacy are numerous. Perhaps the most outstanding factor with enduring implications was the outbreak of the Bolshevik Revolution even while the war was raging. The Russian Marxists, who ended up monopolizing the revolution's direction, openly declared their intention to guide the revolution toward the predetermined goal of instituting a communist world order. This had the immediate implication of stigmatizing communism just as much as republicanism, particularly in those quarters threatened by its global agenda. The czarist regime's overthrow by the Bolsheviks also had an immediate positive implication for self-determination by ending the Allied powers' previous hesitation to support ongoing struggles against their German, Austro-Hungarian, and Ottoman enemies for fear of also destroying their ally, Russia (Musgrave 1997: 16). The Germans were in fact already busy aiding the Irish republicans and Flemish separatists (Musgrave 1997: 15) with a view to weakening the enemy camp. The Austro-Hungarian and Ottoman empires had actually started crumbling with more and more of their subjects declaring independence even before the Allied powers assembled for the Paris Peace Conference (Heater 1994: 47).

The project to forge a socialist federal state out of Russia, in accordance with the previously articulated Bolshevik approach to self-determination, also looked imminent at the time. Self-determination's potency was hence perceived, in the words of Woodrow Wilson, as "an imperative principle of action, which statesmen will henceforth ignore at their peril" (Heater 1994: 44). Similarly, Lenin's writings (n.d.) on the subject indicate his conviction that the pre-emption of self-determination's exploitation by "reactionary" nationalist forces would be a strategy that revolutionaries would ignore at their peril. Self-determination was thus invoked as either a sub-agendum of the global revolution then perceived as necessary and imminent by socialists or as a concession needed to pre-empt socialist revolution. The invocation of self-determination and the divergent state forms for which it was to serve as the midwife continued to be influenced by these competing approaches until the end of the Cold War.

Articulating a Universal or Particular Role

The role of self-determination and nationhood in theorizing the relationship between the universal and the particular also achieved an unprecedented clarity at this stage. Woodrow Wilson envisioned the linguistic community as the only entity that can promote a "detailed community of thought and absolute unity in point of view." He asserted that "It is in this detail that we find the chief differences between *Nationality* and *Humanity*—the thoughts and ideas peculiar to individual nations and the thoughts and ideals common to mankind" (qtd. in Heater 1994: 26). He went on to envision founding global peace on the convergence of humanity's General Will, the sum total of the general will of all democratic nations. As Cobban states, he was confident of the "goodness and power of world opinion, which might be termed the General Will of humanity, and in its identity with the General Will of every democratic nation, [which] enabled him to hold the view that the self-determination of nations, and national sovereignty, was a possible basis, indeed the only possible basis, of world peace" (Cobban 1969: 64). However, not all nations could have an immediate input into this General Will of humanity as some of them needed to first attain "manhood." But Wilson was certain that "Peoples are becoming old enough to govern themselves" (Heater 1994: 27), at which stage they ostensibly could do so.

Despite its negative implication for the so-called immature peoples' (mostly non-Europeans) entitlement to self-determination at that juncture, the vision of a peaceful world ultimately inhabited and jointly managed by more and more adult (and therefore free) nations pointed to a brighter future for humankind.

Lenin too conceptualized self-determination as a principle that would guide humanity to a clearly articulated destiny. It would contribute to global integration, ultimately bringing about humanity's fusion into a single body of citizenry. He proceeded from the Marxist conviction that humanity was inexorably marching towards the ideal communist stage where classes and the state, the institution that their irreconcilable interests necessitate, would ultimately disappear. Every move was supposed to be taken with an eye on this ultimate goal. Hence, he saw the recognition of self-determination as a step in this direction by commenting: "In the same way as mankind can arrive at the abolition of classes only through a transition period of the dictatorship of the oppressed class, so can mankind arrive at the inevitable fusion of nations only through a transition period of the complete emancipation of all oppressed nations, i.e., their freedom to secede." And the ultimate goal of "socialism is not only to end the division of mankind into tiny states and isolation of nations in all its forms, it is not only the rapprochement of nations but also *their fusion*" (Lenin n.d.: 128; italics added). His vision of a future marked with the fusion of nations was qualitatively different from Wilson's more modest expectation of a concert of free nations serving as the pillar of world peace. The former grand vision has become distinctly passé in the post-Cold War period and there is no apparent movement to further develop Wilson's vision. The absence of a more current theorization of the universal/particular relationship hence poses as perhaps the major challenge to imbuing current quests for self-determination with a constructive and emancipatory role.

Conflicting Aspirations Produce Distorted Outcomes

Wilson, the most vocal exponent of the principle of self-determination, had to take into account the conflicting aspirations of his allies. The British preference was to limit self-determination's relevance to continental Europe, to thereby pre-empt its application to their globe-encompassing empire. The French and the Italians went further to aspire confining "it to Utopia" (Cobban 1969: 66) so as to freely pursue their territorial acquisitions in Europe and elsewhere. Even Wilson ultimately restricted the principle's relevance only to the "territories of the defeated empires"

(Cobban 1969: 66). France pursued the agenda of severely punishing one of the defeated powers, Germany, by allocating as much of its territory and people as possible to itself and other members of the alliance (Heater 1994: 55, 58), thereby violating the principle of self-determination in several ways. First, it was predicated on reviving the treatment of the peoples affected by its annexationist agenda as a "mere appurtenance of the territory" that could easily be transferred from one sovereignty to another. Second, it frustrated the German-speaking community's desire to unite and form one great German national state. The desire of Austrian Germans to join Germany appeared evident at the time (Heater 1994: 67). Had the nationality principle been fairly applied, these could have been joined by another 4.3 million German speakers whose settlements touched on the borders of Germany and Austria (Heater 1994: 68). The size and strength of the resulting German state must have been frightening not only to France but also to the other members of the alliance. The frustration, disappointment, and anger of a significant portion of the German-speaking population evidently festered for the following two decades and ultimately contributed to another global conflagration, the Second World War.

Annexation also fomented frustration and disappointment among the victors, who were allocated less than they had claimed. Italy, which entered the war with promises of territorial gain, claimed large swathes of Europe adjacent to it as well as colonies in Africa (Heater 1994: 61). Asia's only rising industrial power, Japan, aspired to inherit Germany's preferential privileges in large parts of China and to take direct ownership of Shantung (Heater 1994: 59). The disappointment of these powers with the gains accorded them contributed to the frustration that simmered for the following two decades, ultimately resulting in their alliance with Germany during the Second World War. Hence, mismanaging the self-determination of cultural and linguistic communities completely negated the agenda of founding sustainable global peace on its recognition. It was primarily the knee-jerk reaction to the abuse of self-determination as a supremacist theme by Fascists that stigmatized its invocation by cultural and linguistic communities in the period after the Second World War.

Smaller Polyglots Replace Bigger Ones

Self-determination as an instrument for creating a clear correspondence between *people, nation, state, territory,* and *sovereignty* proved awkward during this time. This becomes evident from several forms of distortion that accompanied those cases where attempts were made to uphold the right to self-determination. First, consulting the desires of the concerned *peoples* was dispensed with (Cobban 1969: 60) when the Allied powers decided to recognize the new states resulting from the invocation of the principle, such as Czechoslovakia, Yugoslavia, and Romania. Instead, the decision was based mostly on taking the opinions of "one or another group of [mostly self-styled] national leaders as representative of the wishes of each nationality" (Cobban 1969: 67). Plebiscites and the notion of popular sovereignty were evidently not relevant.

Second, these new states were determined to grab as much *territory* as they could without giving any consideration to the views of the affected populations (Heater 1994: 60), prompting Lloyd George to describe them as being "more imperialistic than either England or France, certainly than the United States" (Cobban 1969: 87). At one time during the period, fourteen different small wars were raging between these emerging mini-imperialist countries (Heater 1994: 60). This should not be surprising in view of the track record set by the more "mature" nations of France, Britain, Italy, and Japan, who were already imperialist or aspiring to become so. Their experience had amply demonstrated that the freedom, survival, and glory of one's nation depend on the subjugation of other nations and the negation of their right to self-determination.

Third, most of these new independent entities harboured substantial minority populations. Minorities made up, for example, 30.4 percent of Poland, 34.7 percent of Czechoslovakia, and 25 percent of Romania. The result was the creation of new "Irelands" in Eastern Europe (Cobban 1969: 86), as aptly concluded by one observer. Or, in the words of a participant in the Paris Peace Conference, "the national principle has at last triumphed over the polyglot" Austro-Hungarian state, by giving birth to equally polyglot new states such as Czechoslovakia (Heater 1994: 102). The Italian politician Nitti made an even harsher criticism of the outcome "Before, there was a single Austria-Hungary with its fierce nationalist struggles. Now, Poland is an Austria-Hungary in which the parties have changed place, and the most ignorant peoples claim to dominate with violence the most cultured and progressive peoples; and in the whole of Central Europe and the Balkans new Austria-Hungaries have been created" (Heater 1994: 106). Despite these shortcomings, historians are prone to conclude that the peace settlement "produced a political map more in line with ethnographic principles than ever before" (Heater 1994: 113). Churchill resorted to statistical argumentation to laud the Paris Peace Conference's success by stressing that less than 3 percent of Europeans remained under the authority of governments whose nationality they repudiated (Heater 1994: 103).

CONCLUSION

The initial aim of the French Revolutionaries was to transform the political system of an existing state. They could draw at best only indirect lessons from the following sources in conceptualizing the new order they coveted. First, they had been observing the political order then steadily crystallizing in other adjacent states, particularly England and Holland. Second, their exposure to (and for some even involvement in) the American Revolution might have clarified their political thinking even further. Third, they appeared to be operating in an intellectual climate deeply permeated by the diverse political theories propounded since the Enlightenment. Other than sharing these impressions, the French Revolutionaries lacked consensus on a clear course of action and an ultimate goal. Evidently operating under these influences, however, they hit on the idea of assigning a *state* to each *people* that attains the status of a *nation* by exercising *sovereignty* over the clearly defined state *territory*. This was soon followed by the aspiration to identify people, nation, and culture and language with each other. The attempt to match the state-inhabiting community (*people*) with the politically empowered community (the citizen collectivity called the *nation*) ultimately necessitated envisioning a single cultural community with a similar implication for the identity of the linguistic community. This had the overall result of exposing new incongruities and the emergence of a political order criss-crossed by racial, gender, class, and ethnic border markers due to one factor. France, a multi-ethnic patriarchal state whose realm included numerous overseas slave-owning territories, was in the process of trying on the nation-state garb. Despite the negative implications of this development, the positive implication of pioneering the notion of vesting power in the people had global emancipatory potential.

All subsequent attempts to attain the nation-state status were driven as reaction to and/or as an emulation of French experience. The "nationalization" of France's language and culture motivated European dynastic states to reject French culture and language. Instead they "nationalized" the culture and language of the dominant ethnic groups and proceeded to impose it on their disparate subject populations, with predictable alienating implications. The difficulties emanating from the attempt of the

Austro-Hungarian, Russian, and Ottoman empires to put on the nation-state appearance continued to simmer, ultimately leading to their demise at the end of the First World War. The new states resulting from this breakup could draw lessons from other historical experiences in addition to that of the French Revolution. The Greeks, Belgians, and Italians had paved the way in shaping their independent states by ending rule by powers deemed alien. On the other hand, Germany, a cultural and linguistic community divided by state borders, had moved closer to achieving perfect congruence between the political and cultural community by removing some portions of the divisive boundaries. Meanwhile, all the new post-Napoleonic European "nation-states" (Greece, Belgium, Italy, and Germany) were displaying a determination to turn themselves into empire-owning entities. Not surprisingly, the new entities resulting from the post-First World War events were not troubled to envision their "nation-states" as virtual empires. Even the positive implications of self-determination did not apply to non-European societies as its relevance was presumed appropriate only to ending empires in Europe. This was, however, operating alongside the enunciation that all European political theories and practices had universal application. The very principles celebrated by the Europeans could thereafter be conveniently cited to denounce their imperial domination over other peoples.

INTRODUCTION

THE PRINCIPLE OF SELF-DETERMINATION ATTAINED unprecedented international exposure at the end of the First World War, raising hopes that by upholding it future wars could be averted. The inconsistencies that attended the implementation of the principle, however, partly contributed to the outbreak of an even more catastrophic conflict, the Second World War. And it was the events surrounding this war that gave impetus to decolonization in Africa, ultimately resulting in a number of aberrations. First, the European powers mobilized their African subjects with propaganda vilifying the racial-supremacist ideology of the Fascist powers. This set in motion a process in which "Fascist nationalism produced the opposed reality of anti-Fascism; and anti-Fascism...became antiracism; and antiracism led in due course to an end of colonization" (Davidson 1992: 52). The result was the erasure of European colonial rule from large swathes of the African continent within a relatively short period of time. Instead of dwelling on this sufficiently documented history, we will focus on the aberrations that accompanied the process of decolonization as well as those that followed it.

The struggle against European colonialism was led by people who had to demonstrate proficiency in European languages, history, culture, politics, and law (Davidson 1992: 107). This meant they had "to find their way ahead in languages not their own," contrary to the Eastern European experience, where, "the handful of scholarly men...set themselves to enlarge and standardize national languages" (Davidson 1992: 156). They similarly had to turn their backs on traditional institutions and to undermine traditional leaders. They were helped in this by the colonial rulers, who, having tainted the traditional leaders by employing them as intermediaries, at the eleventh hour came up with the concept of historic rights. Accordingly, they theorized that each people has a particular social order best suited to its own peculiar genius and which could serve as "the starting point of such further freedom as it may hope to attain" (Becker 1953: 265–66). The emerging new political leadership countered by invoking natural rights and thus "insisted that the political functions of 'natural rulers' and other traditional authorities should not include the right to represent their communities in the decisional organs of the modern state. For the purpose of political representation, the traditional community was conceived, not as a corporate entity, *but as a collectivity of individuals,* each of whom is entitled to representation according to the democratic and egalitarian rule of one person, one vote, one value" (Sklar 1985: 9; italics added). Hence, there existed "an ever-widening conflict of sympathy and purpose between the old nationalists, standing for the resurrection of precolonial powers and prerogatives, and new nationalists, for whom the old powers and prerogatives had no more value, but were obstructions to modernizing progress" (Davidson 1992: 73). The conviction of the new nationalists that progress can only be achieved by jettisoning the power of the old kings and chiefs appeared unshakeable. The modernizers came out as the winners of the ideological war with their traditionalist contestants. And as Davidson (1992: 35) concludes, "No matter how much they spoke in defense of the virtues of Africa's cultures, the 'modernizers' were necessarily standing on the ground of European culture." And they set themselves the mission of disseminating European culture while doing everything possible to dispense with tradition.

The fate of the entities in Africa called tribes was definitely sealed by this dismissive attitude towards culture and tradition. The nation-building project adopted by the post-colonial state leaders who drew upon European models demanded that African tribes die in order to be reborn as nations (Keller 1995: 622). At the same time, it indicated that such leaders subscribed to the Western intellectual notion, identified by Ken Saro-Wiwa, that "the tribe was a useless thing; the tribe had to be killed in order to build a nation" (qtd. in Vlist 1994: 183). But whatever its origin, the death of tribes was simply assumed to be the price of modernization and necessary for the ultimate aim of forging black African nations speaking French, English, or Portuguese.

In another sense the prospect of attaining nationhood was doomed from the very outset. The decolonization version of self-determination was based on the following three principles:

1. all dependent peoples are entitled to freedom;
2. the peoples so entitled are defined in terms of the existing colonial territories, each of which contains a nation; and
3. once such a people has come to independence, no residual right of self-determination remains with any group within it or cutting across its frontiers. (Emerson 1964: 28)

This version of self-determination had numerous implications. The concerned entities often did not find it necessary to demonstrate effective legitimate authority in order to gain and retain sovereignty, having earned such authority "simply on the basis of being decolonized" (Herbst 2000: 98). In addition, their regimes often failed to renew the mandate to rule by consulting the wishes of the populace. The drastic rupture between popularly based sovereignty and an externally recognized facade meant that the citizen category was missing, as evidenced by the plausible designation of African countries as "states without citizens" (Ayoade 1988: 100-18). In the absence of the *citizen* category, imagining the nation contradicts the history we have reviewed previously. Matching *people, nation, territory, state,* and *sovereignty* to shape the nation-state was clearly dispensed with in the African experience. An end to the treatment of peoples as "a mere appurtenance of the land" (Sureda 1973: 17), as happened at the inception of self-determination, was not realized in Africa; there, the haphazardly demarcated colonial *territory* became the owner and ultimate definer of the people category.

THE PECULIARITY OF HORN STATES

How to Frame Self-Determination

At the conclusion of the First World War, self-determination was deemed appropriate only for Europe as a doctrine that allowed new self-styled nation-states to be carved out of the dynastic empires that lost the war. Banishing it from the "European arena" (Ginther and Isak 1991: 11) and reducing its role to ending overseas European colonies became the reigning orthodoxy after the end of the Second World War. From ending domination generally its mission was henceforth reduced to strictly ending white European colonialism. A couple of premises underpinning this reduced role affected the politics of the Horn of Africa which made the region distinct from the rest of the African continent. First was the tacit premise that self-determination was unsuitable in redressing domination by non-white, non-European forces. Second was the more explicit premise that intra-African colonial domination was implausible. These premises confronted victims of oppressive African states with a peculiar challenge.

However, the processes that brought into existence the Horn's most important states, the Sudan and Ethiopia, made the rise of movements to throw off domination inevitable. These movements were thus forced to seek a broad range of precepts when articulating their causes. I shall briefly mention some of these (they will be discussed in greater detail later on). The Eritrean position centred on the argument that Eritrea's "borders were fixed and its national identity defined by colonial history, like the rest of colonial Africa" (Berekhet Habte Selassie 1989: 66). The Eritreans thus resorted to the conventional reduction of self-determination as applicable only to the decolonization of European colonies, on the ground that Ethiopian rule was simply a successor to Italian colonialism. The corollary of this position is the exemption of the remainder of Ethiopia from being susceptible to the invocation of self-determination and possible splintering.

The remainder of Ethiopia was meanwhile facing challenges from movements for self-determination drawing on two separate precepts. The Oromos and Somalis justified their liberation struggles by arguing that Ethiopia's colonial domination over them was sufficiently evidenced by the brutal process of conquest that foisted Ethiopian rule on them and by its resulting cultural, religious, and political oppression. (Incidentally, independent Somalia's handling of Ogadeni struggle complicated its images to the outside world in a number of ways as will be elaborated later on.) Other political groups that could not or would not embrace the Oromo/Somali approach resorted to the second alternative of designating their cases as "national question" whose resolution should not necessarily lead to Ethiopia breaking up. All the positions enumerated above were eventually so nuanced that resolutions ranging from strict separatism, to a radical or a modest reconfiguration of the state, and even to the preservation of a unitary Ethiopian state became a menu from which a choice could be made. Finally, due to the events immediately prior to as well as following Sudan's independence, the southern Sudanese were left with the irrefutable impression that the northerners were determined to simply step into the shoes of the departing British. How this was dubbed the continuation of colonialism and served as the cause of the virtually uninterrupted southern Sudanese struggle for self-determination will be discussed later on.

The Role of State Language and Culture

Self-determination's reduction to decolonization was accompanied by another departure from previous experiences. As the history summarized earlier indicates, the role of language in the effort to achieve congruence between the political and cultural community dates back to the French Revolution. Furthermore, language was considered the key defining factor when deciding which entities deserved self-determination at the end of the First World War. Even more importantly, the impact of language choice on mass participation in politics, administration, education, and the administration of justice appears self-evident. The adoption of "European languages-of-state" (Anderson 1983: 104-105) by the states resulting from the decolonization of European holdings in Asia and Africa was a departure from these previous experiences. Coupled with the "Russifying policy-orientation" (i.e., forging a single speech community by the process called nation-building) that these states inherited from the departing colonial powers, this inferred the ultimate goal of forging African or Asian nations speaking European languages. Evaluating the feasibility and justice of this project lies beyond the scope of this work. Its implication that "Africa would be free: except, of course, that in terms of political and literate culture, Africa would cease to be Africa" (Davidson 1992: 38) appears indisputable. Despite this troubling prospect, the adoption of a European language-of-state has the implication of alienating equally all the peoples of the concerned post-colonial state.

The experience of the states of the Horn of Africa deviates from the more general African one in this respect as well. The Sudan, actually black Africa's first post-colonial state, adopted Arabic to replace English as the language-of-state. The Ethiopian Empire was born equipped with Amharic as a language-of-state simply because it was the language of the conquerors who brought the state into existence. Independent Somalia resulted from the merger of former British and Italian colonies immediately after decolonization. Continued use of one or the other European language or both proved quite cumbersome for the resource-strapped state. In the end, Somalia also chose one particular Somali dialect as the language-of-state. How these language policies marginalized some parts of the population and thus fed struggles for self-determination will be discussed in a later section.

Discontinuity of History

Decolonization in Africa deviated from the way self-determination operated in the rest of the world in yet another important respect. In Europe, during the period between the two world wars, self-determination was invoked by entities predating conquest and alien rule. Therefore, the new states that resulted from its invocation in Eastern Europe at that time "were often in some sense old states as well, states shaped and inspired by preimperialist and native histories of their own" (Davidson 1992: 188). Such a retrieval of the historical experience preceding domination in most cases was assumed neither possible nor desirable in Africa despite the relatively shorter lifetime of actual European rule. Instead, decolonization was conceived as a process that brought into being previously non-existent totally new states. Modibo Keita's assertion that "The colonial system divided Africa, but it *permitted nations to be born*" (Cervenka 1969: 14; italics added) epitomizes the common attitude about the genesis of the post-colonial African state. The partition of Africa among European powers deviated even from the Asian experience. While European colonialism allowed the survival of some historically existing units in Asia (Young 1994: 16), it was carried out in Africa with almost total disregard of pre-existing political structures. Furthermore, historically shaped identities were considered irrelevant in Africa. As a result, European colonies in Africa were "formed and governed as though their peoples possessed no history of their own" (Davidson 1992: 10). Like the language policy discussed above, these peculiarities of the African colonial experience treated all African peoples as societies lacking historically shaped identities, cultures, and political structures. In the Horn of Africa, however, the groups that dominated the state were guilty of treating others as peoples bereft of valuable history, culture, or political structure. The response instigated by this measure is truly remarkable. It has made the writing and interpretation of history central in the struggles for self-determination in the Horn of Africa.

INTRODUCTION

THE CONCEPTS ON WHICH THE MODERN STATE is presumably founded are quite clear. The modern state is situated on a *territory* whose borders are clearly defined. It embraces all the *people* living within this territorial space and synthesizes them to create a culturally homogeneous collectivity called the *nation*. And the nation exercises uncontested control and authority, *sovereignty*, over this territory and interacts with similarly organized entities on the basis of equality. The people become the *nation* through cultural homogenization and enter into a compact that legitimates their collective *sovereignty*. Internationally shaped institutions, conventions, values, and procedures carry legitimacy, theoretically, only in so far as they result from consensus among states instituted in a similar manner. And all states are, or will eventually be, characterized by a convergence between the political and cultural community, thus making *nation* and *state* coterminous and synonymous. The nation-state thus became a concept for organizing local, regional, and global affairs. Conceptualizing such a clearly defined correspondence between the *territory*, the *people*, the *nation*, and the seat of ultimate authority (*sovereignty*) was pioneered in Western Europe and spread to the rest of the world. Formulating such a correspondence and lending it legitimacy became the foundational function of the principle of self-determination. Citizens, through the right of internal self-determination, legitimate the state and turn it into an instrument that embodies their collective views and interests. Their collectively held sovereignty is recognized and respected by other states, thus constituting the external dimension of their right to self-determination. How this concept emerged in Western Europe in eighteenth century, spread to the rest of world, and took on divergent forms and content has been touched upon in the preceding sections of this work. We have now arrived at the stage where we can start seeing the context in which it is being posed in the contemporary world.

The post-Cold War world is witnessing a resurgence of demands for self-determination at a time when the correlation between (and the significance of) these elements of modern statehood (the *people*, the *nation*, the *territory*, and *sovereignty*) are undergoing radical shifts. In many cases, however, those demanding (as well as those denying) self-determination are operating without factoring this new reality into their political discourse. Many of them are failing to take into account the changed significance of these elements when defining their ultimate political objectives. If the opposing sides were willing to recognize the fast diminishing significance of these conceptual foundations of modern statehood, however, the very nature of their debate would change. Such a shift in the framework of their debate could stem the exacerbation of the conflict in which they are locked.

Persisting on the current course, however, would only render struggles for or against self-determination completely futile as well as making destruction their only outcome. If the protagonists take into consideration the changes fast unfolding around them, on the other hand, they may be able to see a more constructive way forward for both of them. The zero-sum game in which they are engaged could be turned into its opposite with possible gains for the parties. This will become more obvious as we list the changed contexts within which both those who are seeking and denying self-determination are operating.

The State: No Longer Fully Sovereign

Sovereignty is the defining feature of modern independent statehood. And, naturally, possessing it is the aim of all struggles for self-determination. Those who oppose the invocation of the right to self-determination usually insist that sovereignty has already been achieved and should remain inviolable; no external power should question the manner in which it is exercised or who exercises it. And no internal challenge should entertain the rupture of its wholeness either through the partial sharing of it or through the secession of a similarly endowed entity. However, the fight over sovereignty is often conducted with scant attention to the illusory nature of the concept. Sovereignty is a very complex concept that can mean different things to different people. Krasner believes that the term "sovereignty" has been understood in at least the following four different ways:

1. domestic sovereignty, or the organization of public authority within a state and the level of effective control exercised by those holding authority;
2. interdependence sovereignty, or the ability of the public authorities to control transborder movements;
3. international legal sovereignty, or the mutual recognition of states and other entities; and
4. Westphalian sovereignty, or the exclusion of interference by external actors in a state's domestic affairs. (Krasner 1999: 9)

Krasner, by studying the history of Westphalian sovereignty, concludes that sovereignty is an enduring form of organized hypocrisy. He enumerates cases of violation of the principle from its very inception at the Treaty of Westphalia in 1648 by the interference of powerful states in the domestic affairs of weak states that they supposedly recognized as independent. He asserts that, in comparison, international legal sovereignty has been more widely honoured, despite exceptional cases in which it is extended to undeserving entities while being denied to deserving ones. He cites the Order of Malta as representing the former case and Taiwan as exemplifying the latter. He concludes that the fundamental cause for the hypocritical way in which sovereignty is upheld is the absence of an effective means of enforcement. Hence, in practice, powerful states are, and have always been, more sovereign than weaker ones because they can more easily impose conditions on, or interfere in the domestic affairs of weaker states in numerous open or hidden as well as direct and indirect ways.

There is a growing awareness, however, that the sovereignty of even such powerful states faces numerous forms of challenges in the post-Cold War world. Cusimano (2000: 1–40) discusses how the proliferation of trans-sovereign issues, concerns, and problems are defying traditional ideas of sovereignty. She enumerates these as environmental threats, refugee flows, and contagious diseases, as well as drug trafficking, terrorism, nuclear smuggling, and other international criminal activities. No single state, no matter how powerful, is currently in a position to single-handedly manage all these issues by itself. Neither is the existing world system of states geared to deal with these concerns collectively. The proliferation of trans-sovereign concerns is just one of many factors undercutting the traditional notion of sovereignty.

A number of emerging global concerns are, at the same time, starting to pose a challenge to the very *principle* of state sovereignty. One of these is the growing belief that sovereignty should no longer hinder the extension of humanitarian assistance to populations threatened by famine or other disasters. Similarly, the conviction is growing that respect of state sovereignty should not override the protection of human rights. These two trends in combination are thus threatening to eclipse the traditional notion of respect of sovereignty. But the subordination of the principle of respect of state sovereignty to these other competing ideals is far from being fully operational. The few tentative measures that were taken in the recent past at the expense of traditional sovereignty were unprecedented and could be the start of a growing trend or merely a passing phenomenon. While potential beneficiaries might welcome the emerging trend, it would not be surprising if the authority figures whose power and prestige are affected by this tendency display resistance and discomfort.

In addition, the *practice* of sovereignty is under increasing challenge due to a number of external as well as internal factors. Cusimano discusses at length how the globalizing dynamics of open markets, open societies, and open technologies constitute external trends that pose a challenge to the practice of sovereignty. These are, of course, not totally new but have escalated dramatically over the last couple of decades. They are posing a rising challenge to the principle of sovereignty by circumventing, ignoring, or practically opposing its relevance to their operations. Even the sovereignty of powerful states is susceptible to this challenge.

Cusimano also mentions that rising internal conflicts, growing subnational movements, and the increasing scarcity of resources can pose so great an internal challenge to the principle of sovereignty as to result in state collapse. At first glance this trend seems to challenge only the sovereign rights of weak states. But the growing phenomenon of collapsed states also affects powerful states in at least two different ways. First, collapsed states trigger an exodus of refugees, with some of these succeeding in their efforts to enter developed states despite all attempts to stem such flows. Second, and more threateningly, collapsed states afford safe havens to international criminal groups, such as drug traffickers, unscrupulous toxic-waste-disposal firms, and terrorists. All of these could significantly impact on the security of even powerful states. Hence, Cusimano's conclusion that "In the post-Cold War period, the security dilemma derives not from the dangers posed from strong states, but from the dangers stemming from weak and disintegrating states, and transsovereign activities of nonstate actors" (2000: 34) is quite a sobering observation. The relation between power and security is no longer as straightforward as it used to be. Meanwhile, power itself is on the move.

In the contemporary world, power is diffusing in every possible direction. Susan Strange (1994) lists ten different ways in which state sovereignty is being affected to draw a disturbing conclusion. She argues that power is moving vertically from weak states to strong states, as many states collapse into internal conflict or limp along as "quasi-states"; also that power is moving sideways from states to markets and some power is evaporating, as states abandon certain functions that no new actor assumes. Michael Keating draws a similar conclusion by asserting that "The state is challenged from above by international and supranational trends, from below by new territorial forces, and laterally by the advance of the market and of the self-regulating mechanisms of the civil society. This poses questions about the traditional meaning of sovereignty" (Keating 1998: 39). The traditional perception that power is concentrated in a specific location thus appears increasingly out of sync with reality.

The assumption that the legitimacy of modern states rests on their citizens' exercise of collective power through their elected officials never really applied to a large number of countries. The belief that citizens collectively, and through their elected officials, exercise power and determine the cost of security is becoming increasingly questionable even in states where such processes used to function fairly credibly. This is even more salient when it comes to the citizens' role in influencing economic policy as they are increasingly being asked to "accept the judgment of an international economy in which they have no formal political say" (Horsman and Marshall 1994: 89). This has always been the case for weak or developing countries, but it is now starting to affect even those of the developed world. Direct foreign investment has grown even in the advanced industrial countries to such an extent that it has started to erode their governments' control. Even the US "ceded considerable control over its economy to foreign investors … [holding] the power to keep the US economy growing or to plunge it into recession" (qtd. in Gelber 1997: 52). Loss of control is thus restricted neither only to weak states nor just the economy. The entire international system seems to be spinning out of control, according to Horsman and Marshall, who conclude that "Just as the ability of the state to run the nation has declined, so has the ability of any one country to run the international system of states which is its counterpart" (1994: 104). Scholars from wide-ranging disciplines are thus concluding that sovereignty in addition to being upheld hypocritically is now declining in principle as well as in practice.

The hypocritical practice of respecting sovereignty, so aptly put by Krasner, has in the past stood in the way of upholding the rights of peoples and human rights. Thus, the growing recognition of the hypocritical manner in which sovereignty is upheld and its declining practical effectiveness could have positive implications for the rights of individuals and communities. This evolving trend could give rise to new opportunities for enforcing the respect of rights, including the right to self-determination. An ironic situation in which self-determination is at the same time the exercise of sovereignty as well as its denial used to stand in the way of such enforcement. The regimes of some states love to demonstrate the exercise of their sovereign rights by acceding to international conventions, including those dealing with the respect of human rights and peoples' rights. Once the signing ceremony is over, however, such regimes go on violating these rights with impunity by invoking the same principle of sovereignty. For far too long, the internal dimension of self-determination has lived in the shadow of external sovereignty. Many influential leaders are now recommending that this practice be brought to an end. Boutros-Ghali (1992: 9), as the UN General Secretary, offered in his *Agenda for Peace* the recommendation that "The time of absolute and exclusive sovereignty... has passed; its theory was never matched by reality. It is the task of leaders of States today to understand this and to find a balance between the needs of good internal governance and the requirements of an ever more interdependent world." Dealing particularly with the ironic opposition between sovereignty and self-determination, he offered the following recommendation: "The sovereignty, territorial integrity and independence of States within the established international system, and the principle of self-determination for peoples, both of great value and importance, must not be permitted to work against each other in the period ahead" (Boutros-Ghali 1992: 10). Both of his recommendations, if followed, could easily diminish many demands for self-determination that are fuelled by bad governance and the refusal to devolve power. And the emerging attempt to end the artificial dissonance between self-determination and sovereignty could go a long way to resolve the issue in cases where an internal accommodation becomes demonstrably unworkable.

The State: No Longer Truly National

Modern states are presumed to be national states, or at least national-states-in-the-making. The two terms, "nation" and "state," are often used interchangeably. The practice of treating "nation" and "state" as synonymous terms is, however, now becoming increasingly questionable. One of nationalism's pre-eminent scholars, Ernest Gellner, asserts that culture and social organization are universal to human history and the state and nationalism are not. He defines culture as "a shared style of expression in words, facial expression, body language, style of clothing, preparation and consumption of food, and so forth" (1997: 1). Language (expression in words) could, of course, be identified as the most enduring and central feature and carrier of culture. According to Gellner, nationalism is "the principle that homogeneity of culture is the political bond, that mastery of a given high culture is the pre-condition of political, economic and social citizenship" (1997: 29). The corollary to this notion is that those who do not satisfy this condition must "accept second-class and subservient status" or "must assimilate, or migrate, or seek to change the situation through irredentist nationalist activity." Gellner historicizes the emergence of this notion in the western tip of the European continent at the time of rising industrialization. Even those who disagree with Gellner's modernist view of the birth of nations do accept that several West European states (Spain, France, the Netherlands, Denmark, Sweden, and Portugal) evolved into nations earlier than any others (Hastings 1997: 8). The idea of a state that is also national spread to the rest of the world partly through imitation, competition, and imposition. Achieving congruence between the cultural and the political community thus became an agenda for states around the world to pursue.

Gellner seems to imply that congruence between the cultural and political communities was achieved in Western Europe because cultural homogenization had preceded the birth of the nation-state. He thus appears to agree with Cobban's view that the efforts of mediaeval monarchs had already brought into existence a number of recognizable nation-states in Western Europe by the sixteenth century (Cobban 1969: 28). If the congruence between the nation and state had been achieved in the countries of Western Europe, then why are we currently witnessing demands for self-determination being tabled by parts of their populations? The number of scholars who dismiss the belief that cultural homogenization has been completed in Western Europe is now on the rise. One of them, Oommen (1997), offers such a straightforward dismissal by asserting that "The ideology of homogenization as implied in the notion of the nation-state and in operation for the past five centuries in Europe did not accomplish its avowed objective" (1997: 145).

Oommen analyzes the track record of the homogenization project in three Western European states (Great Britain, France, and Germany) to support this assertion. He describes Great Britain as a veritable multinational state since people who refer to themselves as Welsh, Scottish,

Irish, English, or just British live within its borders (1997: 137). Another scholar, Michael Freeman (1999), offers a similar observation despite sticking to the tradition of using the terms "state" and "nation" interchangeably. He argues that the United Kingdom and Ireland constitute two nations (states more properly). However, "Sociologically, there are at least five (Irish, English, Scottish, Welsh and British)" in the two entities (1999: 45). He goes on to discuss how the precedent set by anticolonial movements encouraged minority nations in the "old states" (the Irish, Scots, Welsh, Bretons, Corsicans, Basques, Catalans, and others) to assert the right to national self-determination in various forms and by various means. And Britain is considered not only the oldest of these "old states" but also the quintessential nation-state in which the state and nation have achieved the highest degree of congruence. The nationalist movements of all the constituent peoples, other than those who call themselves either English or British, testifies to the inaccuracy of this impression.

France, one of those states that followed Britain in pioneering the nation-formation project, continues to harbour distinct cultural communities (nations) such as Bretons, Basques, Corsicans, and Occitanians. Oommen considers that the national movements of some of these, particularly that of the Occitanians, belong to "the great family of Third World nationalism" (1997: 141). Bretons, Basques, and Corsicans also have organizations devoted to championing their national causes. Empirical studies are often used to demonstrate the absence of a fit between the state and nation as implied by the term "nation-state." For example, according to a 1970s study, some seventy-three nations (defined as speech communities) live spread within or across the borders of only twenty-four European states (Oommen 1997: 25). The great majority of the world's independent states (73 percent of them) are actually multinational states (van den Berghe 1992: 193). According to Beiner, only Iceland, South Korea, Japan, and "a few others" out of all the states in the contemporary world are sufficiently national to avoid current or potential demands for self-determination (Beiner 1998: 160).

Oommen concludes with a striking observation of the divide between the conception of the nation-state and the reality. He remarks that "the nation-state was only an aspiration, in fact an unfortunate aspiration, which was never realized *even in Western Europe*, and that, in pursuing this aspiration, numerous nations (usually smaller and weaker ones) within multinational states have been subjected to ethnification" (1997: 136; italics added). Elsewhere, he suggests that "the nation-state as an aspiration and as an ideal ought to be abandoned" (1997: 34). In a deliberately provocative essay, Pierre L. van den Berghe goes much further to denounce the so-called nation-building process as nation-killing, asserting "that the vast majority of so-called 'nation-states' are nothing of the sort; and that modern nationalism is a blueprint for ethnocide at best, genocide at worst" (1992: 191). He too recommends that the attempt to fuse the cultural (national) and the state community must be abandoned. And Duvenhage, by placing the ongoing trend within the evolving world, concludes that "The nation-state as a standardized political institution is going to be replaced (and has partially been replaced) by a large number, as well as a variety (potpourri) of political actors" (1998: 8).

No doubt, a greater degree of homogeneity has been achieved in developed countries like France and Italy. But this resulted from the erasure of the identity of a significant sector of the peoples residing within their borders. According to Guibernau, the number of speakers of Flemish, Basque, Celtic, and German languages in France could have been as high as 6 million (in excess of 20 percent of the total population) at the outbreak of the Revolution in 1789 (1996: 70). Today France is among those countries that qualify as nation-states since only 5 percent of its population habitually speaks a language other than the official one. How did it get to this stage? In the words of van den Berghe, "The *grande nation* only became so by ruthlessly suppressing the languages and traditions of a dozen *petites nations* all around the periphery of Ile de France: the Flemings, Bretons, Alsacians, Corsicans, Basques, and others. The blueprint for nation-building was born: ethnocide (the cultural suppression of ethnic and linguistic diversity), or genocide (the physical extermination of ethnics)" (1992: 196). Similarly, those who used Italian in their day-to-day communication constituted a minuscule 3 percent of the population at the time of the unification of Italy in 1861, according to Oommen (1997: 144). Hence a similar process to that which produced a more homogeneous population in France must have reversed the minority status of Italian speakers over the last century and a half.

The partial success of the homogenization project in these states took place alongside other developments that made it possible. Their economic, cultural, and social life was improving at a rapid pace. In addition, they were pursuing imperialist ambitions in other parts of the world, thus increasing opportunity and making assimilation to the ruling core society rewarding. As Stephen Castles states, "Colonialism was crucial to the emerging nation-states; exploitation of the natural resources and the labour power of dominated peoples made industrialization possible"

(1998: 224). Enhanced self-esteem and an ever-improving lifestyle accruing from industrialization made assimilation less painful in these earlier cases of nation-building. Continuing the same mission amidst rising poverty, dimming prospects for economic improvement, and ever-plummeting individual and collective self-esteem makes the futility of the project elsewhere indisputable. If the mission remained incomplete even where it was implemented under more conducive conditions, its result could only be devastation elsewhere.

In addition, the homogenization project was pursued in Europe at the time when pseudo-Darwinian thinking was more widespread and the extinction of the weak was seen as inevitable and even desirable. However, in the contemporary world the extinction of species is a cause of great concern. Hence, rescuing endangered species of insects, reptiles, birds, other animals and plants from extinction is one of the most emotive current global concerns. Advocating the preservation of non-human species while carrying out or condoning the elimination of human cultural groups thus poses a grave moral dilemma. The extension of ecological principles to humans, in fact, underscores the scientific wisdom of averting the erasure of identities. For example, Nietschmann considers the eight thousand or so language groups (nations) existing in today's world as "the only true or organic group identities and *crucial for the survival of the planet* because these nations have evolved through a harmonious relationship with the local environment" (qtd. in Herb 1999: 14; italics added). No one can guarantee the indefinite survival of all of these groups as distinct entities. In fact, the permanence of their existence seems to be quite unlikely. However, the manner by which they interact with other similar entities, mutate, and give rise to new ones does matter. Pierre van den Berghe makes an apt observation that "languages operate in a sort of marketplace of utility" (1992: 205), where they compete freely and survive, change, evolve, or disappear through a natural process so long as state intervention is lifted. Thus, if left solely to the inevitable process of entropy, such natural merger or differentiation of peoples could conceivably strengthen all of humanity. Their hastened extinction resulting from deliberate state actions could, however, rob humanity of the strains of culture, style of thinking, and other human traits, embodied in their personalities.

Increasing awareness of the incongruity between the state and nation is therefore compelling scholars to increasingly draw a distinction between the two. In his conclusion to an interesting essay on the impact of globalization on citizenship, Stephen Castles, recommends that "At the individual country level, citizenship must be based on the separation between nation and state" (1998: 241). In discussing the reality of the nation-states that make up the European Union, Anderson and Goodman assert that they actually often contain more than one nation (1999: 17). Similarly, Cusimano advises against treating nations and sovereign states as interchangeable (2000: 3). The rising insistence on treating "sovereign states" and "nations" as distinct categories was unthinkable only a few decades ago. The importance of this change cannot be overemphasized, for it is the presumed identity of nation and state that lies at the heart of the proliferating struggles for self-determination. The belief that all states are, or must be, nations has almost inevitably generated an urge to make states out of all nations. Lord Acton identified the absurdity of the nation-state idea when he wrote that "The greatest adversary of the rights of nationality is the modern theory of nationality. By making the state and nation commensurate with each other in theory, it reduces practically to a subject condition all other nationalities that may be within the boundary. It cannot admit them to equality with the ruling nation which constitutes the state because the state would then cease to be national, which would be a contradiction of the principle of its existence" (qtd. in Ryan 1998: 76).

Stephen Castles exposes a similar contradictory picture of the nation by looking at the relation between national identity and citizenship. He asserts that "citizenship is meant to be universalistic and above cultural difference, yet it exists only in the context of a nation-state, which is based on cultural specificity; on the belief in being different from other nations" (Castles 1998: 230). It is in recognition of this contradiction that he recommends that the state and nation be separated. Such reconceptualization of both the state and the nation may not eliminate all demands for self-determination, but it seems to offer a better opportunity for reducing the number of such demands and holds out hope for a less destructive settlement of others. Such reconceptualization will be the subject of the next chapter.

The People

Now we come to the third conceptual pillar of modern statehood, a clearly defined *people* category. The *people* category is experiencing another form of diversification, in addition to the one discussed above, in the contemporary era. Determining just who constitutes the *people* category became the subject of a fierce contest once the notion of sovereignty was detached from the person of the hereditary sovereign and rearticulated as popular sovereignty. The people who voluntarily pooled their inalienable individual rights to shape their collective sovereignty became citizens. Agreeing that all hereditary authority figures need to be excised from the rest of society to define the *people* proved far easier than reaching a consensus on the criteria for inclusion (see chapter 1). In fact, the emphasis was initially more on finding new pretexts for exclusion. Gender was the least controversial criterion for excluding some—that is, all women—from political participation regardless of their competence and wealth. Narrowing the circle of males eligible for political participation, particularly suffrage, was achieved by imposing the criterion of property ownership.

The struggle over suffrage rights in the developed world continued to widen the *people* category first to result in the inclusion of all adult males. It was only after the First World War, however, that women's struggle for inclusion in the *people* category started making advances even in the developed world. The ever-widening embrace of the *people* category has now, at least in principle, culminated in adult suffrage becoming a universal norm. Gender, race, and religion thus should not stand in the way of an individual's participation in the politics of the state. This norm is now enshrined in numerous international conventions, although enforcing it globally has yet to be seriously attempted.

The form and content of the *people* category, however, are undergoing a new kind of evolution in the contemporary world. Two parallel trends are starting to emerge. First, the equalization of rights is narrowing the distinction between citizen and alien in some parts of world. Second, the loss of rights is blurring the distinction between the refugee and the citizen in other parts of the world. The former trend is evidenced by the extension of the right to vote to long-term foreign residents of some democracies. For example, in Belgium and the Netherlands such a practice has been in existence since 1985 (Feldblum 1998: 236). The new concept of *personhood* was thus coined, and it has started to compete with *citizenship* as a criterion for political participation. It became sensible to extend the right to vote to persons who were living and working in a foreign country for an extended period and thus paying taxes. Such a trend seems not only to be on the rise but is also occasioning the entertainment of totally unprecedented ideas about political rights. That Turks in Germany and Mexicans in California are demanding the right to vote in their countries of origin as well as in the states where they are residing would have been unthinkable only a few decades ago. In addition, social services, usually reserved for citizens, are also being extended to asylum seekers and other aliens in many countries, thus further blurring the distinction between alien and citizen (Feldblum 1998: 236–38). The *people* category is thus starting to expand and to become much more than just those persons who are permanently and uniquely attached to the territory of a specific state. The human composition of states has not yet become as diverse as that of the departure lounge of a major international airport, but it is moving in that direction. Mobile persons now tend to be attached to more than one state, an unthinkable idea only a few decades ago.

A similar blurring of the distinction between alien and citizen is taking place in undemocratic states due to the equalizing process of loss of security and other rights. In large parts of the world, undemocratic neighbouring states are engaged in the mutual exchange of refugees. A state that serves as a safe haven for persons from its neighbour often simultaneously jeopardizes the safety of its own residents, thus driving them across the same border crossed by the refugees it is hosting. Insecurity and loss of rights thus objectively equalize the status of both categories. In some cases, refugees end up playing a decisive role in the politics of the host country, affecting the fate of its populace in a dramatic way. The growth of this trend has implications for state and regional security particularly in large parts of Africa.

The most outstanding such case is the involvement of long-term Rwandan refugees in the armed struggle that installed a new regime in Uganda, the host country. This involvement served as a rehearsal—indeed, as a springboard—for the Rwandan exiles to return and capture state power in Rwanda, the home country that most of them left as mere infants. Such experience informs the present regime in Rwanda of the danger posed by exiles living in an adjacent state. Its determination to deny its antagonists any chance of repeating its own strategy to capture power has led it to invade and occupy parts of the Congo. The result has been increasing regional insecurity, prompting other states to interfere. The overall result is pervasive insecurity for states, communities, and individuals throughout the whole zone.

Refugee flow is identified as one of the factors that pose a challenge to the sovereignty of even powerful states, as has already been discussed. The presence of a large number of exiles within their borders could have implications for such states' foreign policy. For example, Germany had to take into consideration the implications of Serb exiles in the country when thinking about participation in the Kosovo intervention. Although it was not the only factor that influenced German hesitation to intervene in Kosovo, it did play a significant role. Looking at another case, the City of Toronto was burdened with an unexpected expenditure of several millions of dollars to police the protracted Serb protest marches during the same event. The result was a contention between the city, provincial, and federal governments over who should ultimately foot the bill. If a brief, internationally sanctioned intervention could trigger such controversies and policy dilemmas, one wonders what would happen in the case of an actual drawn-out war. The internment of emigrants from a belligerent state, as happened during the Second World War in North America, could very well become a burdensome proposition as well as posing a grave moral dilemma.

Regimes that instigate refugee outflows may not necessarily enhance their security with the departure of recalcitrant elements. Support for armed opponents of such regimes may no more be restricted to refugee camps in adjacent countries. Emigrants who have settled in the developed world are following the precedents set by the Irish, the Jews, and the Palestinians in continuing to support their kinfolk in their home countries. Modern transportation and communications facilitate this solidarity like never before. While extending moral and material assistance to their compatriots, such exiles also lobby their host countries to influence policy concerning their home country. Thus, the formal diplomacy of oppressive regimes is countered by the informal advocacy of such groups, who as adopted citizens of democratic states can demand to be heard. The government of Sri Lanka, for example, had to lobby Canadian officials to stem the flow of financial backing to the Tamil Tiger insurgents from Canadian Tamils. In addition, exiles living thousands of kilometres away from the area of initial conflict could (and do) get embroiled in new forms of conflict with other refugees or supporters and officials of the state that drove them out. The most advanced and determined among them could be involved in acts of terror, thus affecting the security of their adopted country.

The *people* category is also changing due to another development. When the notion of the melting pot was predominant, the homogeneity of countries receiving immigrants was supposed to be affected only temporarily. The melting pot idea was of course born in North America at a time when mostly white, Western European Christians arrived there and appeared to melt, within a couple of generations, into the social milieu around them. Stephen Castles identifies two ways in which current trends of migration differ from these previous ones. First, the scale and speed with which it is taking place is higher. And second, current immigrants come from "areas increasingly distant—not only in kilometres but in cultural terms" (1998: 227). The source of immigrants has hence moved to non-white and non-Christian parts of the world and these immigrants are increasingly seen as "the irreducible Other" within societies that are ever more multiethnic. Gelber asks whether this situation is resulting in the replacement of "assimilation" in the US by the "salad-bowl" of "self-consciously hyphenated Americans?" (1997: 70). The melting of these distinct immigrants is bound to prove at least much more gradual than in the past because of other contemporary pressures. The relative ease and speed of transportation and communications is likely to encourage immigrants to sustain contacts with the home country, thus postponing for a longer time their assimilation into the larger society, presuming that it does ultimately take place. The survival of immigrants as ethnic communities, despite their dispersion throughout the society of adoption, could be much more sustained. Ethnic identity is thus bound to survive alongside new identities resulting from residence in a new country and engagement in new professions. Not only are individuals and collectivities bound to have multiple identities, but countries are also likely to become more multiethnic and multicultural than in the past. Hence, Oommen's observation that "the United States of America has become a veritable multi-cultural and poly-ethnic state" (1997: 4) is bound to apply to more and more metropolitan countries. The traditional concept of national identity is bound to shift as a result. The form of the *people* category has thus fundamentally changed. Not only the national diversity of states, but also their ethnic heterogeneity, is bound to increase and prove more enduring than was once expected.

Territory

I shall now make a few brief remarks about the final element out of which modern nation-states are presumed to be shaped: *territory*. I have already remarked on the shifting linkage between territory and citizenship. Territory (i.e., land) used to be one of the most important factors of economic activity. In fact, modern states' obsession with territorial control emanates from this importance. The territory of the so-called nation-states used to be seen as the arena of exclusive economic production and accumulation. However, "national boundaries are no longer barriers to the movements of factors of production, especially capital, because international capital markets are integrated to allow for almost instantaneous movements of funds" (Herbst 1997: 84). This mobility is not restricted to capital, as Cusimano observes that "The means of production, capital and labor are mobile, not fixed" (2000a: 317). Hence, the state's ability to control the economy by controlling the territory is proving increasingly difficult. In addition, the significance of territory as an economic factor is diminishing. In particular, "The new economic system is based on information, technology, services, which is less dependent on the control of territory" (Cusimano 2000a: 317). Moving capital into and out of states as well as moving production to a less expensive labour source, or vice versa, has become so fast and easy that the ability of state authorities to control the process has significantly diminished. Thus, Cusimano concludes "for states with modern, information-based economies, territory becomes passé—as does conflict over territory" (2000: 28).

Herbst enumerates four different ways in which the traditional "economies of scale" rationale for large states is eroding. We shall examine just the one that deals with the size and control of state territory. He posits that the possession of an advanced manufacturing capability coupled with a skilled labour force could create affluence despite the smallness of a state's territory or its lack of natural resources. He concludes that "Countries do not become rich today by mining a vast hinterland or by dint of large labor forces" (1997: 83). He lists Japan, Korea, and Taiwan as states that have managed to achieve spectacular economic development despite having "very little land" and being bereft of natural resources. One could enumerate the converse of this, situations in which large and well-endowed state territories have failed to stem economic stagnation and rising poverty. This fits in very well with Gellner's observation that "everyone knows now that the power and prestige of a nation depends on its annual rate of growth and its economic clout, and *not* on how much of the map it manages to paint with its own colour" (1997: 107; italics added). But the possession of an extensive and well-endowed territory itself alone does not assure a state's prosperity. Without sufficient capital and the necessary technology, human and natural resources could remain untapped, as they often do. Thus, the competition to attract the involvement of capital and technology in the economy of one's country is heating up. State authorities often display a willingness to shape their internal policy with the aim of enticing foreign investment. This willingness is abundantly demonstrated by the behaviour of diverse states and regimes. As Cusimano writes "the Chinese communist system, the Australian parliamentary system, and the Iranian theocracy are all simultaneously undertaking reforms to make themselves more attractive to investors' capital and technology flows" (2000a: 317). According to Scholte, governments now live in terror of being deserted by footloose global capital if they fail to provide sufficiently appealing taxation and regulation environments (1999: 132–53). This has compelled even the normally protectionist governments of Cuba and Myanmar to at least partially accommodate transborder capitalism's intention to intrude into their state territory. According to Scholte's argument, globalization is the growth of supraterritoriality, which is leading to a relaxing of the linkage between social relations and territorial space.

The correspondence that used to seem to exist between territory and identity is suffering similar erosion. Cusimano states that "Identity is becoming less tied to territory. If identity and authority do not stem from geography, what is our new church, our new religion?" (2000a: 318). The rupture between territory and identity is widening due to a number of growing trends. For instance, the number of people who regularly cross state boundaries or who are continuously on the move has never been so great. And for such individuals identity is complex. It is affected by, and in turn affects, the locales where they have stayed and are staying. While they will wish to emphasize some elements of their identity, they will be ambivalent about others. In comparison to those who remain in their places of birth, the number of such persons may be minuscule. But their number is rising, and they also impact on the attitude of those remaining behind. Most of these are of course situated at the bottom of the world's labour market. A similar change is also taking place at the top end of the labour pool. State elites (state policies too) are increasingly transnational, according to Anderson and Goodman (1999: 17). The constituencies of states have become partially globalized, according to Scholte, turning states into "an arena of collaboration and competition between a complex array of territorial and supraterritorial interests" (1999: 140). Globalized interest groups or constituencies may be smaller in comparison to the bulk of the population that remains tied to the nation-states, as Anderson and Goodman observe, but their continued expansion does look quite plausible. In addition, since their economic and political clout more than compensates for their numerical minority, we can expect their desire to shape the world to fit their own identity and interests will have significant implications.

The availability of resources of international importance, such as petroleum, could actually pose a great danger to the survival of communities. We are witnessing the eradication of communities to pave the way for the exploitation of such resources in the Sudan, Nigeria, Angola, Algeria, and elsewhere. In addition, the exploitation of such resources could make state leaders more dependent on transnationals than on the consent of the populace. (For a discussion of Nigeria's case, see Samatar 1999: 23-24.) The recent armed conflicts in Sierra Leone, Liberia, and Angola were sustained by the existence of easily exportable natural resources. Hence, some African states suffer instability as a consequence of being well endowed with natural resources, while others suffer due to their absence.

The Emerging Alternative

The elements out of which modern independent statehood is supposedly constructed (sovereignty, people, nation, territory) are undergoing noticeable changes. Some of these changes are simply the recognition of the imaginary nature of the correspondence between these elements that supposedly underpins the modern state. Other changes are attracting attention now because globalization has risen to new heights. Established concepts and practices often undergo significant changes before they are replaced with their successors. And different facets of those concepts and practices may change at different times and rates. As we are now witnessing, all the component concepts of statehood are experiencing changes at the same time in the contemporary world. Although traditional notions about the state have not yet been overthrown, the growing recognition of change has started to motivate the conceptualization of possible alternatives.

One obviously cannot state with absolute certainty whether the emerging conceptions of the state will eventually replace existing perceptions and practices. Awareness of the fluid nature of the contemporary state is essential especially when its legitimacy and relevance are subjects of contest. Unfortunately, most state authorities and their wannabe successors continue to display a mentality that takes these elements as fixed, and they remain oblivious of the changes that are taking place all around them. They end up fighting over powers and principles that are steadily becoming obsolete. Recognition of this dynamic situation, on the other hand, would enable them to frame their respective positions in new terms and fitting into the unfolding context. Such a reframing of the issues could open up the way for new and innovative resolutions to the struggles regarding the control and projection of states.

Reconceptualizing a number of concepts, including the principle of self-determination, could stem, if not avert, continued meaningless or destructive conflicts over the control of states. The state, the nation, the ethnic community and the principle of self-determination all appear ripe for redefinition, when seen against the changes enumerated above. Reconceptualizing any one of these, of course, has implications on how the others are understood and handled. The intimate interrelation between them makes this inevitable. The following remarks are not, and cannot be, a final and absolute redefinition of these concepts, as the dynamism of the post-Cold War world seems to be just taking off. What I am attempting here should be taken as no more than a tentative suggestion of the direction in which the contemporary world seems to be evolving.

The Architecture of the Emerging State

The concept of the state as the sole repository of authority that demands the undivided allegiance and loyalty of those residing within its clearly delimited borders, and which imposes a single master identity, is undergoing noticeable changes. While state authorities and their political opponents continue to invoke these attributes of the state, a growing number of authorities are grappling with the articulation of alternative ways of conceptualizing the state to bring it more in line with heightened globalization. Numerous authorities from diverse disciplines are recognizing the need to articulate alternative ways of structuring the state to address the diverse challenges accompanying increasing globality. Instead of perceiving the nation-state as the ultimate and immutable framework of social organization framework, it is now increasingly regarded as just one variety of humanity's diverse ways of organizing its affairs. As Cusimano states "Human history is the unfolding story of numerous and varying social organizing frameworks" (2000: 23). The 350-year record of the nation-state as such an organizing framework should not lead us to expect that it could endure for as long a period of time in the future, she advises.

Others believe the model of the nation-state could wisely be superseded by newer forms of organization. Such is the view of the historian Adrian Hastings, who posits "the model of a nation-state, which could seldom fit social reality without grave injustice to numerous minorities, may well be wisely superseded by arrangements which stress both smaller and larger units of power and administration" (1997: 7). His anticipation of its replacement emerges from the recognition of the crimes inherent in the pursuit of the nation-state agenda.

Cusimano's search for an alternative framework for organizing the particular and global affairs of humanity, however, results from her study of trans-sovereign concerns that defy the sovereignty of contemporary states. She enumerates the globalizing forces that are pushing the world in a new direction as open markets, open technologies, and open societies.

Changes in the economy, in the nature of emerging elite groups, and in ideas are accompanying the growth of these globalizing forces. Similar changes had served as a midwife when feudal Europe, after a long period of gestation, gave birth to the modern form of the state. She wonders if history is not repeating itself. Is the contemporary world cohabited by the existing political organizing framework and its potential successor, reminiscent of the circumstance that prevailed during the long, drawn-out transition from feudalism in Europe? She seems to think so by stating that "while no new form of political organization has unseated the sovereign state, new forms are beginning to emerge around the sovereign state that are chipping away at functions previously performed by the state and changing the role of the state" (Cusimano 2000a: 321). Contrary to the drawn-out nature of the transition from feudalism, this new leap could happen much more rapidly due to faster and easier communications and transportation, she believes. Ideas and changes in politics and lifestyles disseminate at a much faster rate, impelling the world's society onto a new stage. Her question as to whether we are entering a new uncharted stage in world history is answered in the affirmative by some authorities.

The future has already arrived; we just didn't know it, say Anderson and Goodman (1999). They go a little further than Cusimano in elaborating the features of the emerging form of the state. Using a neo-Marxist analysis of globalized capital's behaviour, they conclude that a new state structure is already becoming a reality. The "state monopoly" and the current "transnational" tendencies of capitalism should not be conceived as being mutually exclusive trends, they write. Although one of the tendencies might dominate at one particular stage in history the other can, and does, continue to operate alongside it. Transnationalism, which was dominant in the nineteenth century, has been in the ascendant since the 1970s as enterprises have increasingly connected and operated across national (state) boundaries. By basing their argument on the survival of enterprises tied to the territories of existing states alongside the prevailing transnationalism of capitalism, they dismiss the impression that states are in terminal decline (Anderson and Goodman 1999: 19). This stands in stark contrast to Oommen's categorical assertion that "Western Europe, the birthplace of the nation-state has become or is becoming its graveyard, with the emergence of the European Union" (1997: 4). According to Anderson and Goodman, however, the European Union would not lead to the end of nation-states or a federalized United States of Europe "but perhaps instead a process of 'arrested federalization'—an 'intermediate' arrangement which is distinct in its own right rather than transitional to a 'post-national' Europe" (1999: 18). Thus, they believe a more complex form of structure is evolving in response to the ambiguity of capitalism's behaviour as neither purely "transnational" nor strictly "national" during the current phase of heightened globalization.

They believe that states, instead of withering away, are being reconfigured simulating a complex structure that prevailed in medieval times. Such a reconfiguration appears most advanced in developed states, where attempts are being made to adjust to the rising transnational behaviour of capitalism. The "growth of 'common markets,' suprastate bodies, and various functional regimes and political communities not delimited primarily in territorial terms," (Anderson and Goodman 1999: 20) they believe, is reminiscent of what used to prevail in medieval Europe. Political authority in medieval Europe was shared between feudal knights and barons, kings and princes, guilds and cities, bishops, abbots, and the papacy. Power, in addition to being functionally divided into the temporal and spiritual spheres, was also associated with territories that were fluid and discontinuous. Anderson and Goodman believe Bull's 1977 anticipation that growing European integration could herald a partial restoration of a similar order, which he named New Medievalism, is becoming a reality.

Conceptualizing the growing integration of Europe within this context of New Medievalism serves as a convenient tool for clarifying a number of misconceptions and controversies revolving around the process, Anderson and Goodman assert. It affords a new perspective, which reveals an underlying unity between opinions that on the surface appear opposed to each other. The debate between the "realists" who advocate intergovernmentalism and the "Euroenthusiasts" who anticipate the birth of a federal new Europe falls into this category. Both sides are united in adhering to the existing state framework when articulating their respective positions. However, neither a federal Europe nor the continuation of the traditional notion of the nation-state is resulting from the unfolding reality, in the view of Anderson and Goodman. They conclude that "Instead of getting caught up in the debate between 'realists' stressing intergovernmentalism and 'Euro-enthusiasts' stressing federalism, we should recognize that in broad terms 'the future' may have already arrived—neither a simple continuation of the modern system of states nor a federal state in embryo, but something quite different from both, an 'intermediate' confederal form which is distinct in its own right rather than merely transitional'" (1999: 26). The current stage should thus be considered to be "late" rather than "post" modernity, in their view. During this grey period, all we can do is seek analogies for conceptualizing the nature of the coming order. Thus "'medieval' and 'pre-modern' analogies are suggestive of future possibilities, and indeed they highlight the multiple levels and overlaps of territoriality which already exist as the mosaic of nation states and national communities is increasingly overlain with other forms of community and authority" (Anderson and Goodman 1999: 31).

Such an overlap of multiple allegiances and connections is not restricted to the European Union. The trend is noticeable in other parts of the world as well. Elazar believes that the diverse forms of structures created to account for the interdependence of supposedly independent state entities is creating a paradigm shift. He expands the meaning of "federation" to include existing federal state structures such as the us and Canada, confederations, and other confederal arrangements, associated states, special inter-state joint authorities with constitutional standing, and others. Such ways of pooling authority generate the simultaneous conclusion of pacts to institute numerous parallel horizontal as well as vertical relationships. Looking at just one example will help demonstrate the complexity of the trend and the inadequacy of existing terms to define it. The us, itself a federation, has federal arrangements with Puerto Rico and the Northern Marianas. The fifty states of the us constitute a single federal unit that has now formed another type of federal arrangement with these two other entities. What then is a federation? There is another parallel development. Indigenous Indian nations, whose residual sovereign rights were always recognized by the us (at least in principle), are now starting to institute more coherent strategies and structures of self-government. When these associations are seen in combination with all the interstate bodies to which the us belongs, a more complex picture starts to emerge. By analyzing the growth of these kinds of complex inter-linkages, Elazar concludes that "It is not that states are disappearing; it is that the state system is acquiring a new dimension, one that began as a supplement and is now coming to overlay (and, at least in some respects, to supersede) the system that prevailed throughout the modern epoch" (1997: 94). The new trend heralds the end of an era when "every state strove for self-sufficiency, homogeneity, and, with a few exceptions, concentration of authority and power in a single center" and the dawn of a new epoch in which "all states have to recognize their interdependence, heterogeneity, and the fact that their centers, if they ever existed, are parts of a multicentered network that is increasingly noncentralized, and that all of this is necessary in order to survive in the new world" (Elazar

1997: 94). His conclusion comes very close to Cusimano's in one respect and Anderson and Goodman's in another. Like Cusimano, he believes the traditional state system is operating alongside something new. And like Anderson and Goodman, he seems to hint that the emerging structure is overtaking the structure formerly associated with states. Unlike them, however, he does not attach the appellation New Medievalism to the emerging structure.

The emerging New Medievalism has important implications for conceptualizing the process of state integration or disintegration. Anderson and Goodman's description of what is happening in Europe could apply to other similar cases. The evolving New Medieval structure "would not require anything as clear-cut as the 'death' of the nation state, a proliferation of successful separatisms or a federal European 'superstate.' These would simply increase or decrease the number of states, a quantitative but not a qualitative change in the state forms. Instead, a new 'medievalism' would emerge when the pressures on the state 'from above and below' achieved more partial and ambiguous changes: sovereignty undermined and diffused rather than clearly relocated" (1999: 25). Their designation of a federal "United States of Europe" and separatist "regional governments" as merely scale replicas of existing states, the state "writ large" in the former and "writ small" in the latter is of fundamental importance. Bull blamed the "*the tyranny of existing concepts and practices*" for the tendency of both the integrationists and separatists to be "drawn towards solutions which would result simply in the creation of new sovereign states" (1977: 267; italics added). He forwarded an alternative vision, stating that "Perhaps the time is ripe for the enunciation of new concepts of universal political organization which would show how Wales, the United Kingdom and the European Community could each have some world political status while none laid claim to exclusive sovereignty." His prescience is actually being borne out by ongoing attempts to realize such a peculiar relationship between Wales (as well as Scotland and Northern Ireland), United Kingdom, and the EU, as I will touch upon later on. The relevance of framing how demands for self-determination are posed within the evolving political organizational framework goes beyond Europe to apply to all cases. Destructive and quite often avoidable conflicts look inevitable so long as aspirants for self-determination and their opponents continue to frame their positions by adhering to the concepts traditionally associated with the modern state. In Europe, experiments to adjust the state form to incorporate, defuse, or redirect pressures on the existing state are underway. Some of the states that are not experimenting with this kind of adjustment are gradually lurching towards the status of "quasi-states" or are suffering virtually unstoppable atrophy.

Anderson and Goodman promote New Medievalism as the more appropriate description of the trend that is resulting from European integration. Another authority, Ernest Gellner, prescribes the restoration of a similar structure by focusing on the challenges facing contemporary states. He points to two apparently opposite but complementary processes unfolding in the advanced industrial world. First, the ready availability of technology to manufacture nuclear and biological weapons poses a growing security threat that necessitates a centralized control regime. This scenario dictates the creation of a supranational authority. Second, the prospect of local interest groups achieving industrial affluence depends on their ability to successfully organize and mobilize their collective potential. The proliferation of regional interest groups could be attributed to this second tendency. Gellner then proceeds to draw his conclusion: "If these two trends are really in operation, the consequence may eventually be that the advanced industrial world will once again, *like the agrarian world of the past,* be one in which *effective political units* will be either larger or smaller than 'national' units based on similarity of culture. Just as, once upon a time, city-states were sub-ethnic and empires were super-ethnic, so the agencies preventing nuclear and ecological disaster, controlling the drugs and arms trades, and so on, will have to be super-ethnic, while the agency administering the school and welfare system may become sub-ethnic. This is a hope rather than a prediction, but it is not an unreasonable hope" (1997: 107; italics added). He offers the term "cantonization" as a description for this new political organizational framework in which larger political units come into existence simultaneous with the emergence of greater local autonomy.

Gellner is hence suggesting that the project of matching the state and the nation should be revised. Social organization at the local, state, and interstate levels should not necessarily be tied to cultural homogeneity. Such a linkage may be necessary for some functions and not for others. The challenge of instituting such a flexible and functionally determined architecture of states would be quite daunting. Fortunately, the problems that demand such restructuring are confronting the wealthy and powerful as well as the weak and impoverished. Hopefully, the world will mobilize its intellectual and other resources to bring about the necessary changes before being goaded into doing so by some major catastrophe.

The Functions of the Emerging State

Changes in the functions of states are naturally occurring alongside the structural changes discussed above. Some of these changes in the function of states result from deliberate actions of state authorities while others force themselves upon reluctant state officials, and still others just happen. Developed states, in particular, are experimenting with new forms of organizational frameworks, as can be witnessed with the EU in Europe and NAFTA in North America. These are being developed in response to the enhanced globalization of our times.

Other pressures are necessitating the deepening, widening, and entrenching of the trend to pool state power. Among these can be counted the heightened transnational posture of capital, the globe-encompassing impacts of the environment, and the menace resulting from trade in drugs and nuclear materials. At the same time, sub-state entities are demanding more powers over the affairs that impact on their day-to-day lives. Attempts to craft a new kind of state architecture are being made in some parts of the world. Attitudes about state functions are undergoing a similar change.

In such states, some of the functions traditionally monopolized by individual states are being transferred to supra-national bodies. Other functions are being downloaded to sub-state bodies and communities. Some of the states' traditional functions are being privatized. As Cusimano states, "The state, it would appear, is not going away; the state is contracting out…. The state is contracting out functions to a number of actors simultaneously: IGOs [Intergovernmental Organizations], NGOs [Non-governmental Organizations], MNCs [Multinational Corporations] and local governments" (2000a: 317). Not all of these instances of contracting out are necessarily for the better, but occasions where they enhance the direct involvement of local communities in running their affairs should be welcomed and emulated. This would have important implications for the topic under discussion, self-determination.

What Guibernau identifies as the principle on which the EU is based could serve as an ideal guideline when carrying out the measure of "contracting out" to local governments. She says that European integration is based on the belief that nothing should be done at a higher level that can be done more effectively at a lower level. In particular, "Government and services to the citizens should be *controlled* and *administered* as near the point of delivery as possible" (1996: 113; italics added). Guibernau seems to think in conventional terms. Hence, she sees European federalism as the only framework that would afford protection to the non-state nations living within and across the borders of the member states: "A decentralized, federal, democratic Europe would not only respond to sound economic arguments, but would also offer an adequate framework within which nations without a state could preserve and develop their culture" (1996: 113). States and regional suprastate bodies founded on the above principles can afford to recognize non-state nations and allow them to govern themselves. And they can easily carry out constitutional changes that can reconcile national diversity and state unity by conceding a fair amount of autonomy. Decentralization alone would not permanently end tensions and conflicts, however, unless it is accompanied by a redefinition of the role of the joint state, asserts Guibernau. The joint state of the nations making up the multinational entity should be transformed "into a purely administrative device which co-ordinates the policies of its different nations and parts of nations" (Guibernau 1996: 108). States have developed the habit of responding to global problems and concerns of the contemporary world by creating suprastate bodies and intergovernmental organizations. At the same time, however, most of them are less willing to share their authority and sovereignty with internal groups. The effectiveness and legitimacy of the former trend, however, will remain deficient without the latter form of power-sharing. It would also be ironic to prefer pooling sovereignty with supposed aliens while refusing to do so with supposed fellow nationals. Hence, it is only logical for the two trends to coincide and buttress each other than putting them on a course of opposition. The state that reflects the support and inputs of all its constituent nations would need to redefine its function in order to remove traditional state roles that used to impinge on the equality of its nations.

Thus, the functions of the state have to be redefined in order to transform it into a purely administrative device for coordinating the policies of the nations that make it up. One important traditional function of the state has to be abandoned for this to happen. The project of turning all the inhabitants of the state into one culturally and linguistically homogeneous nation needs to end. Only such a condition could resolve the antipathetic nationalism that non-state nations feel towards the multinational states in which they find themselves. If states were denationalized, the urge to turn all nations into states would at least diminish, if not be rendered totally redundant. This is the thrust of Pierre van den Berghe's argument. Just as secularization of the state once helped to dissipate intractable interreligious conflicts, the denationalization of the state could diminish conflicts resulting from identity politics, he opines:

"Ideally, the state should not be associated with any particular group, but should be the neutral common property of all its citizens. I am simply advocating an extension of the principle of secularization in the religious sphere to language and other cultural domains. Much as the state should tolerate all religions but be associated with none, the state should also be 'denationalized'" (1992: 205). The proclivity of homogenization to generate reactive nationalism and the attendant propagation of conflicts should not really come as a surprise since it was present at the birth of Western European nationalisms. The linkage between the rise of nationalism and the project to homogenize societies was pointed out by Treitschke when he wrote that the explosion of nationalism in Europe was due to a "natural revulsion against the world-empire of Napoleon. The unhappy attempt to transform the multiplicity of European life into the arid uniformity of universal sovereignty has produced the exclusive sway of nationality as the dominant political idea" (Guibernau 1996: 12). The states that were created in rejection of "arid uniformity" in turn pursued the realization of the same objectives within their borders to make nation and state coterminous. Two hundred years later, and after tensions within and major wars between them, these pioneers of the nation-building ideal have yet to fully achieve their aspiration.

The time has come to remove nation-building and the homogenization agenda that it entails from the functions of states throughout the world. One of the rationales for nation-building is the conviction that plurality hampers democratic participation and thus stability and prosperity. Oommen, after refuting a linkage between increasing homogeneity and enhanced prosperity and stability, concludes, "If this is really the case, the doctrine of homogeneity and its institutional vehicle, namely, the nation-state, should be given a decent burial" (1997: 197). Giving up the homogenization mission will have implications for the very definition of what the state should be. Oommen's definition, which is consistent with this situation, is that "The state is a legally constituted institution, which provides its residents with protection from internal insecurity and external aggression" (1997: 19).

INTRODUCTION

TODAY'S WORLD IS EXPERIENCING rapidly unfolding change, but has not yet produced a new reality. Hence, concepts, institutions, and practices that are on their way out exist side by side with those that remain pertinent even as new, unprecedented ones are beginning to exert their influence. However, political actors, as is often the case during such times, continue to employ traditional concepts of the state and nation when framing their positions for or against the rising demands for self-determination. State authorities continue to harp on such concepts as sovereignty, territorial integrity, and national independence when in reality they are conceding these attributes of modern statehood, whether willingly or unwillingly, to growing internal and external pressures discussed earlier. Thus, they often appear to be defending powers that they don't really exercise in full. Those who are pursuing self-determination in order to create smaller replicas of existing states find themselves in a comparable situation. They are fighting for powers that they too would not exercise in full. Interdependence, at the regional and global levels, has been on the rise since the end of the Second World War, and it imposes severe limitations on the degree of independence of existing and potential states, as Elazar (1997: 91) notes. This phenomenon has been occurring at a more rapid rate particularly in the post-Cold War period and is likely to continue to do so for the foreseeable future. A qualitative transformation of people-to-state relations would thus appear to be a better response than merely a quantitative growth or a decrease in the number of states. However, this option is often disregarded by those who demand independent statehood as well as those who oppose such a demand. Both sides articulate their respective positions by overlooking the limitations placed on actual independence by the logic of rising regional and global interdependence. They are stuck with traditional notions of the state while the architecture and functions of the state are undergoing major shifts. Thus, the field is left free for the "tyranny of established concepts and practices" to continue to wreak havoc on the lives and livelihoods of more and more societies.

Clearly, those who are working for self-determination can hope to play a progressive role only if they manage to situate their political discourse within the positive aspects of emerging global political trends. Their demands must be articulated in terms that indicate their awareness of the changed architecture and function of the state. As Michael Keating writes, "Since the state itself is changing in form and functions, so must nationalist doctrine and strategy, and we can see the re-emergence of minority nationalism as in part a response to these changes" (1998: 38). One should not underestimate the challenge posed by such a rearticulation of nationalist doctrine and strategy. As Watson remarks, "all too many statesmen, the media and popular opinion glorify independence" (1997: 2). But dispensing with the familiar doctrines and strategies whose emotive power is proven is indisputably very difficult, although it is very much in need.

There is yet another challenge. Political mobilization often demands a simplification of concepts and practices. Unfortunately, the world in which we operate is complex and is becoming increasingly so. Unless this is accounted for, however, the simplistic pronouncements of political actors will not only remain out of sync with reality but will also be untranslatable into constructive practice. The end result will only be the ultimate disillusionment of the concerned constituencies, as has happened in Africa's experience with decolonization.

Identity Formulation: Defining the "Self"

Several points of departure appear necessary when rearticulating nationalist doctrine and strategy in order to render them more resonant with contemporary reality. The first concerns an identity formulation process that takes into account the complexity this entails. Second, such a formulation of identity should be based on respect for democracy and human rights and the willingness to rigorously uphold them. Admittedly, it is much easier to state this than to translate it into practice. As it is, determining the *people* or the *self* that deserves self-determination has always been very contentious. This difficulty stretches all the way back to the tumultuous events that kicked off the French Revolution. Only by learning from that and plentiful subsequent historical incidents can any group hope to avoid repeating the history of struggling for democracy and ending up reaping dictatorship. Struggles for the democratic rights of the "self" that are predicated on withholding the same rights from some "other" (be it on the basis of class, gender, or other forms of identity) have often ended up in instituting dictatorships. The policies, practices, and institutions, required to hold down the repressed "other" often rebound into the sphere of the "self" to erode the privileges supposedly accruing from the act of exclusion. It has often been remarked that "a nation that oppresses another cannot be free." Hence, rights should be articulated in as inclusive a manner as possible. Although such rights ought to address the aspirations of a specific human collectivity, they should be made to serve a more universal role of expanding the horizon of justice, equality, and freedom. Applying this principle to the right to self-definition is indisputably a daunting proposition, but it is imperative if the concerned collectivity and human society in general are to go forward.

There is a growing willingness to accept the principle that "the right to self-determination entails the right to self-definition" (Stavenhagen 1996: 7). Hence, the right to define the "self" belongs to the concerned collectivity. But the exercise of such a right, like any other right, is susceptible to numerous forms of abuse. One form of abuse results from an overextension of this right (the maximalist position), vesting any group with the right to designate itself a people and hence demand self-determination. This is one absurd limit to which the right to self-definition could be stretched. The resulting implications for the principle of self-determination look self-evident. It would demean and devalue the principle as well as turning it into a recipe for chaos and anarchy, as Stavenhagen (1996: 7) aptly puts. The other side of the pole (the minimalist position), insisting that only the collection of individuals residing within an existing state constitute the legitimate people, would amount to a negation of the right to self-definition. It would only serve the purpose of legitimating and sustaining the status quo that is being challenged. The existence of such extreme poles and the absurdity that they represent is, of course, not restricted to the right of self-definition and self-determination. Like many other concepts and principles, these too are liable to abuse. What is required is achieving a reasonable balance between the two extremes in order to turn the right to self-definition into a constructive exercise.

Determining just what constitutes such a reasonable exercise of the right to self-definition should not be left to a single profession, and least of all to government, in the view of Stavenhagen. "Moreover, it cannot and should not be done behind the backs of the peoples whose self-determination is at stake," he asserts. In his view, "What is needed now is a thoroughgoing collective effort to spell out the universal, rigorous criteria by which the defining characteristics of the claimants to self-determination will be accepted as widely as possible" (1996: 7). He joins a number of others in calling for the involvement of the international community, possibly through the creation of a special UN committee or commission, in drawing up these universal terms and other issues related to self-determination.

Definitively cataloguing the universally acceptable formulation of the "self," even by such bodies (if and when they come into existence), may not eliminate all controversy resulting from contests concerning identity. In the interim, and starting from the current position for respect of human rights and other democratic values, we can perhaps venture to suggest just what should be avoided. The urge to define the "self" in order to claim self-determination is often a response to the imposition of a master "national" identity by those who wield power. Thus, what claimants of self-determination should avoid is the common practice of replacing the imposed master identity with another. Denouncing the policy of state officials to build a single monolithic national identity on the graves of other identity types is certainly justifiable. Rejecting the construction of a monocultural state by the imposition of "arid uniformity" is entirely understandable. But aspiring to repeat the same errors of state officials, however, is not only ironic but also self-defeating, as it could serve as the starting point of another round of rejection and denunciation.

There is another side to this issue. While demanding its right to self-definition, a collectivity should remain open to others' invocation of the same right. There are numerous situations, however, that render such a reciprocal recognition of the right to self-definition well-nigh inoperable. Striking a fair balance between acknowledging cultural diversity and shaping a common political community is particularly difficult in situations of mutual hostility and suspicion. The only mindset that can break such a deadlock is the willingness of the concerned communities to accept the principle of a just recognition of each other's identities. "Just recognition" entails acknowledging "the 'inherent worth' of those whose identity is defined in terms different from our own" (O'Leary 1999: 104). The principle of just recognition of the other's inherent worth is particularly apt in divided communities that invoke their identities in a manner that admits little common ground. The absence of a common ground should not, however, preclude just recognition. Only when one side determines that the recognition of the "other" detracts from its own identity in unjust ways does recognition run into difficulties. Hence, any combination of the exercise of self-definition with the recognition of the "other" becomes just only when both sides give up the rhetoric, mentality, and acts of mutual annihilation. In addition, both sides must admit that the "other," just like the "self," deserves a dignified existence. One's dignity cannot and should not be premised on the humiliation of the "other." Only this willingness of communities to reach across cultural divides to grant each other mutual recognition and appropriate respect is likely to disarm extremist elements intent on playing the zero-sum game. Recognition of the complex nature of identity in today's world offers divided societies the best hope for salvation from cyclical conflicts and endless strife. Happily, this principle is starting to be observed is some parts of the world.

Keating discusses how the crisis of the welfare state in the West is generating responses that include identity politics of the older as well as a newer variety. He lists two of these responses as neo-liberalism's emphasis on hyper-individualism (which rejects the relevance not only of self-determination but also of society in the contemporary world) and an identity politics that denies the possibility of universal values or a public good and attributes interests to ascriptive identities. The latter kind of identity politics signals disregard for the principle of just recognition discussed above. It also signals the continuation of the practice to replace one master identity with another. A third response is "the construction of *new forms of collective identity* and action in both state and civil society which *recognize the limitations imposed by current conditions* as well as *the plurality and complexity of contemporary identities themselves.* One form of this is the new territorial politics, including some forms of minority nationalism" (Keating 1998: 40; italics added). This variety of identity politics can become meaningful and constructive because it is conscious of the limitations under which it is operating. For example, it cannot hope to succeed by constructing impermeable territorial or identity boundaries due to the current fluidity of both categories. In addition, it cannot discount the plurality and complexity of contemporary identities and still remain true to its advocacy of democracy and civil liberties. As Colley aptly states, "Identities are not like hats. Human beings can and do put on several at a time" (1992: 374). Aspiring to shape a single dominant master identity would constitute the rejection of this credible reality. In addition, there is a corollary to the principle of just recognition. Reconciling cultural diversity to shape a common political community through a constitutional process requires from the concerned parties the mutual recognition of each other's voices. Hence, the constitutional foundation of the common state should reflect the symbols and languages of all concerned collectivities. This means recognizing the existence of complex publics, thus accepting that "the public sphere is constituted by a diversity of identities, not one shared or uncontested set of understandings that transcend cultural locations" (O'Leary 1999: 106). If by so doing "the core features of citizens' identity are both *recognised by the state and [rendered] recognisable in the state*," then "the legitimacy of the state and its related social, cultural and political institutions" (1999: 92; italics added) can be said to be established.

The context in which the self-identification exercise is being carried out also should not be overlooked. This context is a world that is moving away from the relatively tidy system of nation-states in which the principle of self-determination was first applied, towards a more uncertain period in which national sovereignty is being eroded by pressures coming both from above and from below (Danspeckgruber 1997: 2). This imposes the search for new ways of self-definition, distinct from the previous manner that brought about the so-called nation-states. If carried out within this context, identity politics "may have a strong democratic impulse, seeking to restore popular participation and accountability to the policy process. It may be *guided by a search for new principles of social cohesion* and for a way to insert the society in the global order on terms not entirely dictated from outside" (Keating 1998: 40; italics added). Searching for new principles of social cohesion are direly needed, particularly in states that are verging on collapse. Negotiating more just terms that enhance such a society's ability to influence the prevailing global order, particularly the global economy, may not appear feasible. Awareness of the existence of such terms, however, can be made much more widespread thus averting rising confusion and the entertainment of unrealizable expectations. This could significantly reduce state authorities' fear of dealing with global financial institutions without carrying the public with them.

Keating's discussion of the plurality and complexity of identity results from his study of ongoing cases of struggles for self-determination in the developed world. Oommen arrives at an identical position by looking at the invocation of identity in general. He argues against the practice of concentrating on one master identity, be it class, race, nationality, or ethnicity, and treating other identities as secondary. And he goes on to state that "it is necessary to insist that individuals and collectivities have multiple identities and that *no single one can acquire primacy in all contexts"* (1997: 11; italics added). His argument about the contextual invocation of identity is so important that it is deserves to be quoted at length:

> Individuals and collectivities tend to invoke the appropriate and/or convenient element from their identity-sets, which consist of their total number of identities. It is the invoking of an identity while ignoring the context, that creates problems and raises the issue of legitimacy. That is to say, the idea of one master identity being displaced by another master identity as society "modernizes" or "progresses" is the wrong way of looking at the empirical processes. What often happens is a net increase in the number of identities constituting the identity-sets, even as some older ones become obsolete, as societies become more complex and as inter-societal interactions increase. Many of the contentious issues in the world today are due to the invoking of identities, while ignoring the contexts. (Oommen 1997: 11)

Numerous forms of identity thus intersect to give the individual and the collectivity a distinct personality at a particular time. Out of the set of attributes that compose an individual's or collectivity's identity, some are invoked to shape a political structure, and still others to fulfill other functions. Some would be needed to articulate a common state while others would become relevant for running strictly local or sectional affairs. Although various forms of identity may not always converge, they do not necessarily always compete. The trick is to accentuate the former while keeping the latter to a minimum. But it is well known that the term "identity" evokes the unity of personality as well as the commonality of the past experience as well as the future expectations of the concerned collectivity. In addition, unfortunately, unity is routinely regarded as the negation of difference. As a result, identity politics often harps on one particular type of difference (the one separating the supposed in-group from the out-group) while intending to ignore or suppress others. It tends to reject the construction of one type of "arid uniformity" while endeavouring to replace it with another.

Only by addressing identity politics in a creative way can the contemporary world hope to reduce the negative consequences of rising incidents invoking the right to self-definition and self-determination. While the need to recognize and tolerate difference applies to all states, including democratic mono-national ones, it is even more imperative for states inhabited by numerous nations. The survival of the latter type of states is becoming increasingly dependent on their willingness to handle the issue of cultural and linguistic difference in a creative way. Those demanding self-determination also face an identical challenge.

Difference can be cultivated within certain limits. Through a careful calculation, an equilibrium can be struck between, on the one hand, the acceptance of the structures of the joint state, and on the other, strong sense of identity (Guibernau 1996: 108). The creative handling of difference would situate nationalist movements among global movements working for progress and would thus contribute its share, in the views of one authority.

> Nationalism entails cultural resistance, and challenges modern societies by vindicating what I shall call 'identity politics', that is, *the claim for cultural difference based upon ethnicity*. I consider it crucially important that the nationalisms which are currently showing renewed strength and energy are primarily those which stem from nations without states. Identity politics involves *a progressive element*, and the national movements that represent it stand alongside the peace, ecological or feminist movements in so far as they stand for *the different, the powerless*. They constitute a voice which can no longer be ignored in a world that claims to accept democracy as the prime legitimizing element. (Guibernau 1996: 133)

Nationalism, of course, has stressed difference (i.e., identity boundaries) in previous eras too. While insisting on the difference separating the supposed in-group from the out-group, it has often been hostile to internal differences. While objecting to the homogenization agenda of others, it has often insisted on implementing its own aim of cultivating a single master identity. I am arguing that contemporary nationalist movements must move away from this course.

Seen within the context of the plurality and complexity of identity, what then is the *nation*, the *people* or the *self* that can legitimately claim and achieve self-determination? The *nation* has commonly been defined as any collectivity that, based on self identification, becomes united and aspires to have a state of its own. This definition of nation was first offered by Weber and has been in circulation ever since. The history of self-determination, however, indicates that groups rarely insist on achieving statehood from the very outset. From Toussaint L'Ouverture through Ho Chi Minh and the leaders of African independence, the initial demands of those seeking self-determination was never to break away to form a separate entity. They were pushed to that limit by the intransigence of their rulers. Thus, I agree with Oommen's conclusion that "a nation tends to produce its state when it faces abnormal situations" (1997: 31). The same holds true for the violence that often accompanies struggles for self-determination. The denial of the right to self-determination by state authorities, not its invocation, has always been more responsible for the attendant upheavals and conflicts, as Stavenhagen (1996: 8) notes.

Now, when state and nation may no more be treated as synonymous, it would be ironic to continue with the definition of the nation as a collectivity that wants to become an internationally recognized state. Those who exercise state power and those who demand self-determination could curb the endless fragmentation commonly associated with the principle by assuming a new mentality. Those who hold power should not treat any and all demands for self-determination as an intention to rupture the existing state. Similarly, those who demand the right should be aware of the irony of equating self-determination with secession. The irony lies in the fact that a struggle that is ostensibly about the people can often end up putting more emphasis on territory. Therefore, defining all nations as state-seeking and equating self-determination with secession are not supported by the empirical study of the history of both concepts.

The enjoyment of group political rights of varying types would be the more accurate current definition of the principle of self-determination. In the contemporary context, the focus of self-determination is on enhancing the participation of grassroots communities in the administration of justice and in running common services while having a fair input into central state politics. To put it another way, the focus is on creating a structure that allows the citizens to control and administer services as near the point of delivery, as Guibernau states. Which particular aspects of a collectivity's identity would be relevant for bringing about such structural change would presumably vary from case to case and from region to region. And whether such an aim could be achieved short of secession also depends on the particular situation. Deliberation on such a practical matter with regards to the Horn of Africa will be the subject of a future section. For now, I am just exploring the emerging background picture.

Self-Determination as a Process

A new form of state appears to be emerging. Its evolving architecture and accompanying functions are just starting to be noticed. This state demands a new kind of identity politics that takes account of the complexity and plurality of identity as well as the prevailing thresholds of respect of human rights and other democratic principles. What then are the implications for the principle and practice of self-determination? We have to add a couple of other emerging conceptions in order to start answering this question. First, nation and state are no longer being treated as identical. Hence, the previous policy of shaping a nation out of every state, and its opposing response of aspiring to turn every nation into a state, are increasingly looking out of place. This is imposing a second very important trend, that is, the previous practice of equating self-determination strictly with secession or separation is being abandoned.

Equating self-determination strictly with separation is a legacy of the post-war era of decolonization that by and large has now come to an end. Unfortunately, the immense distortions resulting from the practice of ascribing the right of self-determination strictly to European overseas colonies continue to linger. At least three crucial simplifications emanated from this narrow understanding of a principle so rich in meanings and nuances. First, self-determination became just another term for independence, thus presupposing secession or separation as its only outcome. Second, it focused on territory rather than ethnicity (actually nationality, in most cases), according to Halperin et al. (1992: 20). One consequence of this was to convert a people-centred principle into purely a state-centred affair, according to Stavenhagen (1996: 4). Also, those demanding self-determination often launched their struggles in the name of the people only to end up glorifying territory. Third, self-determination was perceived as having only two dimensions: external, winning freedom from alien domination; and internal, constructing a new governing regime within an existing state. As often as not, however, the latter was subordinated to the former. The result was nothing short of catastrophic, as leaders of independence movements, once ensconced in power, turned against their followers and denied them basic democratic liberties.

Decolonization drew on a peculiarly simplistic distinction between the "self" and the "other." The "other" hailed from across the ocean and was a member of the white race (this was referred to as the theory of "salt-water colonialism"). A black society perceived as being homogeneous in all aspects thus faced a similarly perceived "other." The separation of the "self" and the "other" had both geographical and racial dimensions. And the departure of the "other" was often marked by a simple but very emotive ceremony. The flag of the colonizer was lowered at the stroke of midnight to be replaced by that of the newly independent state. The populace celebrated the birth of "their nation." And the process was considered at an end since "once a people has exercised its right to external self-determination, the right expires" (Cassese 1995:

101). Coupled with the practice of subordinating the internal to the external, the image of self-determination as a one-time process of transformation—the birth of an independent state (nation)—was established. And the external was easily, routinely, and in practice legitimately invoked to deny the exercise of internal self-determination in the most rudimentary manner. Although "at its simplest the principle of self-determination accords people a right to govern their own affairs" (Halperin et al. 1992: 1), demanding such a right was effectively barred as the competing superpowers of the Cold War era sponsored their favourite brutal dictatorial regimes. Studying the contrasting way, with starkly different outcomes, by which white dominions rose to independent statehood would be very informative. In their case, the process was so gradual that pinning down the dates of their independence is much more difficult, according to Clarence-Smith (1999: 121). Gaining independence was thus a protracted process, not the precipitous affair that became common in the post-war decolonization era.

The sponsoring of dictatorial regimes by influential powers sadly has not yet come to an end. Despite the continuation of this unfortunate policy, democratization and fair and free elections are being given more lip service than in the past. Along with this, there is a growing insistence that "self-determination, as other human rights, must be considered an open-ended ongoing process without point of closure" (Stavenhagen 1996: 5). In addition, the belief that the response to demands for self-determination is not restricted to independence but could cover a broad range of policy options is gaining ground. As Stavenhagen (1996: 5) states, "There are numerous means through which human aggregates—whatever their nature and bonds—can pursue the goal to control their own destinies on a day to day basis." Halperin et al. list some of these as follows: "the full exercise of self-determination can lead to a number of outcomes, ranging from minority-rights protections, to cultural or political autonomy, to independent statehood. The principle of self-determination is best viewed as entitling a people to choose its political allegiance, to influence the political order under which it lives, and to preserve its cultural, ethnic, historical, or territorial identity" (Halperin et al. 1992: 47). Two developments in the perception of the principle stand out. First, self-determination should be viewed as an ongoing process. This has implications for treating its external and internal dimensions as separate entities. For self-determination to be enjoyed on a continuous basis, the mandatory interdependence of the two dimensions should be stressed. External self-determination should not continue to enjoy legitimacy unless it is based on internal self-determination in its simplest form: the periodic change of governments through democratic elections. This by itself would reduce numerous cases of the alienation of peoples from the state and its authority figures. Second, even where democratization alone fails to satisfy a people's demand—and there are such cases—the existence of a wide range of responses should not be overlooked.

Bringing demands for self-determination in line with emerging features of the contemporary state and the complexity of identities makes another development necessary as well as possible. Self-determination, in addition to being seen as a process, can (and perhaps in a number of situations should) be viewed as being multi-dimensional. A multi-dimensional form of self-determination becomes imperative as a response to a peculiar challenge facing contemporary states. Contemporary states are proving to be both too large and too small, at one and the same time. "They are too large for full social identities and many real economic interests. But they are also too small for many economic purposes" (Agnew 2000: 16). The acknowledgement of this contradictory nature of contemporary states seems to suggest the need for pooling resources, voice, and energy at various levels. A multi-dimensional model for conceptualizing self-determination is hence being suggested to promote cooperation at various levels. Danspeckgruber suggests such a four-dimensional model for self-determination composed of (1) internal, (2) bilateral, (3) horizontal, and (4) vertical (1997a: 222). This model comes in very handy for conceptualizing the voluntary pooling of authority, energy, and legitimacy at the sub-state, state, and regional levels. This is particularly crucial when multinational states engage in regional integration, which is becoming increasingly necessary for survival. A multi-dimensional exercise of self-determination could serve to legitimate such states as well as the supra-state bodies that they create. First, the internal exercise of self-determination could apply to members of ethnic groups (nations) living within the home area of a particular non-state nation. Second, two such nations living within a multinational entity could enter into bilateral agreements to address issues common specifically to them. Third, all the nations living within the borders of the joint state could enact the instruments that make the entity and its government their common property and servant. Fourth, states constituted on such a principle could more democratically promote regional integration and thus end the practice of turning interstate institutions into, at best, a club for state officials or, at worst, of dictators.

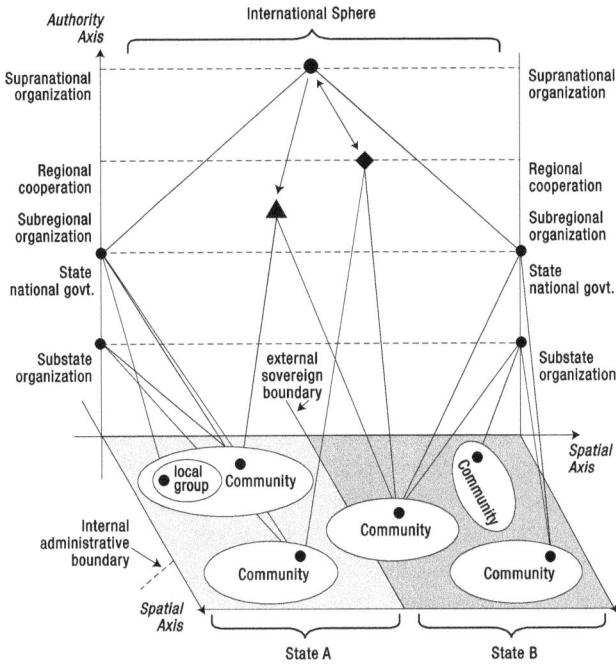

Figure 1: Graphic Representation of Community in Space and Authority. Source: Danspeckgruber 2002:350

Regional integration is, in fact, being offered as one means of reducing the negative consequences of self-determination. Horowitz, who has made an in-depth study of ethnicity (he often uses the terms "nation," "tribe," and "ethnicity" interchangeably), has applied his expertise to self-determination. In a recent essay, he focuses on difficulties commonly associated with secession. First, although secession is often premised on creating a new, more homogeneous state, it routinely ends up birthing a new entity that is just as diverse as the rump state. Reminiscent of what happened after the breakup of the Austro-Hungarian Empire, a smaller polyglot entity often replaces a larger one in such instances. Second, secession is rarely realized without much pain and turmoil and often sows the seeds of future conflict. After discussing these issues, Horowitz goes on to suggest that "international regional integration and the amalgamation of states, is likely to produce far better results in many (though not all) cases of ethnic conflict" (1998: 191). He, however, believes this course is unlikely to be pursued.

India has had a remarkable success in practising pluralist democracy despite the multiplicity of the nations making up its population. Horowitz credits India's diversity for this success. "India is a federal state with so many compartmentalized ethnic cleavages that no single group can be said to dominate the state at the centre" (1998: 198). India is a subcontinent embracing physically diverse geographical regions and a population that has complex and overlapping identities. Horowitz believes India's case vindicates James Madison's writing in the *Federalist* in which he asserted that scale proliferates interests and makes it more difficult for any single interest to dominate. Horowitz mentions two other approaches in addressing problems associated with ethnic (national) diversity. "The first is consociation, a prescription for treating the multi-ethnic state for some purposes as if it is more than one polity and for according to each of the subpolities a considerable degree of veto power and autonomy" (Horowitz 1998: 195). The second one is framing electoral legislation that enables and compels political actors to solicit support across identity divides. Unfortunately, Horowitz does not try to combine one or both of these with his prescription for regional integration. However, this does look possible and could even diminish the shortcomings associated with the latter two prescriptions. In addition, a gradual cultivation of regional integration simultaneous with the devolution of administrative functions to local sub-state entities may reduce the hesitancy that he fears. If sharing power at the regional level while also doing so within the state reduces the burden of the state and produces demonstrable returns, it could start a self-propelling process. This could hold promise in the search for more amenable ways of handling the renewed upsurge of nationalist demands.

International Inputs

States of the premodern world, whatever their sizes, usually came into existence, blossomed, and withered away as autarkies. In the tightly interconnected world of today, however, the logic of the state is not situated purely within itself. Hence, shaping qualitatively new states in response to increasing demands for self-determination cannot succeed without the cultivation of an appropriate global environment. As I have tried to elaborate, the protagonists involved in struggles for self-determination need to search for creative approaches if they are to avert the devastation that would surely follow from the endless replication of existing state types. The US-led international community similarly needs to promote conditions that favour the qualitative transformation of states rather than their proliferation.

The most obvious and contentious issue in this regard is that of international recognition. The recognition of states without due attention to their internal political health has for far too long legitimated the illegal exercise of power. This has only fuelled the alienation and discontent, not only of aggrieved collectivities but also of individuals who have routinely been denied their citizenship rights. State officials have been free to violently repress any demands for group or individual rights with impunity. Their externally rooted legitimacy has allowed them to portray legitimate struggles for rights as not only illegal but as posing a danger to international peace and order. That is why they are always more comfortable with the narrow term "secession" than with the broader content of self-determination. They are thus able to pit legitimate struggles for self-determination against the prevailing interstate solidarity. At its simplest, this is a consequence of opposing the external dimension of self-determination against the internal. Unless this practice is scrapped, many states will gradually collapse or suddenly implode. Implementing UN Secretary General Boutros-Ghali's suggestion that "internal good governance" should be accorded a weight comparable with the sovereign rights of states would appear to be the right place to start. International insistence on internal good governance as the basic credential that allows state officials to speak on behalf of the populace they presumably represent would go a long way to stem the negative consequences of struggles for self-determination.

The people's right to change their governments through fair and free elections should be upheld much more consistently as the legitimating factor of states and the regional, and global bodies that they create. Mere democratization, however, may not answer all questions of self-determination, as many cases indicate. There should thus be a special focus on this particular democratic right. Vague and inadequate principles on how to exercise self-determination were articulated by the international community at the end of the First and Second World Wars. Unfortunately, the manner by which the most protracted global war, the Cold War, came to an end did not occasion a similar deliberation. Hence, ongoing struggles for self-determination were left to simply invoke established concepts or practices or to grope in the dark. The time to rectify this is way overdue. International deliberation on the contemporary exercise of self-determination is very much in need. This is one of the central recommendations of Halperin et al. In addition, the monarch of Liechtenstein tabled a new convention of "Self-government as Self-determination" during his address to the UN in 1992 (Danspeckgruber 1997). We urgently need to replace the earlier instruments that legitimated the demolition of Europe's overseas empires.

There are some commentators who believe that an independent commission composed of eminent persons and experts is necessary to get
such a process started (see Rupesinghe 1996: 352). Halperin et al. would
prefer to situate such a commission within the UN structure. The creation
of such a global organ should be supported. But this alone will not be
enough to address all the peculiarities of self-determination cases. Hence,
a region-by-region or even a state-by-state open and participatory appraisal
of the issues at stake is just as necessary.

Trend-Setting Cases of Self-Determination

A number of factors distinguish ongoing trend-setting quests for self-
determination from more conventional ones. The most important of
these is a stronger emphasis on process than on end result. Another is the
conceptualization of self-determination within an evolving process of
integration at the continental level that takes into account the prevailing level of interdependence at the global level. Naturally, such conceptualization has occurred where continental integration is most advanced,
in Europe and North America. It is against this backdrop that Michael
Keating analyzes the trend-setting nationalist struggles in Quebec, Catalonia, and Scotland.

The European Union (EU), as the most advanced exercise in continental integration, has great impact on how states are conceptualized. The
gradualist process of its institution has also fundamentally influenced
how self-determination is conceived and pursued by some nationalist
elements. Nationalist movements within the countries of the EU are thus
afforded the opportunity "to credit citizens with dual or multiple loyal-
ties and identities, and the capacity to act in different arenas" (Keating
2001: 22). They can act, and are acting, within the state as well as at the
EU level. The result is an emerging picture of politics echoing back and
forth from the regions these movements inhabit to the state within which
they are situated and to the continent of Europe. The resonance of political moves in these diverse spheres is having a remarkable impact. It is
giving rise to a situation in "which European politics are regionalized;
regional politics are Europeanized; and national [i.e., state] politics are
both Europeanized and regionalized" (Keating 2001: 61).

The movement of Catalan nationalism attempts to fit its agenda into
this evolving picture, and thus serves as an exemplary case of contemporary approaches to self-determination. The Catalan nationalist agenda
is remarkable for its ambiguity. The notion of federation is muted, and
outright separation is given even less attention. Although pinning down

the Catalan aspiration could rob it of its intended nuance, one could define it as seeking the status of "a self-governing nation within a weak Spanish state encompassed in Europe" (Keating 2001: 189). Instead of working for a clearly defined end result, Catalan nationalists continuously up the ante according to their slogan "Now for More!" They thus find themselves in the position of responding to criticisms regarding the ambiguity of their agenda by simply pointing to the similarly indeterminate nature of European integration (Keating 2001: 158). What they are practically seeking, in the meantime, has been put thus: "Catalan nationalists seek the degree of self-government required to maintain and advance the interests of their national community and are ready to play in multiple political arenas in order to do this: the local arena; the Spanish arena; the European arena; the Mediterranean arena" (Keating 2001: 195). Thematic concerns as well as spatial considerations have motivated them to cultivate relations both inside and outside the Spanish state as well as the Mediterranean region and even beyond. Catalonia has concluded a special agreement of cooperation with Valencia and the Balearic Islands to develop and enhance the status of their common language (Keating 2001: 168). Its proximity with the Maghreb countries has necessitated engaging them in discussions concerning the economy and immigration, particularly with Morocco (Keating 2001: 193). Contacts have been established with Argentina, the State of Illinois, the World Bank, and the International Monetary Fund to further other interests. Hence, Catalonia, while formally remaining a sub-state entity, is systematically expanding its competence by taking on some functions conventionally reserved for interstate spheres.

The nationalist struggles in the British Isles are similarly influenced by the situation evolving in the European Union. Scotland has a strong nationalist element that is pursuing the agenda of "independence in Europe." Meanwhile, a decades-old demand for the devolution of power has finally culminated in the establishment of a Scottish Parliament in 1999. Scots may thus act at the level of Scotland, Britain, and Europe at the same time and in diverse ways. The picture has become even more intricate after the Good Friday Agreement was adopted to deal with one of Europe's oldest conflicts, that of Northern Ireland. This provides for the creation of the Council of the Islands, adding still another tier to the multiplicity of sites where elements of sovereignty are pooled and shared.

Developments in Wales have followed those emerging in Scotland quite closely. Here too the aspiration to revive Welsh nationalism was premised on fitting it into the evolving continental integration. Thus,

Welsh nationalists "have used the EU as a basic framework for advancing their cause. They have established institutions that focus on the role of Wales in Europe, and they have argued that Wales should have a status somewhere between that of a constituent unit of the United Kingdom and that of a sovereign state" (Murphy 1999: 63). Lost in the process has been the previous practice of one identity necessarily displacing another. Instead, being Welsh, British, or European has become dependent on context and the purpose that is to be served by the identity invoked.

The North American counterpart of the EU, the North American Free Trade Agreement (NAFTA), is still in its nascent phase. It thus figures much less in the political calculation of Québécois nationalists. However, even in this case Québécois commitment to the continental body remains strong alongside demands for more sovereign rights. When we look at the issue of identity it appears clear that being Québécois has replaced being Canadian, at least for the French-speaking majority in Quebec (Keating 2001: 130). Devising a satisfactory relationship between the rest of Canada and North America seems to constitute the issue of contention. Two poles can be discerned in this exercise. First, preserving the federal status quo remains the position favoured by the central government and English-speaking Canada. Second, separation is being aired by elements in the nationalist quarter. Interestingly, not all those identifying themselves as Québécois are comfortable with either option. Between the two extreme poles exists a range of other options. These include (1) sovereignty (with its ambiguity); (2) sovereignty-association; (3) a mandate to negotiate sovereignty-association; and (4) special status within the Canadian federation. It is the existence of this range of options that makes the Québécois struggle for self-determination interesting. Under a similarly relaxed political atmosphere, it is quite conceivable that those who aspire to self-determination in other parts of the world could also entertain a similarly diverse agenda.

PART II

Resonance of Conflicts in the Horn of Africa

INTRODUCTION

IN THE FIRST PART OF THIS WORK I tried to trace the evolution of the nation-state and its presumed midwife, the principle of internal self-determination (*popular sovereignty*) and external self-determination. Self-determination was originally conceived as a vehicle through which the *people* coalesce to constitute the *nation* that exercises *sovereignty* over the *state* whose power over a clearly defined *territory* is presumed unchallengeable both from within and without the designated geographical space. Numerous forms of convergence supposedly characterize the nation-state resulting from this neat correspondence between *people, nation, state, territory,* and *sovereignty.* In particular, the nation-state is premised on the congruence of the political, cultural, linguistic, and economic and physical security community. Achieving the above match and the attendant congruence has proven problematic in the African reality, thus forcing *people, nation,* and *popular sovereignty* to live under the shadow of the *state, territory,* and *external sovereignty.* Although this is the gravest consequence of the mismatch between the relevant categories, problems persisted even where a better fit gradually evolved. Some social sectors found themselves within the state *territory* but outside the cultural and linguistic *nation* due to their peculiar racial, cultural, or linguistic markers. Property ownership and gender often served as the pretexts for excluding even bona fide members of the national/linguistic community from the politically empowered *citizen* category. Progress has been registered in stemming this exclusion in the nation-state's birthplace of Western Europe through the extension of universal suffrage and other political rights. The predicament of those who found themselves within the state *territory* but outside the cultural/linguistic *nation,* however, has proved more enduring. This has necessitated recognizing *nations without states* and their right to autonomous existence within the constraints of prevailing interdependence within states, regions, and the world. How both the state and self-determination are being rearticulated to deal with these issues was the topic of Part I.

In Part II, I will attempt to explore the circumstances that brought the states of the Horn of Africa into existence and how this impacted on their legitimacy. The legitimacy of many African states is deficient, as has been so aptly elucidated by Okafor (2000). Okafor traces the legitimacy crisis currently afflicting African states to political developments that go back to pre-colonial and colonial times, and that persist into the post-colonial era. His observation that European colonial subordination of African peoples was facilitated by the pursuit of the same aspirations by African empire-builders rings particularly true for the Horn, with one particular difference. Unlike other failed attempts in the rest of Africa, Abyssinia's empire-building aspiration was successfully consummated, thus bringing forth the contemporary Ethiopian state. And this peculiar success resulted from the process of the imperial ambitions of a number of European powers and of other local Africans cancelling each other out. Even more remarkable, the events that brought the Ethiopian state into existence and led to its international recognition proceeded in a mutually interactive manner with the processes that resulted in the formation of the other Horn entities. The legitimacy crises of the concerned Horn states went on to manifest themselves in the almost ubiquitous invocation of self-determination. And the Ethiopian Empire is the central actor in the tensions and contests between and within states that have become the hallmark of the Horn region.

This resonance of diverse forms of conflicts, their historical roots, and the central role of Ethiopia are explained in the following manner by Partick Gilkes: "There is a long history of state formation and conflict within the Horn of Africa, largely though not exclusively, centred upon what is now the polity of Ethiopia: ethnicity, religion and control of resources have been at issue within a highly complex region" (1999: 4). The Sudan (the other major Horn state) has also been the scene of interminable conflict involving ethnicity, religion, and control of resources. Somalia was set on the course that ultimately led to the chaos currently reigning there when its irredentist hopes of absorbing almost half of the Ethiopian Empire started dimming. Once this outward orientation was eclipsed by internal self-examination, the supposed homogeneity of Somali society was found significantly deficient in sustaining cohesion.

In the following pages I will try to briefly sketch the interactive process that led to the emergence of the various entities populating the Horn of Africa. These interactive processes stamped the concerned entities with features that negatively impact on their internal legitimacy in a more glaring manner than prevails elsewhere in Africa. These entities that initially came into existence merely as footholds for grand imperial projects started putting on the nation-state garb after the Second World War. The prevailing non-existence of congruence between the historical, territorial, and cultural/linguistic communities, however, practically obviated the assumption of this status, thus generating their crises of internal legitimacy.

CONFLICTING EXPANSIONISM OF EXTERNAL ACTORS

The Horn of Africa region is nowadays defined in various ways. The most common and perhaps historically more appropriate definition would be the area stretching from the border of Chad, in the west, to the Indian Ocean, in the east, and from the Egyptian border, in the north, to the borders of Uganda and Kenya, in the south. The references to Horn of Africa in this writing apply to the area delimited by these borders. This area became the site of fierce expansionist competition during the second half of the nineteenth century, involving forces from within the area as well as those from without. The expansionist agenda of the local forces was driven primarily by a religious-based ideology of domination with control of resources as the ultimate aim. Control of the Red Sea coast (whose strategic importance suddenly rose with the breaching of the Suez isthmus) drew external competitors to the area. I will first discuss how three external forces (Egypt, Italy, and France) succeeded each other in putting parts of the region within pincer movements with the aim of ultimately controlling large swathes of the Horn. The role of the fourth external power, Britain, was focused on frustrating French aspirations and "regaining" the Sudan for itself and Egypt. Although the ambition of local forces will often be mentioned here, I will treat it in greater detail later.

Egypt's Grand Empire

Egypt became the first external power to entertain carving an expansive empire out of the Horn of Africa. Khedive Ismail (1863–79) advanced this ambition by enveloping the entire area within a pincer movement in the mid-1870s. He moved in this direction by first extending the borders of the Sudan westwards as far as Darfur and southwards close to the Equatorial Lakes. He followed this up by occupying Massawa (in today's Eritrea) and parts of its hinterland in 1874. When his troops landed in Zeila (in today's Somaliland) and then advanced inland to conquer Harar (in today's Oromia region of Ethiopia) the following year (Holt 1970: 3), the extent of his imperial ambition was sketched out.

The khedive's grand ambition to connect the whole territory enveloped by these footholds was countered and ultimately frustrated by two local forces. Christian Abyssinia (itself an aspiring expansionist) was the first local power to check Egyptian expansionism. Internal Abyssinian politics was thrown into convulsion at the same time. The Egyptians tried to improve their chances of conquering the targeted area by supplementing their military operations with internal subversion of the then reigning Abyssinian Emperor, Yohannes IV. They found a willing ally in this enterprise in King Menelik of Shawa (the emperor's deadly internal challenger), who opened communications with them. When Egyptian forces started clashing with those of the emperor, Menelik thus saw it as a unique "chance of destroying Yohannes without any military investment, and with the prospect of some free armaments" (Marcus 1975: 37). The Egyptians had their counter-agenda of placing "Yohannes between 'two grinding stones' and later, 'profiting by this enfeeblement of the Ethiopian nationality,' to turn on Menelik and integrate Ethiopia into the Egyptian empire" (Marcus 1975: 39). Incidentally, Menelik's dual aim was neither strange nor new, as the emperor himself had used a virtually identical treasonous dealing with the British to ascend the throne as "King of Kings." Thus, when he was ordered to mobilize for the 1875 battle against the Egyptians, Menelik stayed home citing "a Galla (i.e., Oromo) disturbance" as the pretext. Unfortunately for him, this battle ended with victory going to the emperor's forces. When the Egyptians returned with a larger force early in 1876, "With the notable exception of Shoa, all of Christian Ethiopia supported the Emperor" (Marcus 1975: 41). When this second Egyptian army also suffered defeat, "Menelik's beautiful plans and fond hopes went up in smoke" (Marcus 1975: 42). En passant, had this series of Egyptian defeats not instigated the development in the Sudan that torpedoed their expansionist ambition, their manoeuvre to manipulate and ultimately depose Menelik looked distinctly plausible for one important reason. Moslem Oromo leaders who were then suffering from his aggressive acts (the rulers of Jimma, Innarya, and Goma) were actually appealing for Egyptian protection (Rubenson

1976: 85). Others would have perhaps followed suit in requesting Egyptian help against Menelik's pillaging and subjugation. But let us now return
to the issue at hand, how developments in the Sudan suddenly and permanently ended Egypt's grand imperial aspirations.

Egypt's "indecisive and expensive war with Abyssinia" (Holt 1970: 37)
led to two developments that ultimately brought forth the second local
force that sealed the fate of Egyptian ambition: Mahdist Sudan. First, the
news of its forces' repeated defeats appears to have seriously damaged
Egypt's prestige, thus exposing its vulnerability. Second, financing the
expensive war necessitated levying higher taxes in northern Sudan. Resist-
ing increased taxation in turn served as one of four factors (Holt 1970: 32)
that enabled Mohammed Ahmed al-Mahdi to instigate the rebellion that
catapulted him to power and led to Egypt's hasty withdrawal not only
from the Sudan but also from all its other footholds. Launched in western Sudan in 1881, the success of the Mahdi was capped with the capture
of Khartoum in late January 1885. After suffering a humiliating defeat
by Mahdist forces, Egypt was permanently knocked out of the race to
control large parts of the Horn of Africa. Meanwhile, Lord Cromer was
busying himself acting as the "governor who governs those who govern
Egypt." (Map 1 shows Egyptian lines of advance.)

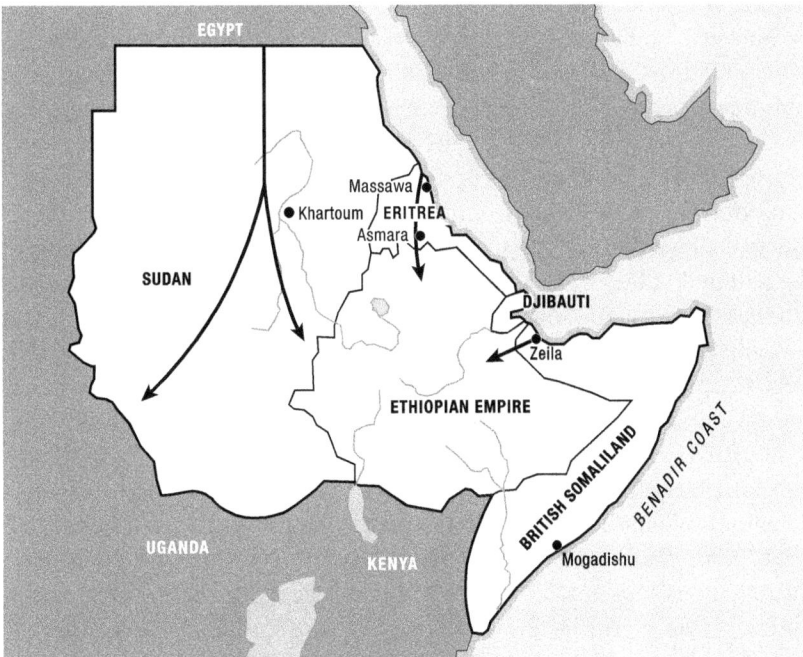

Map 1: Egyptian Lines of Advance

Italy Steps In

At this stage, France and Italy, the latter serving as British surrogate, entered the scene under the impression that a vacuum had resulted from the collapse of Egyptian expansionism. And this occurred at a time when interest in the Red Sea had risen to an unprecedented level due to the prior opening of the Suez Canal. The concerned European powers started transforming hitherto insignificant and dormant trading posts on the Red Sea coast into important bridgeheads for inland penetration and colonization. The Italians already had a foothold in Assab, initially acquired in 1869 by an Italian navigational enterprise called the Rubattino Company (Zewde 1991: 56). The French were poised to expand from adjacent Obock, till then an insignificant fuelling station for their naval forces travelling to and from the Far East. Partly in order to frustrate this French ambition, the British signalled to the Italians (on 15 October 1884) the possibility of occupying Massawa Island and thus replacing the evacuating Egyptians (Gooch 1998: 129). Once they acted on this suggestion and occupied Massawa in early 1885, the Italians started weighing their options. They could either advance directly west to Kassala and thence to Khartoum or march northwest to capture Suakin. Alternatively, they could proceed in a southwesterly direction to capture Adowa and Gondar in Abyssinia (Gooch 1998: 130).

Barred from pursuing the other options by British objections (Gooch 1998: 131), the Italians were left with no choice but to control Abyssinia and the areas to its south and east. Enveloping this target area within a pincer movement necessitated the acquisition of a foothold in another part of East Africa. Thus, within weeks of occupying Massawa, they set in motion the process that would determine the southernmost extent of the area they coveted. The explorer Cecchi was dispatched to persuade the Sultan of Zanzibar to cede to Italy the Benadir Coast and the adjacent Juba valley (in today's southern Somalia). "The Juba would thus mark the extreme southern boundary of our possessions" (Hess 1966: 15), stated Cecchi upon the success of his mission. Thereafter, Italy harboured a determination to connect this area with Massawa by either war or wile; they ultimately failed in both. Remarkably, the Italians repeated the Egyptian tactic of encouraging Menelik to internally subvert Emperor Yohannes. When the Italians started encroaching towards the edges of the Abyssinian plateau adjacent to Massawa, Yohannes was busy quelling the rebellious Moslem Oromos of Wallo, whose rising was inspired partly by the news of the Mahdist victory in the Sudan. Meanwhile, an encounter between the Italians and an Abyssinian force commanded by

Ras Alula ended in Italian defeat at a place called Dogali on 26 January 1887 (Zewde 1991: 57). Menelik was in constant communication with the Italians during this time, sharing with them contents of messages from his Emperor (Marcus 1975: 85). The Italian defeat at Dogali once again put Menelik in a tight corner, as the Egyptian defeats of the late 1870s had done. While "the enthusiasm of the Abyssinians approached to delirium" as a result of Italian defeat at Dogali, Menelik alone "was up-set," according to the report of an Italian agent (Marcus 1975: 87). Menelik in fact started considering requesting Italian protection (Marcus 1975: 88), signalling to the Italians that their plan of linking their northern and southern footholds was within reach. In exchange for five thousand Remington rifles and credit to purchase ten thousand more, Menelik concluded a "secret treaty of amity and alliance" (Marcus 1975: 102) with Italy later in 1887. Paying for more and more arms, of course, meant mounting repeated campaigns against the Oromo and other peoples to the south of Shawa accompanied with the usual practices of pillaging and raiding for slaves.

At this time, Yohannes found himself not between two but three grinding stones: (1) the Italians, (2) the Mahdists, and (3) his arch-rival, Menelik. Pulled in so many directions at the same time and unable to cultivate an alliance with anyone, he ended up fighting all of them. He spent most of his last years hastening from one battlefield to another. After dealing with the Wallo Oromo Moslem rising, he rushed to the Red Sea coast, arriving within striking distance of the Italians in March 1888. News then reached him that the Mahdist dervishes had penetrated Abyssinia, defeated the armies of his vassal (Gojjam's king Tekla Haimanot), and sacked Gondar (Abyssinia's capital for centuries). When his call to his co-religionists (the Italians) to join him against the enemies of his religion (the Mahdists) went unanswered (Gooch 1998: 133), he turned around and rushed to southern Abyssinia first to put down the insurrection brewing there.

The mood of insurrection was spreading as Menelik encouraged Tekla Haimanot to join the anti-Yohannes conspiracy by harping on his grievance that the emperor had failed to come to his rescue during the Mahdist incursion (Marcus 1975: 101). Yohannes thus had to march into Gojjam and then Shawa to secure his rear as a matter of priority but also for a very practical reason. Maintaining his burgeoning army intact necessitated provisions "which were available only in Gojjam and Shoa" since other areas under his direct rule such as "Wallo, Tigre, and Begemder had been exhausted of supplies for quite some time" (Marcus 1975: 103).

While en route, he approached his fellow Africans (the Mahdists) with a proposal to join forces "against the European invaders" (Gooch 1998: 134). This search for alliance also proved futile as the Mahdists demanded his conversion to Islam as the minimum precondition, a prospect that was truly imponderable for a Christian fanatic. Pressed from outside and betrayed from within, Yohannes contemplated abdication at this stage (Marcus 1975: 104).

In this frame of mind, he proceeded to Gojjam "leaving a trail of devastation through Begemder," reaching Gojjam in September 1888 and completely ravaging it (Marcus 1975: 105). Menelik characteristically not only failed to come to Tekla Haimanot's rescue but also tried to blame him for initiating the conspiracy against the Emperor (Rosenfeld 1976: 134). Uncertain whether this would suffice to assuage Yohannes, Menelik asked the Italians for more arms while imploring them to advance to the Eritrean highlands and to thus "deflect the emperor from Shoa" (Marcus 1975: 105). Yohannes's much-weakened army was poised to carry the punitive campaign into Shawa when the Mahdists returned, thus affording him escape from an internal war in which his victory was not quite certain. He thus grabbed the opportunity of demonstrating his staunch "defence of his beloved Christian empire against the infidels" (Marcus 1975: 110), thereby hoping to morally strengthen his position against his challenger. This calculation led him to his death at Metemma on 12 (or 13) March 1889 and the dispatch of his head to Omdurman, which the khalifa (the then Mahdist leader) paraded as a trophy throughout northern Sudan. Yohannes's removal from the scene left the door wide open for Menelik to finally achieve his fondest goal of donning the crown as King of Kings, which he proceeded to do on 3 November 1889 after subduing all other contenders by force.

A few months before ascending the throne, Menelik concluded the (in)famous Treaty of Wuchale with the Italians. Menelik's new empire had become an Italian protectorate, according to the Italian version of the treaty; however, requiring Italian good offices in conducting diplomatic relations in Europe was optional in the Amharic version. Disagreements on the authenticity of these competing translations began to poison the friendship between Menelik and the Italians. The event of this period with enduring implications was Italy's successful occupation of Keren on the second of June and Asmara on 10 August 1889. With the declaration of Eritrea as an Italian colony on 1 January 1890 and Menelik's apparent acceptance of protectorate status, the Italians thought they were putting the final touches to their project of connecting their northern and southern footholds. Meanwhile, controversy with Menelik regarding the exact content of the Treaty of Wuchale was heating up. At this critical juncture, Menelik found in France an alternative ally and source of arms. And when he concluded that nothing short of war would settle the controversy with Italy, he "cleared his flank by reaching an agreement with the dervishes" (Gooch 1998: 140). The Italian military's preparedness was even more inept than their diplomatic manoeuvres, resulting in their resounding defeat at the battle of Adowa on 1 March 1896. Thus, Italy's aspiration to link its two colonies in the Horn of Africa (Eritrea and Italian Somaliland) had to sit on the back burner for another forty years. Meanwhile, Italian defeat had immediate repercussions for the Sudan, and for the British and the French. But we will first look at how the French attempted to repeat the failed Italian trick of swindling Menelik into a protectorate status.

France Replaces Italy

In tipping the balance in Menelik's favour at the battle of Adowa, French diplomatic support and provision of weapons played a considerable (if not a decisive) role. Firearms had being pouring into the empire in the two decades preceding the war, estimated to total a staggering one hundred thousand by one Russian reporter (Pankhurst 1967: 108). As Italy and Menelik edged closer to war, France continued to frustrate joint Anglo-Italian diplomatic efforts to stop this flow of arms. On the contrary, they allowed the open importation of firearms through their port, Djibouti. Some eighty thousand Russian-made repeater rifles (a gift of Czar Nicholas II) and sixty thousand French firearms passed through Djibouti in the first half of 1891 alone. A ship loaded with thirty tons of war material (partly purchased with Russian funds) destined for Menelik's court left Marseilles later the same year (Pankhurst 1967: 108). French support went beyond facilitating the importation of firearms to include active diplomatic intervention on Menelik's behalf. For example, they scuttled an Italian plan to attack Menelik from the southeast by firmly objecting to their request to pass through British-controlled Zeila (Pankhurst 1967: 113). The French ingratiated themselves with Menelik in this manner because they were about to revive an idea originally entertained by one of their countrymen in the 1840s.

A Frenchman by the name of Rochet d'Héricourt happened to be one of the earliest Europeans who showed up at the court of Menelik's grandfather (Sahle Sillassie) in the 1840s. Like the Italians of later decades, Rochet considered different alternatives that would enable him to realize "French Abyssinia." He could initially arm Sahle Sillassie to expand his kingdom only to subsequently overthrow and replace him as the ruler of a large swathe of Africa. Alternatively, according to Rubenson (1976: 151), he "was *even* prepared to unite and use the Galla (i.e., Oromo) tribes" and thus by "raising 200,000 Galla troops to unite his French Abyssinia with the French possessions on the Senegal river" (italics added).

The collapse of Egyptian imperial ambition in East Africa followed by that of the Italians after the battle of Adowa suddenly rendered the revival of this original French aspiration more feasible than at any previous time. France was planning the Marchand expedition to the Upper Nile when the Italian debacle at Adowa took place. Another expedition from the Red Sea coast was also being put together to serve as the other arm of the pincer movement that would enclose the area targeted for French conquest. The Marchand expedition destined for Sudan's Upper Nile left Brazzaville (on the Atlantic coast) in March 1897. The governor of French Somaliland, Lagarde, travelled to Menelik's capital in the same month to solicit the Ethiopian Emperor's cooperation in launching the second arm of the pincer movement. Lagarde was entrusted with the mission of persuading Menelik to extend "his frontiers to the right bank of the Nile" (Lewis 1988: 125). French territorial offers to Menelik were quite generous. They signalled their desire that "Ethiopia reclaim and extend its ancient frontiers, from Lado in the south as far north as within two hundred miles of Omdurman and Khartoum" (Lewis 1988: 125), obviously at the expense of their British rivals. Menelik was, however, much more interested in pushing his territorial claims eastward at the expense of the French. Menelik succeeded not only in this but also in humouring Lagarde to such an extent that his "self-congratulatory dispatches depicting Ethiopia as a virtual French satellite were convincing" (Lewis 1988: 126). At the very moment when their manoeuvres to oppose and frustrate Italian aspirations became a success, the French thus exposed their own intention of repeating Italian tactics. (See map 2 for the Italian north-south line of advance and the French east-west line of advance.)

Britain Takes Two Actions

The British now had to step forward and implement two interrelated measures to frustrate this French dream: speed up the "reconquest" of the Sudan and recognize the "independence" of the Ethiopian Empire. The "reconquest" of the Sudan had to be launched within days of Italian defeat at Adowa for three reasons. First, a European colonial power suf-

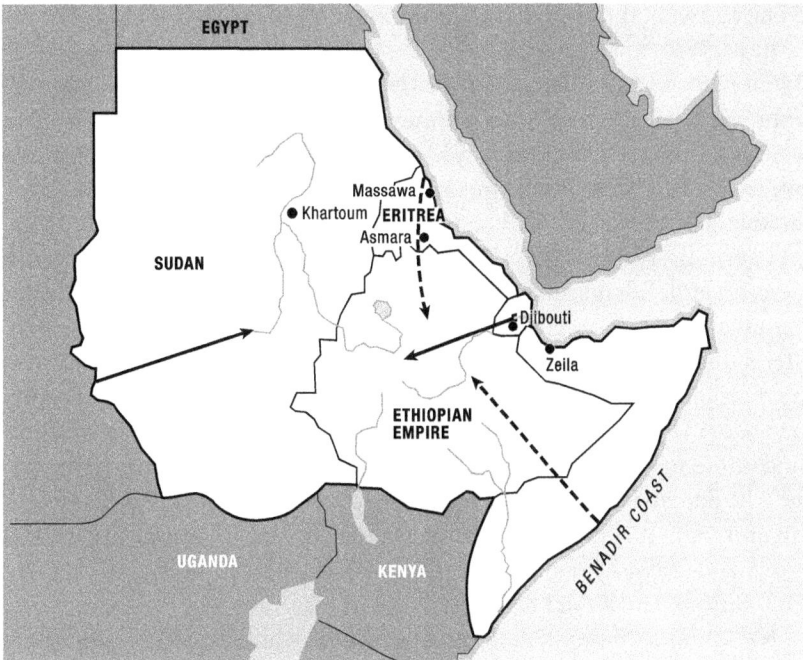

Map 2: ———→ French Lines of Advance; ------→ Italian Lines of Advance

fering defeat at the hands of an African kingdom was one thing, but the annihilation of its army was another matter altogether for it could encourage other Africans to emulate the act. In fact, speculation was then rife in Europe that the wiping out of the entire Italian army could serve as "the first revolt of the Dark Continent against domineering Europe" (Lewis 1988: 120). Second, there was also a distinct impression that "the Abyssinian and Mahdist armies were working in alliance" (Holt 1970: 223). According to an Italian newspaper report, Menelik had in fact dispatched a message to the khalifa saying "I have beaten the Italians at Adwa, it is now your turn to conquer them at Kassala" (Lewis 1988: 121). A domino effect thus appeared to be in the offing. Third, the French attempt to link their actual and potential possessions in the Horn with others in the Senegal valley (then underway) required a British response in speeding up the "reconquest" of the Sudan. The plan to "reconquer" the Sudan was thus put into effect within days of the Italian debacle at Adowa. The demise of Mahdist Sudan, whose emergence was instigated by developments in neighbouring Abyssinia, was once again triggered by yet another development in Abyssinia. Ever since, events occurring in one corner of the Horn have tended to set off others in yet another zone of the region.

The second measure that the British took to frustrate French colonial ambition resulted in the most attractive deal for Menelik. The British assumed the role previously taken by the French as defenders of his empire's autonomy. A contingent bearing the message of British preparedness "to live with an independent, neutral Ethiopia" (Lewis 1988: 128) actually showed up in Menelik's capital while Lagarde was still there. Lagarde's scheming to eventually turn Menelik's new empire into a protectorate was thus countered by the much more appealing British offer to recognize its "independence." As with the French, Menelik used the moment to extend his territorial claims eastwards into what had by then become "British Somaliland." Declaring that the Somalis had since time immemorial been nothing else but the "cattle keepers of the Ethiopians," he demanded at least a half of all British possessions, eventually settling for "a hefty third" (Lewis 1988: 130). According to another article of the agreement he concluded with the British, he promised to prevent arms shipments to the khalifa.

Meanwhile, Menelik neither opposed nor wholeheartedly supported a joint Franco-Abyssinian expedition to rendezvous with Marchand at Fashoda. While the French laboriously proceeded to this destination from two directions, Menelik was busy snatching Beni Shangul from Mahdist Sudan despite having sent friendly letters to the khalifa. The military manoeuvres that resulted in this annexation were portrayed to the French as part of their grand joint exercise. In the event, a contingent of Abyssinians accompanying a couple of French officers reached a wrong spot on the White Nile (on 22 June 1898), planted French and Abyssinian flags, and immediately withdrew prior to Marchand's arrival at Fashoda (on 10 July 1898). The British (who had driven the khalifa out of Omdurman and rushed southward) and French forces under Marchand stood eyeball to eyeball until diplomatic deals resulted in France backing down (weakened as it was at home by the Dreyfus controversy). The khalifa spent the year after this incident running to Kordofan and back east as a fugitive until meeting his death at the final battle near Kosti on 24 November 1899 (Holt 1970: 243).

We can now enumerate the geopolitical entities that came to constitute the Horn of Africa when the curtain finally dropped on this intricate drama.

1. The demise of the Mahdist state led to the emergence of the peculiar colony of Anglo-Egyptian Sudan.

2. The other British-owned colony in the region was British Somaliland.
3. The French remained restricted to their minuscule enclave of French Somaliland (later Djibouti).
4. Italy remained in possession of Eritrea and Italian Somaliland to once more attempt connecting them, at the expense of the Ethiopian Empire's survival, in the 1930s.
5. Situated in the middle of these European colonies was the peculiar African empire of Ethiopia.

In the 1990s, the borders of these entities reverted to what they had been roughly a century earlier. They still remain in the grips of conflicts driven mostly by the desire to achieve a better fit between *people, nation, state, territory,* and *sovereignty.* Remarkably, these conflicts continue in a manner reminiscent of the interactive process that brought the concerned entities into existence. How to situate the resolution of these conflicts within the contemporary context of increasing interdependence at sub-state, state, regional, and global spheres is the fundamental aim of this work.

THE EXPANSIONISM OF INTERNAL ACTORS

Christian Abyssinia

The two local actors, Christian Abyssinia and Mahdist Sudan, share the common feature of subscribing to religious-based ideologies. Evincing a primordial identity and subscribing to a religious-based ideology of domination have, however, endured for much longer in Abyssinia. The self-perception of the Abyssinians as a people destined to rule their neighbours is noted by a number of scholars. One of them states that "the Abyssinians consider[ed] themselves entitled to subject and enslave other people" (Kaufeler 1988: 197). Similarly, Christopher Clapham (2002: 10) asserts that "The possession of a long-established and politically dominant state ... promoted a set of attitudes or ideologies, compounded of Orthodox Christianity, a set of historical mythologies and a written language, which defined its members in their own eyes as being more civilized than their neighbours and in turn *fostered a sense of manifest destiny in their claims to govern surrounding territories*" (italics added). The mythology that Clapham alludes to was first recorded in a medieval piece of literature known as the *Kibre-Negast* (The Glory of Kings). The fundamental message of this writing is that the Abyssinians are superior not only to the surrounding so-called Hamitic peoples (already denigrated in the Scriptures) but also to other Semites and Caucasian Christians, according to Levine (1974: 92–112). This supposedly resulted from God's decision to revoke his original covenant with the other descendants of Abraham (Moslem Arabs and Jews) and replacing it with a new one solely with the Abyssinian Orthodox Christians. Other Christians are discredited for deviating from the true orthodox faith. The overall result was the elevation of the Abyssinians to the status of "the sole authentic bearers of Christianity, the only people in the world now favored by the God of Solomon" (Levine 1974: 107). The result was the entrenchment of Abyssinian self-perception as being superior "to the Jews and other Christians; and a fortiori to all who were not of Semitic descent or Christians" (Levine 1974: 107). Integrated into the teachings of the Orthodox Church, this myth has been drummed into the minds of ordinary Abyssinians down through the centuries until the supremacist thinking has become accepted as a given.

This Abyssinian supremacist conviction was perhaps viewed with benign curiosity by neighbouring societies before modern firearms started flooding into the region in the second half of the nineteenth century. Coupled with the realization of the centuries-old Abyssinian obsession with the acquisition of firearms, this supremacist belief thereafter spelled utter disaster for numerous adjacent societies. Its religious-based ideology of domination also made conflict with the other religiously motivated local power (Mahdist Sudan) inevitable. We will return to these issues later on. What should be underlined here is the elevation and entrenchment of Abyssinian supremacist belief subsequent to Italian defeat at Adowa and the resultant Abyssinian success in lording over numerous previously independent communities.

Mahdist Sudan

The rise of Mahdist Sudan was also driven by a religious-based ideological conviction, as has already been stated. Mohammed Ahmed's rise to leadership resulted from his successful assumption of the status of the Mahdi, the Expected Deliverer whose arrival was prophesied in Islamic literature. One could become a Mahdi on the grounds of descending from the Prophet Mohammed (i.e., being of the *ahl al-bayt*), preferably reinforced with personal and hereditary piety. Mohammed Ahmed fulfilled both qualifications, for "[H]is family claimed to be Ashraf, descendants of the Prophet, and one of his ancestors had been noted for piety" (Holt 1970: 45). Once he managed in persuading a core group of committed followers to accept his "divine election" based on a series of visions (Holt 1970: 45), he was well on his way to successfully assume the Mahdiship. However, it was a series of military victories that he scored against the Egyptian forces starting in 1881 that more than anything else became the pivotal factor that persuaded groups from within the Sudan and elsewhere to rally to his cause. As one victory followed another, the morale of his adversaries rapidly ebbed, enabling him to capture Khartoum on 26 January 1885. This set in motion the collapse of Egyptian rule not only in the Sudan but also elsewhere in the Horn of Africa, as has been noted above.

The news of Mahdist victory reverberated throughout the neighbouring Moslem world. But within six months of rising to such prominence, the Mahdi died, on 22 June 1885, before he could transform this prestige into the project of conquest that he had promised to extend as far east as Mecca and Damascus (Clark 1998: 207). He was succeeded by his earliest and most committed disciple and able lieutenant, Abdallahi bin Mohammed, whose succession was not uncontested. Unlike Mohammed Ahmed, Abdallahi could not trace his origins to Arabia, let alone claim descent from the Prophet—indeed his roots were in West Africa (Holt 1970: 51). Hence, he had to come up with an alternative rationale to override the opinion of those who believed that succession belonged strictly to the Mahdi's relatives. He came up with a story of a chain of communications existing between him and the Almighty with the Mahdi as one of the intermediaries:

> Al-Khidir saith unto me, "The Mahdi has said to you that God informed Gabriel, and Gabriel informed the Prophet, and the Prophet informed the Mahdi, and the Mahdi informed me that I should inform you that God has made you a guidance in the earth from the east of it to the west; and he says, 'He who loves you and follows what you say has accepted the guidance from Us. He who has accepted the guidance from Us is accepted of Us and is safe from the punishment of God. He who does not love you and does not hear what you say is amongst those who have gone astray, and the abode of him who goes astray is hell-fire.'" (Holt 1970: 139)

Despite his relative success in having this story accepted by many of his immediate subordinates, including even a few from the Mahdi's kinfolk (the Ashraf), he was never confident of the latter's unreserved loyalty and had to exercise maximum vigilance. He moved some of the Ashraf to Omdurman for better surveillance and demoted those in positions of key command. Abdallahi's security, however, rested on maintaining "the momentum imparted to the Mahdist movement by its founder" (Holt 1970: 147), more than on anything else. He thus stepped up his predecessor's practice of issuing ultimatum to powers near and far to either convert or face the jihad. Yohannes IV received such a message while he in turn was busy instructing Wallo Moslem Oromos "to renounce their faith and embrace Christianity or face confiscation of their land and property" (Zewde 1991: 48). Their competing sources of legitimacy and posture as zealous apostles of their respective faiths alone would have sufficed to pit these two powers against each other. It was two other developments, however, that speeded up this impending clash. First, the presence of prominent Sudanese refugees, including the sheikh of the Hamran tribe, Salih Idris, in western Abyssinia, became a cause for friction. (The presence of one entity's asylum seekers in the other would remain the cause for mutual suspicion a century later.) Second, and even more importantly, the Abyssinians (in collaboration with the sheikh's followers) raided al-Qallabat in August 1884 to carry out Yohannes's agreement with the British to facilitate the evacuation of Egyptian contingents besieged there (Holt 1970: 168). The decision of the Abyssinians to side with the anti-Mahdist camp was significant for it relieved the khalifa of the Prophet's stricture "Leave the Abyssinians alone, while they leave you alone." Hence, the prevailing reluctance of Sudanese Moslems to fight the Abyssinians was thereby dissipated.

I have briefly sketched how Yohannes had to conduct war simultaneously on two fronts: against internal challengers and external aggressors. The khalifa's situation was no different as he had to subdue numerous internal revolts while fighting Abyssinia and trying to expand into Egypt. The Rizayqat, Kababish, and Darfur of the west were in rebellion for most of 1887. A self-styled Nabi Issa—"the Prophet Jesus who was to come after the Mahdi" (Holt 1970: 171)—also staged a rebellion among the forces stationed at al-Qallabat facing Abyssinia. This coincided with the rebellion by one of the riverine tribes (one of the earliest communities to rally to the Mahdi's cause), the Rufai Al Hui. After they were defeated by a contingent of the Khalifa's forces, they "were dragged off to Omdurman where they lived in abject misery and destitution" (Holt 1970: 171). The khalifa's preoccupation with these rebellions and fighting the Abyssinians relieved southern Sudan of much attention. Raided rather than ruled (Woodward 1994: 82), southern Sudan hence was for practical purposes outside Mahdist Sudan.

THE DAWNING OF EVIL DAYS

Were my account to stop here, the history of war among local and external powers competing to control large parts of the Horn would paint a misleadingly romantic picture. Seen through the eyes of the affected common folk, however, those indeed were "evil days," as noted by several contemporary foreign observers (Pankhurst 1967: 163, 168). For the multiple conflicts that raged in the Horn of Africa in the second half of the nineteenth century spelled catastrophe for ordinary people. Even ordinary Abyssinians, whose leaders were emerging as local imperialists, suffered immensely. But the peoples conquered and subjugated by Abyssinia suffered even more. Mustering and arming large armies required resource mobilization to an unprecedented extent. For example, the size of Menelik's army at the time of the battle of Adowa was estimated at one hundred twenty thousand fighting men (Pankhurst 1967: 114). The term "army" is perhaps a misnomer as this force "did not consist of fighting men only; there were women, grandfathers, lame people, babies, priests, lepers … it is the transplanting of a whole people" (Pankhurst 1967: 33). Since each combatant was accompanied by at least three supporters/dependants, the population on the move must have exceeded three hundred thousand. And this migrating humanity depended on locals for all its provisions. Observers were at loss to find proper ways of describing the impact of this horde's passage on the affected society and the environment. One likened it to a "trail of brown ants … eating up everything" while Pankhurst (1967: 175) himself states that the soldiers "destroyed the country in much the same way as locusts." He concludes that "The fighting and troop movements of 1895 and 1896 were as destructive as any on record" (Pankhurst 1967: 167). The Adowa area was littered with the skulls of men and bones of animals (Pankhurst 1967: 168). The country was stripped clean of trees for firewood and defensive purposes and even bird and animal life was absent. Not surprisingly, the locals took arms from the Italians to protect their property (Pankhurst 1967: 169). The environment around Adowa and the immediate vicinity perhaps never fully recovered from the devastation that took place at this time, thus perhaps setting the stage for the recurrence of famine in the area during the subsequent decades.

The non-Abyssinian peoples conquered by Menelik during this time were deliberately treated even more brutally. Writing of the area around Didessa, one observer noted that "three quarters of the male population had been killed" (Pankhurst 1967: 173). The Borana Oromo pastoralists were raided for cattle no fewer than seven times during the same period. Keffa was raided by the army of Gojjame king Tekla Haimanot in November of 1890 "more to obtain food than to conquer," as stated by one source (Rosenfeld 1976: 146). Whatever livestock escaped these raids was wiped out by the rinderpest epidemic that suddenly arrived on the scene. The resulting catastrophe was immense, with the Oromos areas "immediately adjacent to the northern highlands" losing up to 75 percent of their population (Marcus 1975: 144). Although ordinary folks of the conquering and conquered societies suffered, the Abyssinians were treated preferentially in three ways. First, they remained owners of the land they tilled while the conquered societies were mostly turned into landless tenants of the conquerors. Second, living on their own land as tillers of the soil, "nearly all" of these (northerners) possessed "modern breechloaders and plenty of cartridges," in the words of a foreign observer. As a result of such pervasive possession of firearms, "Northern Ethiopia had in fact become an arms-owning society" (Pankhurst 1967: 121). The Abyssinians were apparently telling each other "Seek ye first the firearm and all other things shall be added unto you." All an armed individual needed to do was to migrate to the conquered areas if he wished to become a landlord benefiting from the sweat of the subjugated peoples. Third, the conquered areas were raided for grain and cattle to establish granaries in many Abyssinian provinces, including the not so popular Tigray (Marcus 1975: 139), to feed famine victims. The overall result is put succinctly by Harold Marcus: "As King of Shoa, Menelik had exploited the south and south-west to purchase weapons; as emperor, he used its wealth to bolster the north's sagging economy, and to ensure the continuation of Amhara-Tigrean political and cultural hegemony" (1975: 140).

The picture concurrently emerging in the Sudan was not perhaps so grave but it was also bleak. Sustaining recurrent internal military operations alongside thrusts into neighbouring countries necessitated maintaining high levels of taxation. Renamed in Islamic terms as *zakat, ushur,* and *ghanima,* taxation continued with the *awlad al arab,* "the western Sudanese brought to Omdurman by the Khalifa Abdullahi" as collectors, while the bulk of the burden fell on "the *awlad al balad,* the merchants and cultivators of the Nile valley" (Clark 1998: 209). *Ghanima* was the Islamic notion of war booty that results from the expropriation of the property of anyone declared an enemy of Allah, which was rendered synonymous with opponents of the Mahdia. Clark depicts a truly vicious cycle when he writes that "The threat of confiscation became a weapon for control, but as the state's demands grew and costs rose, the number of potential opponents increased" (Clark 1998: 210). Bogus accusations of apostasy were used to raid the peoples of Beni Shangul merely to provision the Qallabat garrison, although their rulers were among the earliest converts to the Mahdist cause (Triulzi 1981: 151).

CONCLUSION

The years between the rise of the Mahdi in the Sudan in 1881, which occasioned the collapse of Egyptian expansionist ambition, and the defeat of Italy in the battle of Adowa in 1896, were truly momentous ones. Two neighbouring entities (Abyssinia and the Sudan), pursuing expansion inspired by their respective religious beliefs, confronted each other while quarrelling with and being manipulated by (as well as manipulating the rivalry of) European colonial powers. Developments within and between these two local powers tended to impact on each other in a mutually reciprocal manner, as they continue to do a century later. Despite failing to withstand direct European (and nominal Egyptian) re-occupation, Mahdist Sudan achieved the status of being described as the first independent Sudanese state (Woodward 1994: 81). And that state's presence was concentrated at the central and northeastern parts of the Sudan (Woodward 1994: 82). British investment in social and economic development was also concentrated in the same area. Hence, the elite groups that took over the post-colonial Sudanese state and championed the task of nation-building arose from this core area. Southern Sudan, which was "not effectively part of the Mahdist state" (Holt and Daly 1979: 10), remained marginalized both under the condominium and during the independence era.

On the other hand, Christian Abyssinia not only avoided Sudan's fate of falling under European domination but actually became a party to the scramble for Africa to emerge as the Ethiopian Empire. As so aptly put by Erlich (1986: 4), "While rebuffing imperialism successfully in its north, Ethiopia managed to practice it to the south." This, of course, resulted fortuitously from the impasse of inter-European rivalry rather than from a peculiarly cohesive state putting up resistance. Regardless, Abyssinia's luck in avoiding the fate of many African societies had one important implication. Coptic Christianity and the related mythical writings of the *Kibre Negest* were further reinforced and continued to serve as the basis of supremacist thinking. The persistence of this belief would later stand in the way of forging a state that acknowledged the equality of its citizens. On the other hand, Mahdism's ability to inspire the same level of supremacist thinking was severely damaged by the reconquest. However, the Mahdi's meteoric rise to power testified to Islam's mass-mobilizing potential. The resultant British manipulation of pro-Mahdist as well as anti-Mahdist sentiment inevitably stamped northern Sudan's political culture. The politicization of Islam that manifests itself in diverse forms could thus be traced back to Mahdist period and the subsequent British era.

Finally, all the entities that today make up the Horn of Africa came into existence as temporary affairs when competing grand ambitions to bring the whole area under one dominion were aborted. That such grand ambitions weren't realized was primarily due to rivalries between European colonial powers and the obstruction of similar local aspirants. The actors engaged in this process were seeking an alliance on the basis of religion and race. Domestic conflicts within the Sudan and Abyssinia and their conflicts with European powers as well as with adjacent African societies overlapped in a seamless manner. The process that gave birth to all other entities in the Horn of Africa was also operating as Christian Abyssinia was transformed into the Ethiopian Empire and Mahdist Sudan was restored to the status of the Anglo-Egyptian condominium. Italy's temporary footholds, Ertirea and Italian Somaliland, and the British and French Somalilands came into existence during the same period. In none of these entities was it necessary to articulate cultural, political, or other bonds between the rulers and the rest of society except the principle of effective occupation. Hence, the cultivation of such new bases faced insurmountable difficulties when it became necessary in the period after the Second World War. The sustainable existences of the concerned entities began to have a mutual and negative impact on each other then and continue to do so to this day.

INTRODUCTION

THE INTERACTIVE PROCESS that brought the various entities of the Horn of Africa into existence has been summarized in the previous chapter. Their status as tentative footholds for grander imperial territorial acquisitions has also been discussed. I will now proceed to briefly summarize how even their *territorial* definition remained susceptible to change well into the 1950s. Prior to this period, some of these entities appeared destined to disappear by being absorbed into adjacent ones, resulting in the expansion of the absorbing entities. The potential territorial alterations perhaps impacted minimally on the day-to-day existence of the concerned populace. Nevertheless, as Rubenson (1989: 406) states, "Ideas, plans and proposals, once expressed publicly or institutionalized in government departments and agencies, seem to hold on to some kind of life of their own, more or less dynamic, sometimes hibernating as it were for a longer or shorter period of time." Rubenson then traces developments in the Ethiopia of the 1970s and 1980s back to various proposals to partition the Empire during the decades after its emergence. The same could perhaps be said regarding simultaneous political developments in Somalia and Sudan. The repercussions of the proclaimed or implemented proposals by themselves would not have perhaps endured. Couching them in terms that appeared to recognize the rights of numerous *nations* was what imbued them with lasting implications. The notion of ascribing certain *territories* to the *nations* inhabiting them started to emerge during this time, permanently affecting the politics of the region.

THE ETHIOPIAN EMPIRE'S UNCERTAIN FATE

The Ethiopian Empire was merely a quasi-independent entity, as seen by the powers owning contiguous colonies. "The most obvious expression of recognized statehood was then the ability to gain access to imported arms," according to Clapham (2002: 11). Each concerned European power upheld the right of Abyssinian rulers to acquire arms either as a first step toward the Empire's annexation or to frustrate a similar agenda of its competitor. The aberrant existence of Ethiopia as an independent entity in an otherwise completely partitioned Africa was widely expected to be temporary. The ease with which the concerned powers subsequently deliberated on partitioning the Empire attests to this expectation.

Spheres of Influence

As Emperor Menelik's health started failing in the early 1900s, the concerned powers (Britain, France, and Italy) found it necessary to revisit the fate of the Ethiopian Empire. They had divergent appraisals of what could follow a chaotic succession, if Menelik died without naming an heir. France and Italy looked forward to the Empire's disintegration, hoping to extend their adjacent colonies. Britain, however, preferred supporting "a neutral, weak, indigenous Ethiopian Government than to allow the country to be divided into spheres of influence" (Marcus 1964: 30). After a series of complicated diplomatic negotiations, they ultimately concluded the Tripartite Treaty of 1906. Despite agreeing to maintain "intact the integrity of Ethiopia" (Ghebre-Ab 1993: 17-19), they proceeded to assign each other spheres of influence. The Nile basin was assigned to Britain while France was granted the area through which ran the railway then under construction from its colony of Djibouti. The lion's share was allocated to Italy in order to afford it a "territorial connection between Eritrea and Italian Somaliland" (Barker 1968: 22-23) through a corridor passing to the west of the imperial capital. Kitchener ultimately drew up the 1913 proposal based on the relevant articles of this treaty (see map 3). It was succeeded by yet another proposal apparently discussed during the grand territorial bazaar held in Paris after the First World War (see map 4). (Both maps are from Rubenson 1989.)

Appeasing Fascist Italy

Britain and France returned to the issue of the fate of the Ethiopian Empire in the mid-1930s when they wished to entice Italy away from entering into alliance with Germany by bribing it with territorial conces-

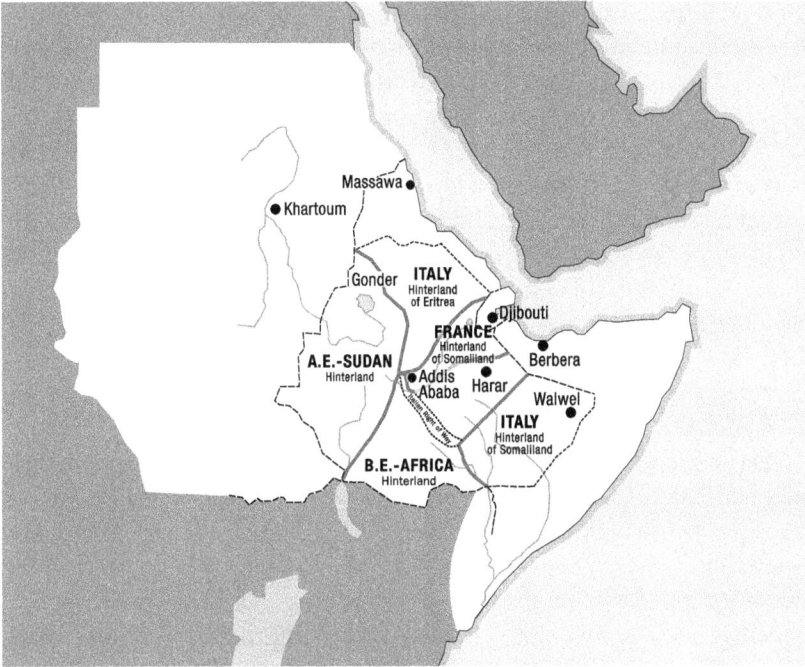

Map 3: Tripartite Partition: Kitchener Scheme of 1913 (PRO. MPK 430—S.R. 1934)

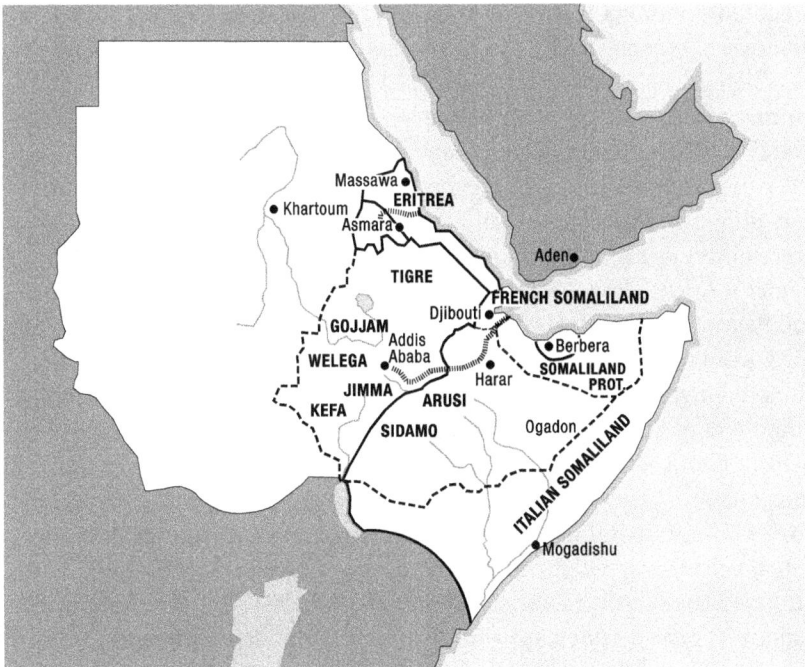

Map 4: Anglo-Italian World War I Partition Scheme (PRO. MR 1932—S.R. 1934)

sions at Ethiopia's expense. Consequently, they began cajoling "Haile Selassie into handing over large portions of Ethiopian territory to Italy" (Barker 1968: 191). "[H]ow little would Italy take; how much would Ethiopia yield; how far could a solution be imposed without incurring an outcry" in Britain and France was all that remained to be sorted out (Barker 1968: 193). Italy was told it could annex the whole of Tigray to Eritrea and the Ogaden to Italian Somaliland. Furthermore, it was also to enjoy special economic rights in large parts of southern Oromia (the Oromo homeland) adjacent to the Ogaden. (For a sketch, see Barker 1968: 195.) The Ethiopians "helplessly watched while great powers negotiated their fate" (Salwen 2001: 75) without even informing them, thereby implying the "acceptance of Italy's position that Ethiopia was not an independent nation" (Salwen 2001: 91).

These gestures ultimately failed to achieve their intended aim, perhaps because Fascist Italy desired to avenge the defeat of 1896 as much as it wanted territory. It therefore went ahead and invaded the Ethiopian Empire in late 1935, completing its conquest the following year. As war clouds gathered over his realm, however, Emperor Haile Selassie was evidently seeking pretexts that would avail him the protection of a significant power. With this in mind he signed an agreement with the mostly British-staffed but American-owned African Exploration and Development Corporation on 30 August 1935. This agreement accorded the Corporation "the sole rights to oil, minerals, and other natural resources, over half of the Empire for 75 years." The expectation was "to draw the United States into the Italo-Ethiopian conflict, hoping that the United States would be committed to defending its economic interests." When the Americans dismissed the prospect of engaging in "dollar diplomacy," this ploy came to naught (Salwen 2001: 202). As the invading Italians were converging on his capital both from the south and north, the emperor made a last-ditch effort to salvage something from the impending fiasco. He sent "private communications to Mussolini expressing his willingness to cede large portions of his country" (Salwen 2001: 96), thus displaying flexibility concerning the territorial integrity of his empire. Undeterred by even this offer, the Italians pushed on with their plan of conquest. Once they had completed the conquest, the Italians integrated the Empire with their other colonies, thus creating their grand Africa Orientale Italiana. In the administrative arrangement they instituted, Eritrea was redefined to include Tigray and Italian Somaliland to embrace the whole of the Ogaden (Sbacchi 1985: 85). The fate of the Empire appeared sealed as even the Emperor and his crown prince were outbidding each other to recognize Italian rule, during their time in exile (Sbacchi 1985: 121–26). One secret negotiation exercise was actually about to result in settlement when the British stepped in to quash it (Sbacchi 1985: 126). The decision of the Italians to side with Germany ultimately pushed Britain and its allies into the war that resulted in Italian expulsion from the Horn of Africa. Italian administrative divisions are shown below.

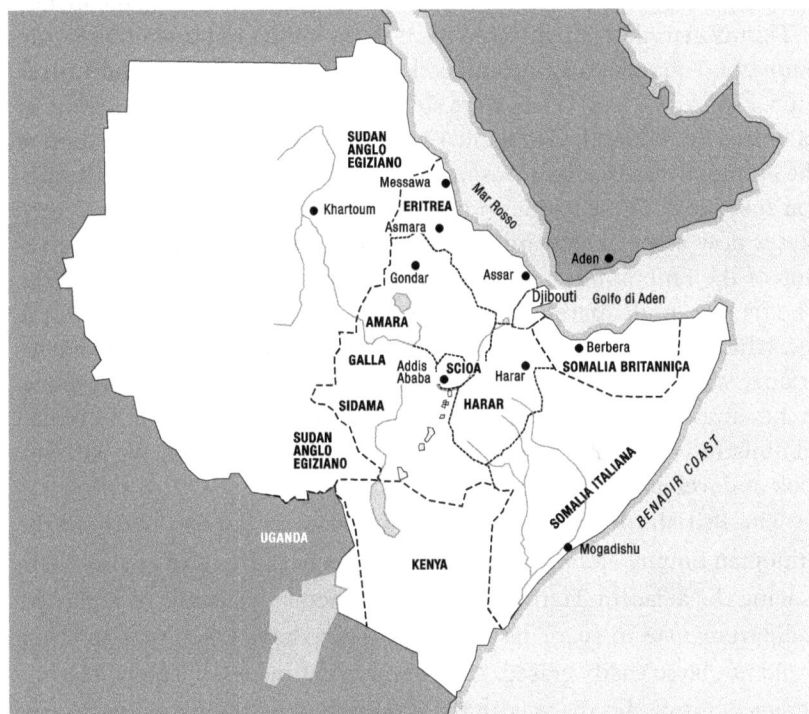

Map 5: Italian Administrative Divisions

Going from Doom to Boon

Haile Selassie's empire, which looked doomed in the late 1930s, actually appeared poised to extend to the shores of the Red Sea and the Indian Ocean by 1940. This is evidenced by the fact that, as he was re-entering his realm, the Emperor called on the Eritreans and "Italian" Somalis to come and dwell under the shade of the Ethiopian flag (Markakis 1987: 280). He later requested British permission to visit Mogadishu, displaying "an interesting symptom of Ethiopian imperialistic dreams embracing territory from Massawa to the Juba," (Rubenson 1989: 404) in the words of a British official. He then started "creating and supporting an irredentist movement for the incorporation of Eritrea and Italian Somaliland into the Ethiopian State" (Ellingson 1977: 261). These targets of his irredentist claims were bound to respond in kind by claiming the Empire's provinces inhabited by their kinfolk. Irredentism and counter-irredentism thus began to confront each other in large areas of the Horn.

Meanwhile, the British were considering a number of options concerning the Empire's fate. Their evident interest in maintaining the merger of Tigrinya speakers manifested itself in their offer to crown Ras Siyum (Emperor Yohannes's grandson) as king of a united Tigray and Eritrea (Rubenson 1989: 404). They were similarly talking about the creation of "a united Somaliland, Gallaland (Oromoland), and the amalgamation of the Nilotic tribes that live West and North West of Lake Rudolf" (Rubenson 1989: 405). These various proposals were scuttled because the United States now stepped forward as the supporter not only of the preservation of the Empire but also the extension of its borders to the Red Sea. The US role in ultimately railroading resolution NO. 390(v) through the UN, which linked Eritrea with Ethiopia through a federal arrangement, is fairly widely known to need much elaboration here. Meanwhile, movements interested in preserving the national unions resulting from Italian administrative arrangements started appearing on the scene. We will first look at developments in Eritrea.

The British ultimately restored the pre-1935 borders between the Ethiopian Empire and Eritrea. The definition of Eritrea as a territory embracing the adjacent Tigrinya-speaking Ethiopian province of Tigray (as it did from 1936 to 1940), however, appears to have taken root and thus could not be so easily erased. A movement calling itself Tigray-Tigrinie emerged during the 1940s with the intention of working towards the independence of such a Greater Eritrea. The leaders of this movement argued that "The geographic position, its culture, its history and its trading are clear proof that Tigray is part of Eritrea—as it was before the Italian occupation of 1889 and in the years 1935-45" (Abbay 1998: 42). The idea of a united Tigrinya-speaking *nation* was destined to resurface in the initial manifesto of the Tigray People's Liberation Front (TPLF), souring its relations with the Eritrean People's Liberation Front (EPLF). The 1998-2000 Ethiopia-Eritrea war partly resulted from TPLF frustration with failing to entice Eritrea back into some form of association with Ethiopia, as I argue elsewhere (Lata 2003). Thus can ideas floated decades earlier influence attitudes much later on.

Had the Eritrea of the 1940s and 1950s achieved independence (with or without Tigray), it in turn would have faced separatist demands by some of its diverse communities. The appearance of a group advocating the separation and ultimate independence of the western province (homeland of the Beni Amer pastoralists) in the 1950s attests to this possibility (Markakis 1987: 67-68). Similar simultaneous pressures for fission and fusion appeared in various parts of the Horn and at different times. The Emperor's irredentism ultimately prevailed over that of the Eritreans, thereby paving the way for Eritrea's outright annexation in 1962. The Emperor cited numerous historical, cultural, religious, and economic reasons for making his case regarding Eritrea. The fear that an "independent Eritrea would be a magnet and refuge for dissidents in Tigrai" must have also figured in the Emperor's calculation, according to Markakis (1987: 63).

The Imperial Ethiopian Government was not so lucky in achieving its irredentist claim of the adjacent Somali-inhabited European colonies. The regime's problems started when the British delayed restoring the Empire's pre-1935 borders with Italian and British Somaliland. Territorial loss appeared threateningly possible once the British plan of permanently amalgamating all Somali-inhabited areas was publicized (Markakis 1987: 53). External powers once again came to the Empire's rescue when the US, USSR, France, and Italy joined forces to scuttle this plan, paving the way for the resumption of Ethiopian rule over the Ogaden, Haud, and Reserved Areas. This did not happen, however, without the seed of Somali irredentism taking root. The aspiration of ingathering all Somalis into one state had grown so widespread and so strong that the merger of former British and Italian Somaliland appeared inevitable once they attained independence. The Emperor, meanwhile, continued to fight irredentism with irredentism. Dismissing the viability of even a Greater Somalia, he advised the Somalis to emulate the Eritreans by "rejoining" their "Mother Country" (*Ethiopia Observer* 1956) as late as 1956. This was at a time when irredentist sentiments had become pervasive throughout Somali society, ultimately becoming the sturdiest foundation of Somali national consensus.

THE SUDAN'S EQUALLY UNCERTAIN FATE

The fate of the Sudan was similarly under consideration during this same period. Its supposed joint rulers, Britain and Egypt, engaged in a competition to win "the hearts and minds of the Sudanese" (Daly 1988: 188). The British were keen on thwarting the Sudan's permanent reversion to unilateral Egyptian rule. They found invoking the Sudanese "right to self-determination" a convenient rationale to advance this agenda. Thus, by harping on "the historical Sudanese mistrust of Egypt," they started encouraging those Sudanese who had raised the slogan of "Sudan for the Sudanese" (Daly 1988: 188). Meanwhile, they also instituted the policy of insulating southern Sudan "from the destructive influences of the northern, Arab, Muslim Sudan" (Daly 1988: 194). Nevertheless, the policies of detaching Sudan from Egypt and southern Sudan from the north were subordinate to the policy of "ensuring the British position in the eastern Mediterranean" (Daly 1988: 192). The overriding nature of this policy limited the extent to which Britain could go in confronting Egypt.

At the time when they were shielding southern Sudan from Arab and Islamic influences, the British were also considering whether to annex it to one of their "East African colonies" or to allow it to emerge "as an independent state." Egypt's objection combined with Britain's superior interest there ultimately forced (in 1947) the latter to abandon this "policy of separate development for the South" (Deng 1997: 338), a mere nine years before a united Sudan's independence. How Sudan's ascension to independence was accompanied with the outbreak of violence, which has continued with a brief hiatus from 1972 to 1983, will be discussed in a later section.

The Sudan that avoided fracturing in fact appeared poised to gain more territory in its northeastern and southeastern borders in the 1940s. This was to result from Britain's other considerations regarding the future of Eritrea and Somalia. A plan, under discussion in the Foreign Office in mid-1943, involved ceding highland Eritrea to Ethiopia in return for Ethiopia relinquishing areas adjacent to Somalia, Kenya, and the Sudan. The Empire was hence being asked to "relinquish the whole province of Ogaden with parts of Harar and Bale, a strip of territory along the Kenya frontier near Moyale, and the Baro triangle in the west" (Yohannes 1991: 63). Had this British policy been implemented, the Sudan would have thus gained Ethiopia's Gambela province as well as the whole of lowland western Eritrea.

Sudan's disappearance by absorption into a much larger Egyptian state also remained a distinct possibility during this time. Only a fluke consequence of the 1951 Nasserite revolution saved it from this destiny. The revolutionary government "abandoned Egyptian claim to sovereignty" over the Sudan (Daly 1988: 190), perhaps counting that unionist sentiment would prevail. British advocacy of the Sudanese right to self-determination ran the risk of proving hypocritical once the Egyptians stood aside and left the choice of unity with Egypt or separation to the Sudanese. Left with no other alternative, Britain was hence forced to conclude the 1953 Anglo-Egyptian Agreement, which provided for "elections to a Sudanese parliament and an elaborate timetable by which power would be transferred and the Sudanese themselves would determine the question of union [with Egypt] or independence" (Daly 1988: 191). Union was doomed for two reasons. First, the Ansar (the followers of the Mahdi) were staunchly opposed to it. Second, the stance of the pro-Egyptian unionist forces was, in all probability, merely tactical.

CONCLUSION

The *territorial* definition of the Horn's two major states, the Sudan and the Ethiopian Empire, was not stabilized until the second half of the 1950s. Sudan's separation from Egypt and the unification of the north and south had then become a reality. During the same period, the Ethiopian Empire had achieved its irredentist claim to Eritrea. What remained was to undo the anomalous federal arrangement that had served as a convenient compromise both in Eritrea and at the United Nations. The only irredentism that refused to go away was that of the Somalis. After British and Italian Somaliland precipitously merged immediately after independence in 1960, Ethiopia became preoccupied with frustrating a united Somalia's claim to the adjacent parts of the Empire. The fate of the French colony of Djibouti remained suspended as its two neighbours fought over territory.

The unquestionable international recognition of the Ethiopian Empire's independence was also accomplished in the period after the Second World War. The growing international proscription of colonial domination was pivotal in making this possible. The same current was responsible for the Sudan and other concerned entities gaining independence from European colonial rulers. Along with the growing belief that made this possible, the original haphazard territorial claims had come to an end. From then on, at least paying lip service to the idea of government by consent became an indispensable foundation of modern statehood. Hence, thereafter the concerned Horn states faced the challenge of replacing the original basis of "effective control" with its modern counterparts, popular endorsement and the cultivation of a single national identity. This became the main content of the nation-building exercise that will be discussed in the following pages.

INTRODUCTION

THE ERA AFTER THE SECOND WORLD WAR witnessed the emergence of the nation-state as supposedly the only appropriate structure for organizing local and global affairs. Empires were subsequently impugned as illegitimate since "Fascist nationalism produced the opposed reality of anti-Fascism; and anti-Fascism...became antiracism; and antiracism led in due course to an end of colonization" (Davidson 1992: 52). This view helped facilitate the attainment of independence by European colonies in Africa. Casting the emerging independent African states in the nation-state mould, however, proved a highly daunting proposition. Shaping nations out of the entities in the Horn proved even more challenging than in the rest of Africa due to a number of factors. First, the history of the *nation* and *state* was commonly assumed to commence with decolonization in most parts of the rest of Africa. In the Horn of Africa, however, the *states'* official history was reduced to that of the dominant groups and traced back into antiquity. Those who found themselves within a state's *territory* but were left unmentioned in these official histories were practically treated as nations without history. Hence, contests over the interpretation of history commonly accompanied the articulation of self-determination in the Horn. Second, most African countries adopted the departing European colonial powers' languages as the medium of administration and education. In the Horn of Africa, however, the languages of the dominant groups were accorded official status. The result was the politicization of language to a degree rarely witnessed in the rest of the Continent. Culture and language were to ultimately figure in the conceptualization of many Horn peoples as *nations*.

The Horn states would all try to overcome the undeniable mismatch between *nation* and *state* in an interactive manner and ultimately fail.

The Somalis invested heavily in extending the state *territory* to embrace the entire homeland of the Somali *nation*, obviously at Ethiopia's expense. Once this dream began to dim Somalia was put on the course that eventually resulted in the disintegration of its state and society. Meanwhile, the Eritrean struggle, wholeheartedly supported by the Somalis, was capped with success, resulting in Eritrea's emergence as the only African State that attained independence by breaking away from another. After this took place in 1991, the borders of the Ethiopian Empire reverted to what they had been from around 1900 to 1952. Even the rump of the Empire was forced to abandon the project of continuing to shape a monocultural nation-state. The Sudan's position lies somewhere between that of Somalia and Ethiopia with large parts of its *territory* remaining outside the control of central state authorities from the early 1980s onwards. Whether mere decentralization, a reconfiguration of its identity, or even its breakup would ultimately result from the decades-long armed struggle is hard to predict at the moment.

The lessons that could be drawn from the above process of ongoing fragmentation are sadly escaping the concerned state actors and their opponents. The nation-state model's continued dominance in their thinking seems to stand in the way of drawing the required lessons. Hence, Eritrea displays a determination to succeed in its nation-building exercise despite the failure of this project in the immediate environs and elsewhere. The ongoing process of resolving the Sudan's decades-old conflict is premised on giving it another chance to successfully coalesce into a *nation*. If this proves impossible, northern and southern Sudan are expected to emerge as separate *nations*. That the difficulty may rest more with the inappropriateness of the nation-state model in the case of Africa is in the process completely overlooked. Meanwhile, a strong current within the southern Sudanese movement continues to equate the achievement of self-determination with gaining independent nation-statehood. In Ethiopia, some opinion makers are working to revive the practically discredited agenda of shaping a monocultural nation out of the Empire by demonizing the post-1991 federal arrangement as "ethnic politics." They are, of course, capitalizing on the incumbent regime's abuse of federalism as a divide-and-rule tactic, which has resulted in sporadic intercommunal clashes. Dismay at this abuse and at "anti-ethnic politics" ravings is pushing some self-determination movements to react in an understandable but nevertheless outdated fashion. They are increasingly convinced that nothing short of independence would restore their constituencies' right to self-determination. This work aims to explore the conceptual frameworks that could put these contests within the evolving global and local context.

PROJECTING ETHIOPIA AS A MODERN NATION

The Aim: Shaping a Nation Out of Empire

How to describe the state created by Menelik and later on expanded by Haile Selassie with the annexation of Eritrea has been the subject of continuous debate, not least among "Ethiopians." The Somalis used the concept of "Euro-Abyssinian colonialism" (Greenfield 1965: 108) to define Ethiopia as an empire no different from that of the Europeans. Oromo scholars in due course developed the concept of dependent colonialism (Holcomb and Ibssa 1990) to designate Abyssinia as the local surrogate of Western imperialists. The assertion that one entity (Ethiopia) colonized another (Eritrea) predominates in the Eritrean discourse. The designation of Abyssinians as colonialists is, however, refuted by the Tigrean scholar Adhana Haile Adhana (1993: 12–29). He does this by arguing that a historico-politico-religious *state-nation* (distinct from a linguistic and secular-cultural *nation*) called Abyssinia existed in the region for many centuries. He believes a mutation emerged, however, when the Shawan Amhara sector of this *state-nation* first created the *empire-state* by expanding southwards under Menelik. And this Shawan-dominated *empire-state* subsequently succeeded in subordinating the other components of the *state-nation*. Hence, all the inhabitants of the contemporary Ethiopian state are portrayed as victims of domination by the Shawan Amhara aristocracy, according to Adhana. Abyssinia will hereafter be used in reference to the *state-nation*, the Orthodox Christian societies of the Horn of Africa composed of the speakers of Tigrinya and Amharic languages.

One fact appears indisputable regardless of whichever description one subscribes to: subordination characterizes the Ethiopian state, which clearly obviates its status as a *nation*. Concealing this subordination was not necessary in the days of Menelik, as empires outnumbered nation-states then and being an imperialist accorded one a dignified status. By the 1960s, however, the direct opposite was emerging, signalling that the days of empires were numbered. Disclaiming the existence of internal subordination and projecting Ethiopia as a modern *nation* became increasingly mandatory thereafter. The distortions resulting from this projection, however, impacted differently on the members of Adhana's *state-nation* and the rest. The measures that Emperor Haile Selassie's Imperial Ethiopian Government (IEG) took to qualify Ethiopia as a modern *nation* are numerous, but only the following will be briefly discussed in this work:

1. historicizing Ethiopia as an ancient *state* and a cohesive *nation*;
2. centralizing administration and imposing ostensibly uniform laws; and
3. imposing a single official language and state religion, Orthodox Christianity.

An Ancient Nation

Contemporary Ethiopia assumed its current territorial definition only at the end of the nineteenth century through the process discussed earlier. Officially, however, the IEG started projecting its existence as a *nation* back into antiquity. Former prime minister Aklilu Habte-Wold, for example, once announced at an OAU conference that "Ethiopia has always existed in history for centuries as an *independent state* and *as a nation*, for more than 3,000 years" (Habte-Wold 1963: 34; italics added). School textbooks similarly projected the history of the contemporary Ethiopian state back into antiquity. This official Ethiopian history was, of course, nothing else but the history of Adhana's *state-nation* or Abyssinia. And it was completely silent about other peoples who found themselves situated on Ethiopia's *territory* but outside the *nation* glorified in this official history. The practical presumption that these non-national inhabitants of Ethiopian *territory* have "neither their own history nor their distinct cultural personalities" (Kebede 1999: 14) was highly alienating, prompting them to inquire into their past. The esteemed personalities glorified in the official *national* history textbook were none other than the butchers, plunderers, and enslavers of their ancestors, they found out.

Centralizing Administration and Imposing Uniform Laws

Concentrating sovereign power in a single central location is the other aspect of modern *nation*-statehood. As part of projecting the empire as a nation, Ethiopia's rulers started avidly embracing "the universal norms of centralized government" (Zewde 1994: 35) from 1940 onwards. Centralization had been rising in Abyssinia since the middle of the nineteenth century, according to Teshale Tibebu (1995). "[T]he process of transformation from parcelized to centralized sovereignty" (1995: 31) was, however, completed only during the time of Haile Selassie. Thereafter, the ages-old Abyssinian tradition in which the Emperor (King of Kings) reigns over other monarchs came to an end. Care was however taken in assigning local notables as administrators of Abyssinian provinces, as attested to by the following figures: "from 1944 to 1966, 72% of the governors of *awrajas* (counties) in Tigre were Tigrean, 68% in Wollo, 52% in Gojjame, 83% in Shoa." Outside Abyssinia, on the other hand, "the highest offices were held by the Shoan nobility, middle-level posts by Amhara colonists, while local elites occupied—sometimes—only posts at the lowest level, that of the *woreda* (district)" (Lefort 1981: 17). Consequently, the ruled and the rulers rarely shared a common history, religion, language, and customs in the non-Abyssinian provinces. Their identity was thus neither recognized nor rendered recognizable by state organs and their functionaries.

Another aspect of the imperial regime's centralization exercise was the imposition of a uniform system of taxation. The previous *gabar* system of tribute exaction in the southern areas was, ironically, revoked by the Italian fascists and could never fully be reimposed. Instead, "the physical labor services of the gabbar system were transferred to equally exorbitant monetary rent payments and exploitation, where peasants were required to give up to 75 percent of their produce to the landowners" (Baissa 1998: 86). The increasingly onerous exaction of tribute could not be shrugged off as the misfortune of living under the rule of an outsider. Hence, permanent loss of land ownership rights coupled with a higher level of monetary exaction triggered a series of rural uprisings starting soon after Haile Selassie's return. The northernmost Oromos (the Raya and Azebo) rose up in 1943 to avert "fusion with other peoples into a single exploited peasantry" (Tareke 1991: 96). Similar uprisings occurred in Hararghe the same year and again in 1948 (Hassen 2000: 123). During the latter year, the highly Amharized Yejju Oromo "peasants rose after appeals against alienation of their land were ignored" (Zewde 1991: 213). Another major rural uprising in 1958 rocked large parts of Wallo province when the Muslim Oromos of Dawwe rose up to defend their land and religious rights (Hassen 2000: 124). And rising "economic exploitation...coupled with the degradation of their culture" (Zewde 1991: 218) instigated the Gedeo people's uprising of 1960. Discussing the specific situation among the Oromos, Mohammed Hassen (2000: 123) concludes that "Between 1941, when Emperor Haile Selassie was restored to power, and 1974 when he was overthrown, there had never been a decade which was not characterized by Oromo resistance and revolt somewhere in Oromia." The same could be said about many of the other colonized peoples.

High taxation also triggered resistance by the peasantry of the Abyssinian provinces. However, they had an additional grievance. The imposition of uniform taxation implied their demotion to the status of the southern peoples conquered by their ancestors, which was unacceptable. Peasants in Gojjam, for example, rose up partly in reaction to being treated just like the peasants of the areas conquered by their forefathers. "In their view, if southerners had been disinherited, it was because they were colonized peoples" (Tareke 1991: 166). In fact, the Gojjame peasantry could credibly argue that since their "fathers helped in the conquest of those (colonized) territories ... to contemplate governing Gojjam like them is not only to deny the contribution of our fathers but to institute a system of oppression in our land." The rebellions motivated by this kind of thinking and led by the disaffected nobility took place in 1942 and 1944 and were repeated in 1950 as well. A peasant rebellion supported by the local gentry broke out in Gojjam once again in 1968. While brutally dealing with concurrent resistances in Eritrea, Bale, and the Ogaden, the imperial regime "dare not quell this resistance [of Gojjam] violently," and the tax reform had to be shelved (Kaufeler 1988: 111).

Religion and Language Policy

One of the consequences of the nineteenth-century conquest of the south was the incorporation of people who did not practise Orthodox Christianity. In fact, Christians had become a minority after the expansion (Erlich 1980: 406). Regardless, the imperial government continued to describe Ethiopia as a purely Christian nation (Markakis 1987: 73). Christianity has traditionally served as "the most profound expression of the national existence of the Ethiopians" (Ullendorff 1965: 97), while Islam was seen as "the antithesis of Ethiopianism" (Markakis 1987: 74). Since this made the notion of "Ethiopian Moslems" absurd, the phrase "Muslims living in Ethiopia" (Tibebu 1995: 49) had to be coined to officially speak about the Moslem inhabitants of Ethiopian *territory*. The size of the population so publicly alienated was further augmented with the annexation of Eritrea and the return of the Somali-inhabited province. Naturally, these communities were inevitably inspired by the adjacent states' (Somalia's and Sudan's) articulation of their own nationalism as the obvious antithesis of Christianity.

Projecting the Empire as a *nation* necessitated adopting the language of the dominant Amharas as the national language. And "broadcasting, teaching and printing in other languages" was hence declared illegal (Donham 1999: 128). The true Ethiopian was thereafter an Amharic-speaking Orthodox Christian. This had the unintended implication of consigning Tigrinya-speaking Orthodox Christians to the status of "less Ethiopian." The implication that speakers of Oromo, Somali, Wallayita, and other languages were "un-Ethiopians" was discernible. Where being a non-Amharic speaker coincided with being a Moslem, the status of "anti-Ethiopian" was practically implied.

Structures drawing on supremacist thinking have a penchant for ranking peoples; witness the experience of apartheid South Africa. The above ranking, resulting from the imperial regime's language policy, displays the imposition of such strict hierarchical ordering. As Leforts (1981: 36/37) asserts, the "system allocated each people a precise and almost unalterable position." And Tibebu (1995: 32) depicts this ranking of peoples in regional terms as "Center-North-South, in descending order." By the centre he means traditional Shawa and by the north he means the rest of the Abyssinian-settled areas. Contrary to the supposition that *nation* results from the levelling of hierarchies, shaping the Ethiopian *nation* reinforced hierarchies resulting from conquest and introduced them where none existed previously, among the Abyssinians.

One more issue must be touched upon before we pass to other matters: the issue of *sovereignty*. Since the Emperor was *sovereign* in the style of Louis xiv, popular sovereignty was imponderable. Even allowing minimal district-level self-administration was deemed dangerous, for it could fan separatist tendencies. Hence, when a bill suggesting such a devolution of power was sent to the rubber-stamp parliament in 1967, it was rejected outright on the ironic grounds that "while it is clear that Ethiopia has existed for the last 3,000 years ... it is also known that Ethiopia is composed of different tribal groups which were far from regarding each other as members of the same nation, viewing each other as outsiders, having different outlooks and with no free intermingling: to create separate and autonomous *awrajas* (districts) before the people know one another would be encouraging separatist tendencies" (Erlich 1978: 34–35). If the supposed three thousand years of existing within the same *state* was insufficient to introduce the inhabitants of Ethiopia's *territory* to each other, one wonders how much more time was deemed necessary.

The Means: Assimilation

A number of scholars are convinced that the imperial government was determined to integrate Ethiopia's inhabitants into a cohesive *nation* through assimilation. Christopher Clapham (1988) is the most prominent proponent of this theory of assimilation. There are practical reasons, however, why the pursuit of assimilation by a dominant privileged group should be viewed with a high degree of scepticism. First, dominant privileged groups do not normally assimilate their subordinates, as merging them into a uniform society would negatively impact on their privileged status. Hence, it is commonly the underprivileged that work for assimilation; witness the experience of African-Americans. Second, the visible racial distinctiveness of some sectors or the religious beliefs of others renders their assimilation highly improbable. The Nilotic inhabitants of Ethiopian territory seem to fit into the first category and peoples professing Islam into the second. More importantly, the melting-pot notion has proven unworkable in today's world even where it once functioned with relative success, as in the US and Western Europe (as we discussed earlier).

There are, however, scholars who refute that assimilation was taking place under the imperial regime. For example, Lefort (1981: 36-37) asserts that "at the base, the assimilation of the conquered peoples was no more than a myth: it was not even attempted. They retained their language, their religion—the Coptic Church was not in the least interested in proselytizing—and their culture." Let us grant the proponents of the hypothesis of assimilation that efforts were made to assimilate members of the Christianized Oromo elite who rose to positions of power and influence. The experiences of two such individuals, Emmanuel Abraham and General Tadesse Birru, demonstrate the true intentions of the rulers and the self-defeating ultimate outcome.

Emmanuel Abraham is an educated Protestant Oromo from Wellega who served the Emperor in various high posts, which made him an object of envy by his Amhara colleagues. In his autobiography, he cites a litany of complaints brought against him by these "grandees" to discredit him in the Emperor's eyes. One such complaint, lodged when he was the director general at the Ministry of Education and Fine Arts (the minister was the Emperor himself), was that, "Amanuel educates only Gallas" (Abraham 1995: 64). Greatly disturbed by this favouritism, the Emperor decided to conduct his own research to verify the complaint. He found at one school that those who claimed Amhara identity constituted 71 percent of the student body. He then ordered Emmanuel to provide a more comprehensive breakdown of school attendance. Emmanuel writes, "In April, 1947, 4,795 students attended Addis Ababa schools. Of those, 3,055 said they were Amharas and the remaining 1,740 were from the other ethnic groups. Of these, 583 said they were Gallas" (Abraham 1995: 64). The Oromo student population ratio was no more than 12 percent.

When one takes into consideration that Oromos constitute the single largest identity group in the Empire, the degree of Oromo under-representation in the school system becomes clear. It is conceivable that the minister from then on took every precaution to keep the number of Oromos in schools as low as possible to pre-empt further accusations of favouritism. Assigning Oromos as heads of government personnel departments in due course became the most effective way of denying Oromos employment opportunities. This had two implications. First, the so-called assimilated Oromos were not the embodiment of Oromo participation in the state but an effective instrument for obstructing it. Second, the privileged group's natural tendency to curb assimilation is evidenced by the denial of educational and employment opportunities, supposedly the most important avenues to assimilation.

While some "assimilated" Oromo officials perhaps continued playing the roles assigned to them, others reacted differently. The experience of the Amharic-speaking devout Orthodox Christian General Tadesse Birru is a case in point. He was a renowned patriot who fought against the Italians in his youth, ending up in detention outside Mogadishu. He participated in foiling the 1960 coup attempt, thus demonstrating his unflinching loyalty to the Emperor. He was also an activist who worked to spread literacy among Oromos living the rural areas. None other than the emperor's prime minister, however, (mistaking the general for an Amhara), cautioned him by stating "We are leading the country by leaving behind the Oromo at least by a century. If you think you can educate them, they are an ocean [whose wave] can engulf us" (qtd. in Hassen 2000: 131). The general's attempt to "create an Ethiopian nation based on the equality of all Ethiopians" thus ran against the official policy of permanently subjugating the Oromos and others. Shocked by his discovery of an official discriminatory policy, General Tadesse Birru decided to join an Oromo self-help organization (the Metcha and Tulama Association), which he had previously refused to do, arguing "I cannot participate in tribal politics." He later presided over the formation of the Oromo Liberation Front (OLF) and is now widely acknowledged as the father of Oromo nationalism.

STRUGGLES WITHIN STRUGGLES

Ethiopia was the scene of pervasive grievances in the last decades of the Emperor's era. This period was punctuated by sporadic rural uprisings, mostly in the areas of Ethiopia outside Abyssinia, although they did occur there as well. Urban resistance would also make its debut during this time. Ultimately, the urban and rural components of resistance would converge, leading to the country's breakup and the reconfiguration of the remainder ostensibly to address demands for self-determination. Before this convergence was effected, the diffusion of ideas and organizational techniques from Sudan and Somalia would give impetus to the rural struggle.

Diffusion of Ideas and Techniques

When it was federated with the Empire, Eritrea had already experienced a democratic order for about a decade, "complete with political parties, elections, free press, and a growing labour movement" (Markakis 1987: 92). Either the political order in the rest of Ethiopia had to move in a similar direction or democracy had to be stamped out in Eritrea. The latter option obviously fit better in an imperial system that vested absolute power in the Emperor. The imperial regime thus started "the gradual dismantling of the federation" further heightening the "apprehension of anti-unionist circles" (Markakis 1987: 106) who were opposed to the federal arrangement from the outset. Into this ever-growing gulf between Eritrean society and the imperial system stepped the pioneer of Eritrea's liberation struggle, the Eritrean Liberation Movement (ELM). The ELM drew its founding members mostly from Eritrean lowlanders living in exile in Port Sudan. They formed their movement in 1958 by emulating the clandestine organizational technique of the Sudan Communist Party, to which they were exposed while in exile. They started their covert work with the expectation of a positive reception from at least the anti-unionist Moslem sector of Eritrean society. They were, however, surprised with "the depth of political alienation they discovered [even] among Christians" (Markakis 1987: 106). Encouraged, they decided to extend their clandestine recruitment to urban Christians as well. They managed to gain recruits from even among the Eritrean police and security forces at a time when the imperial regime was fast undermining the federal system. Hence, the ELM entertained staging a coup d'état by using its contacts within the police and security forces to pre-empt the abrogation of the federation. When it failed in achieving this aim it tried to launch a rural armed struggle in western Eritrea. This attempt was, however, foiled by the Beni Amer-based Eritrean Liberation Front (ELF), incurring six casualties (Markakis 1987: 109). Thus commenced the saga of internecine fighting that later on became the hallmark of Eritrea's struggle. Meanwhile, the imposition of Amharic by outlawing Tigrinya soon after Eritrea's annexation heightened the resentment of even "the most ardent Eritrean supporters of Ethiopia" and alienated "en masse the Eritrean student population who now had to master two foreign languages—English and Amharic—in order to complete secondary education" (Markakis 1987: 113). This alienated sector would ultimately furnish the leadership that succeeded in undoing the annexation.

As subversive ideas and techniques percolated across the empire's borders with the Sudan, a whirlwind of influence was gathering force in the east. The independence and immediate merger of British and Italian Somaliland to create the Somali Republic in 1960 would have by itself impacted on the attitude of the Somali-speaking inhabitants of the Ogaden province. An Ogadeni uprising was rendered inevitable and immediate, however, by two factors. First, the inhabitants of the Ogaden had been exposed to pan-Somali politics during the decade following the end of the Second World War. Second, the Ogadeni's natural tendency towards resistance was inflamed by the imposition of tax collection and the Amharic language. When the Emperor exhorted Ogadeni chiefs to hurry up and achieve full-fledged Ethiopianness by learning to speak Amharic (Markakis 1987: 174), they could perhaps afford to be ambivalent. Attempts to turn them into his regime's tax collectors, however, were another matter altogether. Since pastoralist communities are inherently averse to taxation even by their own state, one imposed by a regime they perceive as alien was clearly unacceptable and would be endured only under severe duress. When they were ordered to start collecting a head tax in February 1963, the Ogadeni chiefs hence had no doubts that "the measure would be resisted violently by their people" (Markakis 1987: 177).

The armed rebellion that inevitably erupted took on a new dimension due to the existence of an adjacent independent Somali state. Cornered into practically demonstrating its adherence to its declared policy of bringing all Somalis under one state, the young Somali Republic prematurely got embroiled in conflict with Ethiopia by channelling arms to the rebels. This involvement fit into Ethiopia's intention of portraying the rebellion as a purely "foreign" instigated affair. On this pretext, Ethiopia took the war to the Somali Republic by attacking border posts and bombing key Somali towns. With more prominence given to its interstate dimension, the fighting was declared over once the two countries signed an agreement in Khartoum a year after the fighting broke out. Hence, addressing the Ogadeni grievances that triggered the rebellion was sidestepped. From that time, the Ogadeni struggle for self-determination would increasingly be subsumed under the interstate manifestation. And Somalia's vulnerability to intimidation by Ethiopian air and ground forces would necessitate ever-rising investment in the military, ultimately turning Somalia into one of Africa's most militarized states. In fact, Ethiopia and Somalia would continuously push each other in such a direction to the detriment of investment in much-needed social and economic development.

As the Ogadeni struggle started to subside, another one by the adjacent Oromos of Bale and Sidamo provinces was actually heating up and spreading. In this case also, rising taxation and pervasive alien bureaucratic intrusion into society served as the triggering factors. Land measurement to fix taxation levels was, as usual, manipulated as a pretext to dispossess the local tillers. This pretext enabled the government to grant close to 1.5 million hectares "to dignitaries from the civil and military services" (Tareke 1991: 132). At the time, these northern Christian officials were vying to resettle members of their respective communities with the dual aim of diluting the area's Moslem Oromo demographic composition and cultivating a rural power base. Even the established custom of allocating a third of the measured land to local notables was violated in this case, thus heightening this social sector's alienation. An administrative reform proposal to appoint them merely as deputies of Amhara officials was "foiled by the settlers [Amharas], who had the full support of state officials in Addis Ababa" (Tareke 1991: 137). Their awareness of the "political changes in the Horn" [meaning Somalia's independence] combined with their tiller kinfolks' growing restiveness inevitably motivated the local notables to be at the head of their people's revolt. The sentiment that led to the revolt was poignantly put by one participant as follows: "In our own country we have lived as aliens and slaves, deprived of our lands and discriminated against on grounds of our tribal and religious identities" (Tareke 1991: 134). The fighting that broke out in 1963 went on for the next seven years, allowing news about it to spread far beyond the southern parts of the Empire. That the struggle could be sustained for longer than many of its antecedents was due to the people's determination, the locality's conduciveness to hit-and-run tactics, and the provision of some antiquated rifles and ammunition by neighbouring Somalia.

The protracted armed struggle by the Oromos of Bale and Sidamo provinces could easily be identified as the turning point in the struggle against the imperial system for a number of reasons. As it dragged on it increasingly came to be viewed within the larger picture of changing the state and even within the context of contemporary contests at the global stage. The educated youth that was becoming increasingly radicalized started seeing the struggle within the context of contemporary rural-based revolutionary armed struggles elsewhere. The news of gallant Oromo peasants standing up to the imperial army was particularly uplifting to the minority Oromo members of the student body. Combined with an urban-based Oromo contemporary social movement in the form of the Matcha-Tulama Self-Help Association, it enabled them to start imagining an alternative to enduring permanent humiliation. More importantly, exposure to developments elsewhere enabled participants in the struggle to situate theirs within the context of other contemporary revolutionary struggles. One participant's remark to the authorities saying "the conflict between us and you is just like that between the Vietnamese and the Americans" (Tareke 1991: 155) bears testimony to this development. The combination of power change in Somalia in October 1969, sustained military onslaught against civilians and their livestock with British and Israeli backing, and the offer of amnesty brought the armed struggle to a halt in 1970. While many surrendered, others sought asylum in Somalia to bide their time, only to return six years later under the guise of the Somali-Abbo Liberation Front (SALF). More on this later on.

The Debut of Urban Politics

Urban politics made its appearance in the imperial capital in December 1960. The event that occasioned this development was a student demonstration in support of a coup attempt that ultimately failed. "Ethiopian" students from then on became increasingly mobilized and radicalized. Demystifying the imperial system of rule by subjecting it to relentless criticism and ridicule would in due course become their main vocation. They would eventually go on to distinguish themselves as "the imperial regime's political nemesis" (Markakis 1987: 100). News of the diverse rural armed struggles was then percolating into the urban sector and affecting the thinking of the populace, particularly that of the students. Coupled with other factors, such information launched the students on a course of ever-rising radicalism. One of the other factors enumerated by Balsvik (1994) is exposure to Marxist and Leninist literature. Couching all pronouncements within this ideological framework became customary after even scant exposure. Having thus discovered in Marxism-Leninism the magical recipe for ridding the country of backwardness, many students then became determined to transform the empire into an ultramodern socialist state by skipping the "bourgeois democratic" phase and the associated gesture of vesting sovereignty in the populace.

The student body was by no means monolithic, but "its social and ethnic origins were more diverse than those of the ruling class" (Markakis 1987: 99). The Amharas predominated with Tigreans coming second (Kaufeler 1988: 106). As in everything else, the descending centre/north/south stratification applied also to the composition of the student population. For most of the 1960s, the students were united in seeking out and exposing everything that would embarrass the imperial regime. From among such issues, however, that of "Land to the Tiller" (the slogan initially aired during a public demonstration in 1965) came to gain a permanent status. An even more sensitive and related issue, the right of the oppressed societies dubbed the "National Question," was added in 1969 (Gashaw 1993: 149). The dual mission of ending the tillers' landlessness and their treatment as non-Ethiopian *nationals* inhabiting its *territory* came to constitute the core of the student radicals' political agenda.

United in their conviction that revolution was both desirable and imminent, the students focused on debating what shape it should take and more importantly who should be at its helm. Defining the most scientific and thus proper relationship between class and national struggle ultimately became the most contentious issue in this debate, in which three arguments crystallized. First, the majority of those from the centre and from the north (outside Eritrea), were insistent that the eradication of national inequality and oppression would be the automatic by-product of the elimination of class privileges. Second, the minority from the same background (particularly some Tigreans) stuck to the position that national oppression could have primacy under certain situations. And third, most of those from the south and Eritrea saw the colonized people's struggle for the right to self-determination as the natural and appropriate response to Ethiopia's imperial domination. Those supporting the first argument later on crystallized into the two ostensibly countrywide Marxist-Leninist parties, the Ethiopian Peoples Revolutionary Party (EPRP) and the All Ethiopia Socialist Movement, better known by its Amharic acronym, MAESON. The Tigray People's Liberation Front (TPLF) came to represent those who subscribed to the second argument. The people who later on led the Oromo Liberation Front (OLF), and those who led the struggles of other southerners, came from those who supported the third argument. The leaders of Eritrean independence held a view closer to the third but with some distinctive features, which will be discussed later.

From Urban to Rural

Eritrea's experience best demonstrates the relationship between the articulation of revolution within the educated urban milieu and the prosecu-
tion of the mostly communal-based rural armed struggle. The precedent
set by the pioneer Eritrean clandestine movement, the ELM, turned out
to be misleading. The Front that was formed in 1960 to launch the rural
armed struggle, the Eritrean Liberation Front (ELF), did not uphold the
ELM's practice of eschewing religious and other forms of sectarianism. ELF
leaders were not only "deeply distrustful of Christians" (Markakis 1987:
108) but were also determined to cultivate the Beni Amer as their power
base. The Front's earliest leader, Idris Mohammed Adam, being "a Beni
Amer from the western lowlands," appeared determined to found his
power base on his community's loyalty. Moreover, the Front adopted an
Arab/Islamic posture primarily to accomplish two aims: first, to enable
the Front to portray itself as the imperial regime's natural antithesis; and
second, to open up opportunities to mobilize material and political support from the Arab/Islamic countries. But such an approach unambigu-
ously alienated the Christian sector at a time when it was also being
increasingly alienated by the imperial regime. Cultivating the western
lowlands as the leader's power base meant the Beni Amers were to be
more favoured and trusted than even other Moslems, thus alienating
them too. Additionally, stamping Eritrea's Arab/Islamic national identity
with a heavy Beni Amer accent was definitely unpalatable to other
Moslem communities, let alone the Christians. While these deviations
from the precedent set by the ELM were gathering momentum in the
field, even the Christian Eritrean student radicals started supporting or
joining the ELF, probably under the impression that it was merely the
successor of the ELM. When they realized that they were being viewed as
potential government spies, the few who took the risky step of actually
entering the field were shocked, bewildered, and angered. Young Isaias
Afewerki entered the field with the impression of the ELF as a magical
organization. Dismay set in when he realized that people like him were
suspected as potential agents of the Ethiopians (Connell 1997: 79). Those
who remained behind in the cities, however, were unaware of these difficulties and thus continued to extend its clandestine urban networks
and to send recruits to the field under the impression that it is a progressive organization.

The trickle of youthful recruits both from home and abroad that began
in the mid-1960s became a flood towards the end of the decade due to

developments within the Empire, the region, and the world at large. Wolde-Yesus Ammar (1997) lists these contributory factors as follows:

1. actions and developments within Ethiopia such as the lowering of Eritrean flag, the regression of Eritrea's economic and political situation, and the 1960 coup attempt in the Imperial capital;
2. achievement of independence by African states, many of them "at least as small and as 'un-viable' as Eritrea," through wholesale de-colonization;
3. the impact of exposure to Arab nationalist politics and that of other Third World societies; and
4. the desire to duplicate the international publicity of the Ethiopian University Student's "Land to the Tiller!" demonstration of 1965.

As a result of these developments, "the first Christian highlander recruits to join the ELF army were not peasants or workers but mainly 'secondary school students in Eritrea and university students in Addis Ababa'" (Ammar 1997: 75). These recruits immediately got embroiled in the struggle to end the ELF leadership's clear sectarian orientation in order to realize their vision. Under rising internal pressure, the movement ultimately splintered into factions roughly coinciding with Eritrea's religious and linguistic divide. The ELF, under a new, younger leadership and with a more progressive political agenda, tried to survive at one end of the emerging political spectrum. A group of Christian fighters, who chose to project themselves as the antithesis of the traditionalist ELF leadership, started the process of creating what ultimately became the Eritrean People's Liberation Front (EPLF). All the remaining tendencies were drawn to one of these poles at one time or another without ever merging with either. In the expensive internecine fighting that followed, the EPLF finally prevailed when, in collaboration with its TPLF ally, it drove the ELF out of Eritrea in 1981. The ELF then suffered further fragmentation with one faction actually reverting to its original Beni Amer roots. The EPLF's political and military strategy roughly corresponded with that of other revolutionary national liberation struggles, such as the one in Guinea-Bissau. After making the arena of armed struggle its exclusive preserve, the EPLF then focused on winning Eritrea's independence, eventually achieving it by defeating the Ethiopian army in late May 1991. Having ensconced itself as the sole ruling party, the EPLF thereafter got down to shaping an Eritrean national identity with a heavy Tigrinya accent, as some would contend.

Despite generating unwelcome complications, endowing Eritrea's cause with an Arab and Islamic content was pivotal in sustaining the survival of the armed struggle in the critical early years. Soliciting and gaining the support of such Arab nationalist states as Syria, Iraq, and the Gulf States in the form of funding, training, and weapons provision would have perhaps been impossible without it. Even more importantly, transporting such personnel and materiel through the Sudan would have been at least more cumbersome without its government's acquiescence. Support for the Eritrean cause was not restricted to the incumbent Sudanese regimes but embraced the whole political spectrum from the communists to the Moslem Brothers (Markakis 1987: 113). Moreover, the cousins of the Beni Amer, particularly members of the Beja Congress, argued that they were duty bound to support the Eritrean revolutionaries due to kinship and religious affiliations. Pressured by these internal supporters and externally persuaded by pro-Eritrean Arab and Islamic states, successive Sudanese regimes hence were never completely free to barter the Eritrean cause in their diplomatic dealings with successive Ethiopian regimes. Ethiopian regimes, however, routinely demonstrated an eagerness and freedom to trade the southern Sudanese cause in their dealings.

Situating the EPLF

Countering the official projection of Ethiopian nationalism as the antithesis of Islam by articulating the Eritrean identity and cause as the antithesis of Christianity was, of course, a tempting simplification. Such a simplification must have significantly reduced the burden of mobilizing the lowland local Moslems in the initial years. The leaders of the EPLF could not resort to a similar simplification since their constituency shared culture, history, and Coptic Christianity with the adjacent Tigreans and the Amhara rulers of the Empire. Subscribing to Marxism-Leninism and anti-sectarianism did help in projecting the EPLF as the antithesis of the traditionalist ELF leadership. But this convenient contrast was soon lost as the reformed ELF started to increasingly couch its political pronouncements in Marxist-Leninist terms while denouncing the sectarianism of the former leadership. Meanwhile, Marxism-Leninism was adopted also by a sector of Ethiopian leftist groups who recognized Eritrea's right to self-determination with the aim of preserving Ethiopia's unity (Markakis 1987: 101).The TPLF also came into existence by embracing Marxism-Leninism and intending to realize an independent Greater Tigray, which was to include the Tigrinya-speaking Eritrean highlands. Distinguishing the EPLF from other Eritrean fronts and disentangling Eritrea's leftist politics from that of its counterparts in the rest of the Empire thus posed a great challenge to EPLF leaders.

A number of approaches evolved to enable the leaders of the EPLF to distinguish their movement from other Eritrean fronts and the various Ethiopian leftist groups. First, Eritrea's existence as a distinct entity was reinterpreted as stretching back to pre-colonial times, thus signalling the rejection of Eritrean highlanders' centuries-old historical, cultural, and religious affiliation with Abyssinia (the *state nation*). The Eritreans were not, of course, alone in adapting history to serve political purposes. The Imperial regime's eagerness to seal a union with Eritrea was premised on the decision to dismiss the fifty-odd years of European colonial rule as an aberration, thus overlooking the significant impact that experience had had on Eritrean attitudes and lifestyles. The Ethiopian regime's determination to write off this fifty-year period was responded to by the policy of the EPLF leaders to do the same to the highland constituency's centuries-long association with the *state-nation*. This served the purpose of disentangling EPLF politics from those of its other leftist Ethiopian counterparts. Also, the EPLF carried out more daring and spectacular military operations to outclass its Eritrean rivals and to therefore distinguish itself from other Eritrean fronts. Hence, the EPLF's political and military performance was focused on demonstrating that it was the only reliable, determined, and capable front to deliver the unconditional independence of Eritrea. The Front was immensely successful in living up to this image. Implementing this agenda, however, required drawing a clear distinction between Eritrea's struggle for self-determination and those of others against the imperial regime and its successor.

Contemporary notions about entitlement to self-determination and the accompanying definition of *nation* enabled the EPLF (indeed, all Eritrean factions) to achieve this end. As was universally understood during the decolonization era, the sole function of self-determination was "bringing independence to people under alien colonial [European] rule," as has been discussed earlier. And "the peoples so entitled [i.e., to independence] are defined in terms of the existing colonial territories, each of which contains *a nation*," (Emerson 1964: 28; italics added). Any deviation from this dual convention was further stigmatized subsequent to Biafra's disastrous attempt to secede from Nigeria. The Eritreans thereafter found it necessary to argue that "Eritrea is no Biafra" since its "borders were fixed and its *national identity defined by colonial history*, like the rest of colonial Africa" (Habte Selassie 1988: 66; italics added). Meanwhile, the EPLF's leftist counterparts in the rest of the Empire adopted Stalin's definition of nationhood and Leninist approach to self-determination. Accordingly, they defined the nation to be "a historically evolved, stable community of language, territory, economic life, and psychological make-up manifested in a community of culture" (Stalin 1947: 8). Similarly, Lenin's admonition that struggles for self-determination are legitimate only when led by a proletarian vanguard party and that, rhetoric notwithstanding, such struggles should not lead to the breakup of the state was treated as gospel truth. In the event, despite at times making diplomatic pretensions, the so-called countrywide Marxist-Leninist parties were never genuinely persuaded by the Eritrean argument. Likewise, few of the nationalist forces operating in other parts of the Empire accepted the Eritrean assertion that Eritrea and Eritrea alone deserved independence and nothing short of it. Neither did the world community buy the Eritrean argument until the imminence of EPLF military victory in 1991 made premising the recognition of Eritrea's independence on its colonial past a convenient pretext.

However, the EPLF (and all other Eritrean fronts) had to make one exception to the insistence that all other peoples' right to self-determination should be sought within the context of preserving the unity of the remainder of Ethiopia. The price of applying the same to the Somali case would have meant foregoing the Somali Republic's generous and extensive diplomatic and other support and thus had to be avoided. Hence, the Somalis and Eritreans became very reliable allies, despite arguing against each other's positions in their presentations at international venues. While the Eritreans invoked colonial experience and the sanctity of boundaries set by European colonialists to legitimate their pursuit of nationhood and independence, undoing divisions resulting from colonial partition constituted the core of the Somali agenda.

Oromo–Somali Relations

The Somalis too made one particular exception to their consistent policy of extending support to any group fighting against either the Ethiopian state or its government. This was the Oromo struggle for national self-determination as articulated and led by the Oromo Liberation Front (OLF). The Oromos and the Somalis had much in common particularly in the way they articulated their status and political agenda. Designating the process that led to the two communities' incorporation in the Ethiopian state as colonialism was one. Advocating the self-determination of identity communities whose settlement pattern defines their homeland *territory* was another.

The similarity of their political views could have served as the foundation of a close alliance between the Oromos and Somalis. The attitude of the Somalis, influenced partly by a particular way of reading history, averted the cultivation of such an alliance. The Somali elite appropriated the history of the sixteenth-century Islamic warrior Imam Ahmed Ibrahim bin-Ghazi, which had implications for how they portrayed their conflict with Ethiopia. Portraying their contemporary struggle as the continuation of the Imam's legacy, the Somali authorities wished to duplicate the Moslem unity that supposedly prevailed at that time. They thus wished to support and lead the struggles of all adjacent non-Somali Moslem societies. In order to reconcile the invocation of the centuries-old precedent of Moslem-Christian conflict with the modern concept of self-determination, they simply designated the concerned communities as hyphenated variants of the mainstream Somali. They thus renamed the neighbouring Oromos the Somali-Abbo and the Afars the Somali-Hyeka, and created a surrogate front called the Somali-Abbo Liberation Front (SALF) for the former. The territory they named Western Somalia embraced not just the Ogaden but also the homelands of these hyphenated Somalis, thus signalling Somalia's intention of extending its territorial claims all the way to the Great Rift Valley. The OLF's articulation of a secular nationalist politics and aspiration to speak on behalf of all Oromos inescapably put it on a collision course with the Somali Republic and its surrogate organizations. The Oromos and Somalis, who invoked similar principles, were thus unable to strike an alliance, unlike the Eritreans and Somalis. The opportunities that were lost as a result of the Oromo-Somali dispute will never been known. But it is safe to speculate that the defeat of the Ethiopian regime in 1991 by the EPLF, OLF, and TPLF (made possible with the Sudan government's pivotal support) would have perhaps been achieved as early as 1977–78 had Somalia correctly handled the Ogadeni and Oromo struggles for self-determination.

Vanguard Party: The Empire's Saviour

The Oromos and Somalis, of course, were not alone in being at loggerheads despite subscribing to similar political principles. This situation applied perhaps even more to all the other forces that started appearing on the Empire's political landscape in the 1970s. In fact, those with barely distinguishable political platforms and ideologies turned out to be each other's deadliest enemies. Such a drama worked itself out after the Emperor's regime was unseated by the creeping coup d'état of 1974. Goaded by the EPRP and cajoled by the MAESON, the military committee (the Derg) that gradually took over was forced to adopt an increasingly Marxist-Leninist posture. The distinction between the pronouncements of the Derg, MAESON, and EPRP became blurred as their resort to Marx-ist-Leninist rhetoric grew in competition. In addition, these groups were all united in seeking the preservation of the Empire's unity. Furthermore, they were all determined to continue the Imperial regime's policy of con-verting the Empire into an Amharic-speaking *nation* despite paying lip service to the equality of nationalities. And they all believed that this could be achieved only under one condition: the success of a single authentic Marxist-Leninist vanguard party in carrying out a thoroughgo-ing class liberation, which would render potentially divisive national liberation struggles not only redundant but also reactionary and thus deserving to be stamped out. The competition of these three groups to emerge as the sole vanguard party inevitably triggered the catastrophic triangular warfare that claimed hundreds of thousands of lives. The Derg, after its victory in 1977, went on to rename itself the Workers Party of Ethiopia in 1987.

The resulting overall polarization of the Empire's politics can now be laid out. The centralist trio (Derg, MAESON, and EPRP), discussed above, constituted one wing. The movements of the Oromo, Eritrean, Somali, and other southern peoples, who invoked the right to self-determination by articulating their cases as being colonial, occupied the opposite end of the spectrum. The TPLF's flexible and ever-shifting political agenda situated it somewhere between these two poles. The TPLF began its polit-ical career by designating (in 1976) the Tigray question as a colonial one to be resolved by the independence of the Greater Tigray nation which was to embrace the Tigrinya-speaking Eritrean highlanders. Three years later, it switched to defining the Tigray case as a national question to be settled within Ethiopia, mostly in response to EPLF pressure. As the TPLF grew stronger, it took to arguing that referendum was the only legiti-mate mechanism for the resolution of both questions, thus starting to blur "the distinction between the colonial and national question" (Tirvelli 1999: 11). The TPLF went on to argue that "if the future of Eritrea is to be truly democratic, it will have to respect the right of nations and nation-alities to self-determination up to, and including, secession" (Young 1996: 112). The resulting souring of relations with the EPLF lasted until 1988, when the TPLF openly endorsed Eritrea's right to independence in order to resume cooperation with a view to hastening the defeat of the Derg regime.

As the TPLF's stand grew increasingly indistinguishable from that of the centralist trio, its relations with other nationalist forces deteriorated. Meanwhile, stepping up the vilification of the Derg and the EPRP (the only other active member of the trio) and the military operations to liquidate them remained indispensable. The defeat of the incumbent Derg regime was necessary for the TPLF to replace it as the sole vanguard party. Meanwhile, pragmatism impelled it not only to downplay disagreements with the other nationalist groups but also to harness their cooperation. It thus entered into an alliance with these future enemies in the run-up to the overthrow of the Derg regime in May 1991. It then proceeded to invite some twenty political organizations to a conference in July, to ratify the Transitional Charter. The Charter espoused democratization in general and the adoption of a federal structure for Ethiopia with a view to settling all outstanding demands for self-determination. In the event, the Charter and the accompanying formation of the transitional government were used as a ruse to allow the TPLF to consolidate its hold on power. Once that was accomplished, the TPLF unleashed a reign of terror against all other autonomous political groups. The systematic exclusion of these groups from official politics and administration made TPLF rule to increasingly look like that of the Derg, with the Tigreans replacing the Amharas as Ethiopia's new masters. Roughly a century after Emperor Yohannes lost his life, the descendents of his lieutenants had taken power. With the rise to power of this northernmost sector of Abyssinian society, the form of Ethiopia's imperial character changed, but its content remains. The TPLF merely replaced the Amhara policy, which resembled the French colonial policy of assimilation, with something akin to the British home-rule approach, as I have argued elsewhere (Lata 1998).

Monopolizing access to Ethiopia's official politics and resources was necessary for the realization of the TPLF's other agenda of enticing Eritrea back into some kind of association with Ethiopia. Eritrean support was indispensable to consolidate such monopolization of economic and political power. Richard Trivelli best captures the expectations underlying the extension of economic privileges to the Eritreans: "The TPLF leadership...hoped that the benefits of the economic privileges given to Eritrea and Eritreans would ultimately induce or even force the Eritrean leadership to re-enter into some form of political union with Ethiopia" (Trivelli 1999: 17). When, contrary to heeding this signal, Eritrea decided to complete its sovereign existence by issuing its own currency, the Nakfa, relations between them was put on the slippery slope that ultimately led to the 1998 war. Thus, hopes that Eritrea's independence would remove one cause of the conflicts raging in the Horn of Africa were dashed.

CONCLUSION

The transformation of the Ethiopian Empire into a modern nation state necessitated the cultivation of an array of new approaches, institutions, and social forces. It was these social forces that started vying for influence and exacerbated conflict. The promoters of modernity were divided along communal, religious, regional, and ideological lines. When they assumed a more coherent organizational form, these tendencies proliferated conflict, with violence the most intense among those harbouring virtually indistinguishable ambitions. At the same time, developments within the state and in neighbouring countries resonated with each other. In the end, it was a section of the *state-nation* that managed to break away and form an independent state. Even the rest of the Empire could not continue to press ahead with the failed policy of achieving cultural and linguistic homogeneity. Hence, decades of nation-building led to the breakaway of one region of the country and the reconfiguration of the remainder with the intention of undermining any lingering demands for self-determination.

INTRODUCTION

THE SIMILARITIES BETWEEN ETHIOPIA's and neighbouring Sudan's nation-building projects have been discussed by many scholars. As Markakis notes, "what the ruling groups in Ethiopia and in Sudan perceived as the 'national' identity was their own ethnic identity writ large" (1998: 112). This signalled a departure from the common African experience in which "the association between ethnic identity and the nation was typically indirect" (Donham 1999: 128) and incidental. In Sudan and Ethiopia nation-building consisted of little more than coercive assimilation to forge the rest of the populace into the ruling groups' "ethnic identity." However, "forced assimilation not only was rejected by subordinate groups, but also encouraged them to invoke their own cultural symbols, most often religion and language" (Markakis 1994: 226). Hence, homogenization triggered the contrary process of increasing particularization in both the Sudan and Ethiopia. In the Sudan, however, only the role of religion in projecting the nation and its historical roots served as the causes of controversy. Language did not seem to pose a problem as even John Garang (the leader of Sudan Peoples Liberation Army) declares *"Arabic...must be the national language in a new Sudan and therefore we must learn it"* (1992: 133; italics added). The view of grassroots communities may, of course, be to the contrary; elite political actors rarely seem to take them into consideration.

ISLAMIZATION IS ARABIZATION

Conversion to Islam did not lead to the assumption of Arab identity in most of black Africa. Only in North Africa did Islamization result in Arabization as well. However, contrary to what prevails in adjacent Moslem

139

black Africa, "Northern Sudanese Muslims...see themselves as Arabs despite the African element in their skin color and physical features" (Deng 1997: 337). Their determination to create the rest of the Sudanese in their own image was bound to lead to endless trouble. Members of the northern Sudanese elite often used imaginative metaphors to describe their role and position in Africa. The Sudan is described as "a geographical spearhead of the Middle East into Africa, south of the Sahara" (Deng 1995: 360), according to Mahgoub, a famous northern politician. And the mission of this spearhead stuck in the heart of Africa is holy, according to Assadiq al-Mahdi, the Mahdi's great-grandson. He emphatically declared that "the failure of Islam in southern Sudan would be the failure of the Sudanese Muslims to the international Islamic cause. Islam has a holy mission in Africa, and southern Sudan is the beginning of that mission" (Malwal 1981: 41). This mentality lent urgency to a revocation of the former British policy that sought to curb the dual processes of Islamization and Arabization of southern Sudan, and achieving such a revocation commenced immediately after independence and was pursued with ever-increasing vigour. The achievement of precipitous Islamicization and Arabization meant that the more common gradual and personal conversion to Islam had to be dispensed with, and it now had to be a state-driven process. Coercing "southern chiefs and state employees...into taking Muslim names," derisively called "government" names (Markakis 1987: 72), became the most absurd distortion resulting from this urgency. Christian southerners naturally responded by clinging to their faith while hastening the conversion of remaining adherents of traditional African beliefs.

Pre-Colonial Sudan

Competing interpretations regarding "national" history emerged also in the Sudan, as happened in neighbouring Ethiopia. This was due to another departure from approaches to "national" history in the rest of Africa. The history of the post-colonial state is rarely equated with that of the pre-colonial empire or other form of state in much of the rest of Africa. The birth of the nucleus of a Sudanese *nation-state*, however, is frequently traced back to the Mahdist era (Hurriez 1989: 89) in the northern Sudanese discourse. Some scholars go further to state that "the followers of the Mahdi created both an Islamically identified political system and the first independent Sudanese 'national' state" (Esposito and Voll 1996: 78). The projection of contemporary Sudan's history to the Mahdist era has generated a number of implications.

First, a number of developments prompted the northern and southern Sudanese to outclass each other as having a more ancient existence as a people. One thing can be inferred from some of the Mahdi's pronouncements. His proclaimed intention of ultimately conquering and cleansing Mecca and Damascus indicates his self-perception as the heir to, and restorer of, the glorious Arab and Islamic civilization dating back to the seventh century. Northern Sudanese elite commonly claim that legacy. The southern Sudanese are now responding with their version of history which projects their people's existence to even earlier times. For example, the "tall, black, smooth-skinned, beautiful people" mentioned in Isaiah chapter 18 is "an unambiguous description of present-day southern Sudan," according to John Garang (1996: 7). Claiming competing primordial and perennial identities thus emerged in Sudan's experience as in neighbouring Ethiopia. The Ashraf's claim of descent from the Prophet Mohammed was thus out matched by Garang's assertion of a lineage stretching back to the foggiest past of the Old Testament. What this had to do with the sordid here and now, of course, passes understanding.

Second, and more importantly, the projection of contemporary Sudan's history back to the Mahdist era tended to polarize even the northern Sudanese elite. Their traditional divide-and-rule tactic led the British to manipulate the lingering rivalry between the descendents of the Mahdi's supporters and their opponents. Hence, whenever the British found appeasing the Ansars (descendents of the Mahdi's followers) necessary, they promoted the stature and fortune of the Mahdi's son, Abd-al-Rahman al-Mahdi. At other times, they favoured Ali al-Mirghani (descendent of one of the Mahdi's staunchest opponents) to ingratiate themselves with his followers, members of Khatimiyya sect. And the British were engaging in this exercise at a time when they were installing Moslem monarchs in the Middle East or allying themselves with extant ones. Perhaps encouraged by these precedents, Abd-al-Rahman at one time aired his ambition of being crowned king of an independent Sudan (El-Affendi 1991: 31). Ali al-Mirghani's response was immediate and categorical: "he would [rather] have Haile Selassie as king than Abd al Rahman al Mahdi" (Woodward 1990: 69). How this reaction was framed seems to indicate the persistent perception of neighbouring Christian Ethiopia as the natural negativity of the Sudan since the Mahdist era.

Third, the precedent set by the Mahdist movement influenced attitudes towards political mobilization among the northern Sudanese political elite in numerous ways. Those "Sudanese nationalists" who glorified it "as the national revolutionary movement par excellence" (El-Affendi

1991: 152) wanted to rekindle Islam's potential for mass mobilization. In addition, opposing or supporting the legacy of the Mahdi and the aspirations of his descendants came to assume a central place in northern Sudanese political life. Overall, the "'religionization' of nationalism and politics" (Esposito and Voll 1996: 82) in northern Sudan became the most significant and enduring implication of the Mahdi's legacy.

STRUGGLES WITHIN STRUGGLES

Attitudes towards the legacy of the Mahdi and his descendants stamped northern Sudan's politics with the enduring reality of struggle within struggle. The Umma is the Sudan's oldest political party, having come into existence in 1945, its followers drawn mostly from the Ansar. Descendants of the Mahdi have succeeded each other as the leaders of this party since its formation. The National Unionist Party, the antecedent of the current Democratic Unionist Party (DUP), was the Sudan's second political party. DUP followers come mostly from members of the Khatimiyya sect, the traditional opponents of the Ansar. Descendants of Ali al-Mirghani have led this party either directly or through persons they sponsor. These two parties are commonly called traditional sectarian parties, and they have always played a dominant role in Sudan's civilian politics. Although they share a sectarian social basis, they are each other's deadliest rivals.

The Moslem Brotherhood, which in due course emerged as the National Islamic Front, could be placed to the right of these sectarian parties. Its main preoccupation is excelling the Mahdi's achievements in tapping Islam's potential for political mobilization. The Sudan Communist Party constitutes the extreme left end of the political spectrum. Their ideological orientation renders these two parties also as each other's deadliest enemies. Competition between these four civilian parties is premised on each party that is not in power doing everything possible to bring down its major opponent's administration. Any form of aggregation is resorted to in pursuing such an aim. The military stands outside this circle despite on the whole sharing with these forces a broad range of political values and often membership.

This configuration has imparted a permanent instability to northern Sudanese political life. The civilian parties routinely worked hard to make each other's rule ineffective, thus ultimately inviting the military to take power or rendering such a measure necessary and welcome. Then the civilian parties would pool their influence and pressure to bring down military rule. Civilian administrations, subverted from within, and military regimes permanently challenged, either jointly or separately by civilian parties, have replaced each other three times since 1958.

A wider gulf separates these five northern political forces from the southern Sudanese movements. Regardless, the same absence of principles characterizes the interaction of these northern groups with the southern Sudanese. Whether to ally oneself with the southerners or not often depended on purely whether one's arch-rival was in power. Similarly, whether to support or denounce a proposed resolution of the southern question depended on whether it was supported by one's arch-rival. Driven by these calculations, all of the five northern forces enumerated above have struck an alliance with the southerners at one time or another. The resulting impasse has contributed to the intractableness of conflict in the Sudan.

Struggles within Struggles within Struggles

The fact that southern Sudan did not figure much in the Mahdist state has been discussed earlier. The British policy of insulating the south from Arab and Islamic influence has also been touched upon. Once "pacification" was considered achieved, "British policy moved to isolation, which meant in effect a minimal state presence trying to relate to, rather than crush, indigenous communities" (Woodward 1990: 71). This minimal state presence manifested itself in giving Christian missionaries a greater role in the provision of education and even administration than elsewhere. And the south, which was left far behind the north in cultural and economic development, was reunited with the north only nine years before independence.

Southern Sudanese participation in the negotiation that led to independence was insignificant. The few southerners who were consulted ultimately supported the process that led to independence on the basis of a vague promise that the south would enjoy a federal status. The nature of political rivalry among northern political forces was destined to stand in the way of even discussing this promise. As the day of independence approached, leaders of the Moslem Brotherhood, who were determined to outclass the others as champions of Islam, declared their advocacy of a unitary Islamic republic. They even submitted a model draft constitution reflecting this vision. Although this model Islamic constitution was rejected, the leaders of the sectarian parties were cornered into issuing a joint statement asserting that "It is our opinion that the state in Sudan should be an Islamic Parliamentary Republic, and that the heavenly Shariah should be the source of legislation in the country's constitution" (El-Affendi 1991: 58). Pushed by this rising intra-northern competition "those in power [ultimately] not only went back on the federal pledge but came to equate it with separation" (AbdelSalam 1989: 48). The few reluctant southern participants in central state political life could only look on with rising frustration.

North and south were put on a definite course of rising mutual suspicion and violence by the equally rushed and insensitive process of Sudanizing the bureaucracy and the military. The disparity in appointments resulting from hasty Sudanization of the civil service was immense: eight hundred northerners to only six southerners (Daly 1988: 195). This might have fed southern apprehensions that the northerners were simply interested in stepping into the shoes of the departing British. This impression was perhaps further reinforced when all the departing British commanders of southern troops were replaced by northern officers. Simmering discontent erupted into violence when troops stationed at Torit mutinied on hearing that they were about to be transferred to the north (Markakis 1998: 112). The violence that thus began in 1955 was to continue to this day with the exception of the short hiatus of 1972–83.

The history of the southern Sudanese travail since independence has been sufficiently elaborated by other writers to need much coverage here. What I will attempt in this work is to summarize how local, regional, and international contests intersected over the struggle of the southerners. The following brief sketch of the intricate web of internal and external interests that contributed to the intractability of Sudan's conflicts will hopefully become clear.

Civil to Military to Civil Rule

Suppressing the Torit mutineers and pursuing those who fled into the countryside became the major preoccupation of the civilians who took over from the British upon independence. The mutineers who were apprehended were summarily executed, feeding the apprehension of even those who were not involved in the insurrection. Flushing out those who took refuge in the countryside or in neighbouring countries involved military forays into the rural areas. The attendant harsh treatment of rural civilians spread animosity even to this social sector, which was not very much involved in the mostly urban political contest. While trying to contain rising restiveness in the south, the first civilian administration was gradually sinking into an inter-party quagmire that seriously undermined its effectiveness. However, it was ultimately the "political impasse created in the South [that] prompted the Sudanese military to seize power in 1958" (Deng 1997: 338), headed by General Ibrahim Abboud.

General Abboud's military regime now faced the dual task of containing dissident civilian parties and of stepping up operations against the southern rebels. He did not succeed in either task, as discontent continued to escalate in the north while armed strife in the south proved impossible to eliminate. Failure to resolve the conflict in the south coupled with rising northern grievances was capitalized upon by the civilian parties to instigate the popular uprising that unseated Abboud in October 1964. Deng (1997: 338) mentions the escalation of the conflict in the south to "full-fledged civil war in the 1960s" as one of the factors that instigated the popular uprising. An interim civilian government was installed to replace the military regime overthrown by the popular uprising. This government tried to resolve the conflict in the south by removing one deficiency of Sudan's political system: the absence of a permanent constitution. A twelve-man committee was thus created to start discussing principles that could meet southern aspirations while preserving Sudan's unity. Some southern intellectuals, of course, thought this was an opportune time for the northerners to honour the promise given at the time of independence. While wrangling went on at the round-table conference, developments elsewhere were deepening and lending increased coherence to the struggle in the south.

The southern soldiers who escaped into the rural areas after the Torit mutiny were gradually coalescing into a guerrilla group called the Anya-anya at this time. And their rank was growing as more former soldiers, policemen, and prison guards were pushed into joining them by their growing sense of insecurity. Anya-anya armed bands were initially organized along "ethnic" lines and operated in their own districts with little communication among them. Their agenda was also vague, at least initially, and mostly concentrated on denouncing the Arab and Moslem domination of Christians. While Anya-anya strength was gradually increasing, two powers stepped forward to further bolster their capability. Ethiopia and Israel came to the Anya-anya's assistance to further their own interests in the region. The Ethiopian government of Emperor Haile Selassie started extending assistance in order to "pressure Khartoum to close its borders to the Eritreans" (Markakis 1998: 118). The Anya-anya also won the favour of Israel due to the Khartoum government's rising anti-Zionist posture. With Israeli arms reaching them mostly through Ethiopia (some also through Uganda), Anya-anya units were growing stronger both in quality and in numbers in the 1960s. The coherence of their political agenda and their organization was also improving at this time, ultimately agreeing on separation from the north as their aim.

Meanwhile, the parliamentary government that replaced the interim civilian administration was becoming increasingly dysfunctional due to the usual inter-party bickering. The round-table conference had already reached a deadlock because of the ability of al-Turabi (future leader of National Islamic Front) to employ "his articulate logic and legal talents" to scuttle "the first sincere effort by Northern and Southern Sudanese to resolve their differences" (Collins 1997: 12). The die was ultimately cast when elected Communist Party delegates were expelled from the Parliament in total contravention of even the transitional constitution. The military once again took over in May 1969 with General Numairy at its head and with the backing of the Communist Party. The Communists were perhaps the most vocal party advocating the political resolution of the conflict in the south. While their rise to power thus appeared promising, it also raised apprehensions in strongly pro-Western Ethiopia. This state of affairs, however, did not last as the Communists soon fell out with Numairy and staged an unsuccessful coup to unseat him in 1971. Numairy thereafter started seeking a new social basis for his regime and became interested in defusing Sudan's tense relations with Ethiopia. The search for a new social basis led him to conclude the 1972 Addis Ababa Agreement, brokered by Emperor Haile Selassie. Based on his actions of later years, some came to believe that "Nimeiri only wanted to use the South as a countervailing force against the North" (Garang 1992: 11) when he concluded this agreement.

Military to Civil to Military Rule

The signing of the Addis Ababa Agreement is unique in the region's political history for it is "the only instance of peaceful conflict resolution in the Horn" (Markakis 1998: 119), despite proving a temporary one. As the implementation of the agreement got underway in the early 1970s, Numairy's northern opponents were coalescing into the United National Front, embracing particularly the Umma Party and the Moslem Brotherhood. They then conducted a sustained campaign denouncing the agreement as a sellout (Woodward 1990: 143). They eventually tried to unseat Numairy in 1976 by infiltrating their armed supporters (trained in Ethiopia and Libya) into Khartoum, where they actually succeeded in occupying some government installations. Although they were ultimately overpowered by government troops, their near success exposed Numairy's vulnerability to northern insurrection. Numairy subsequently adopted two policies to shore up his position. First, he started to fully and openly support armed opponents of Ethiopia's revolutionary government while at the same time assuming the posture of the main anti-communist power in the Horn. Second, he opened dialogue with his northern opponents, ultimately signing the 1977 Reconciliation Agreement with them. These were forces that had denounced the Addis Ababa Agreement as a sellout, and thus were interested in undermining it by all possible means. Hence, many believe that the course that ultimately led to the 1983 decision to nullify the Addis Ababa Agreement began with the enactment of this Reconciliation Agreement.

In any event, difficulties surrounding the implementation of the Addis Ababa Agreement were bound to provide the required pretext to start unravelling it. Allegations by some sectors of southern Sudanese society that members of the Dinka ethnic group were dominating the Southern administration (Woodward 1994a: 88) was on the rise at this time. Perception of the majority Dinkas as the south's potential "northerners" was evidently increasing. Even southern students, who used to be united in their common anti-northern sentiment, started engaging in "inter-ethnic" as well as "intra-ethnic" clashes (Arou 1989). The rising dissension within the south provided the pretext Numairy was evidently looking for to unilaterally divide the south into three regions, in total contravention of the Addis Ababa Agreement. With the presidential decree of 5 June 1983 which enacted this redivision, the 1972 Agreement had been consigned to the dustbin of history.

Evidently in preparation for the proclamation of this decree the Numairy regime had decided to transfer some southern troops to the north. The result was a repeat of what happened in 1955, a series of mutinies. When troops garrisoned at Bor and Pibor mutinied in May 1983, a former Anya-anya leader, John Garang, happened to be at Bor (his hometown), thus emerging as leader of the mutineers by leading them over the border into Ethiopia (Woodward 1994: 89). While Garang and his fellow mutineers were busy transforming themselves into the Sudan People's Liberation Army, Numairy provided them with the cause that cemented the southern consensus by healing the rifts resulting from the controversial division of the south. This was the proclamation of the September 1983 law that made Sharia the law of the land. He took this latter step, of course, to appear to be more Islamic than the Islamicists and to thus head "off the [Moslem] Brotherhood by stealing their clothes"

(Woodward 1986: 4).The southerners, despite engaging in periodic intra-south bloodletting, have remained united in their rejection of the Sharia to this day.

While the north-south rift was steadily re-emerging and growing in the early 1980s, some remnants of the Anya-anya (who rejected the Addis Ababa Agreement) were already engaging in low-level guerrilla activities in parts of the Upper Nile. Their number was increasing as more mutineers and defectors from the Sudanese army continued to trickle to their base camp near the Ethiopian border. They renamed themselves Anya-anya II, with the revival of the previous Anya-anya's agenda of separation as their aim. "The Marxist regime of Mengistu Haile Mariam tolerated their presence but offered little material support. Fighting his own war against secessionist rebels in Eritrea and Tigray, Mengistu could hardly have been expected to support the main political objective of the Anya-anya II" (Hutchinson 2001: 310). There was an additional cause for the Ethiopian regime's reluctance to support this group. The leaders and most members of the Anya-anya II were from the Nuer ethnic group, whose settlement straddles the Ethiopian-Sudanese border.

These causes for the Ethiopian regime's hesitation, however, did not apply to the 1983 mutineers for two reasons: their leader was Dr. John Garang, from the Dinka ethnic community; and Garang was prepared to work for the realization of a socialist-oriented New United Sudan. Thus, the SPLA that emerged from the 1983 mutineers was preferable to Anya-anya II on both grounds. Armed conflict ultimately broke out between Anya-anya II and the SPLA and continued into 1984. Thus commenced the second round of the armed struggle with intra-southern bloodletting; attaining mammoth proportions after 1991. Eritrean armed struggle also commenced under similar circumstances, as has been mentioned.

No other liberation front in the region, and perhaps in Africa, matches the SPLA's successes in obtaining massive amounts of financial assistance and numbers of weapons within a short time. Socialist allies of the Ethiopian regime were willing to provide arms and training, including flying some SPLA recruits to Cuba. Arab regimes opposed to Numairy (Libya the most prominent) were ready to pay for arms or donate them from their formidable arsenals. Western countries lobbied by Christian churches provided extensive relief aid, including food, clothing, medicine, and logistics. A movement that enjoyed the backing of these diverse external actors was bound to neglect seeking grassroots social support, which is exactly what happened. Furthermore, the same advantage impacted negatively on the SPLA's internal structure as well. It allowed

Garang the freedom to adopt "the heavy-handed militarism and auto-cratic leadership style of his Soviet-supported host" (Hutchinson 2001: 311).

The result was a preponderance of military operations in SPLA activities with almost no attention given to developing political institutions and extending meaningful social services in the zones under its control. And both Garang and his host were eager to bring about a speedy regime change in Khartoum. A combination of factors ultimately led to the second civilian uprising that brought down the Numairy regime in 1985. These included rising defence expenditures to contain the SPLA; civilian discontent with rising inflation; Sudan's isolation after Sharia law was proclaimed; and finally, Numairy's attempt to curb the rising influence of al-Turabi's National Islamic Front.

Elections were held one year after Numairy was overthrown by the civilian uprising. The civilian parties once again renewed their time-tested habit of paralyzing each other's administration. Regardless, a breakthrough in negotiating a settlement with the SPLA started looking promising due to one development. A coalition embracing some political parties, representatives of labour unions, and professional associations called the National Alliance for National Salvation (NANS) was instrumental in bringing down Numairy. This alliance initiated talks with the SPLA immediately after the change of government. This process led to the adoption of the Koka Dam Declaration on 24 March 1986, which laid down conditions and procedures that would lead to the convening of a National Constitutional Conference in the Sudan with the SPLA as one of the participants. Repealing the September Sharia laws was one of the preconditions the SPLA insisted on to participate. Elections were conducted before any moves were made to implement this declaration, with the Umma Party's leader (Assadiq al-Mahdi) winning the post of prime minister.

The prime minister's Umma party, as a member of the NANS, was a participant in the process that led to the adoption of Koka Dam declaration. When al-Mahdi came to power, however, he had to enter into coalition with either NIF or DUP, both of which were not adherents of the Koka Dam declaration. Furthermore, as the foremost champion of Sharia, the NIF was successful in holding the "other two parties hostage on the issue of Sharia" (Garang 1992: 148), thus stalling any progress with peace talks. However, a breakthrough appeared on the horizon once again when the DUP "went to the clearest commitment in November 1988 making an agreement with the SPLA by which both agreed on freezing of the sharia criminal code pending the proposed constitutional conference" (Woodward 1994: 94). Even the prime minister started distancing himself from NIF at this stage and showed interest in the peace agreement concluded between the DUP and the SPLA. However, the military staged a third coup on 30 June 1989, on the very day the council of ministers was to discuss this agreement, possibly approving most of its provisions.

Fronts against Fronts

While this drama was taking place in the Sudan, the Ethiopian regime was suffering defeat after defeat in its fight against three liberation fronts: the Eritrean People's Liberation Front (EPLF), the Oromo Liberation Front (OLF) and the Tigray People's Liberation Front (TPLF). Out of the three, the latest to start using the Sudan as a gateway to the rest of the world was the OLF, which began its armed activities initially in the eastern Oromo highlands adjacent to the Ogaden. As has already been mentioned, the OLF had tense relations with the Somali regime of Siad Barre and the fronts it was backing, the Western Somali Liberation Front (WSLF) and the Somali Abbo Liberation Front (SALF). In the event, the OLF ended up clashing with these fronts, which meant it would have to fight on two fronts as it was also engaging the Ethiopian regime. Hoping to avoid such a complication, the OLF opened a new area of operations in the Oromo-settled areas bordering the Sudan in 1981. Between 1981 and 1983, OLF guerrillas occasionally bumped into armed southern Sudanese, who were possibly members of Anya-anya II. Although they did not talk to each other, both groups chose to avoid each other as much as possible, and the OLF never informed the Sudan security forces of its encounter with these armed southerners. This situation was to undergo a radical change with the arrival of the SPLA on the scene after 1984.

The SPLA spent most of 1983 and the early months of 1984 organizing itself and fighting Anya-anya II in the southeastern Upper Nile region. During this time the OLF succeeded in establishing a relatively secure base area on the escarpment much further north and east from where these intrasouthern Sudanese conflicts were taking place. In the summer of 1984, however, a large contingent of SPLA fighters suddenly entered the OLF base area. Since OLF messages to impress upon the SPLA the futility of fighting each other were ignored, clashes inevitably ensued. These clashes recurred with increasing frequency and ferocity until 1990, when a joint OLF-EPLF operation drove the SPLA from Asosa altogether.

The Ethiopian and Sudanese governments were both experiencing internal convulsions while coming under increasing pressure from their armed opponents during 1989. The coup of 30 June 1989 was successful and thus brought to power the NIF-supported regime of General Omer Abbashir. An earlier similar attempt to topple the Mengistu regime on 17 May 1989, however, ended in failure and resulted in the killing or execution of some of the regime's most able commanders. Whether the gravely shaken Mengistu regime or the newly installed one of Abbashir would be the first one to go had serious implications for the movements they were hosting. The Derg was experiencing severe setbacks in 1989, having withdrawn completely from Tigray on 27 February, thereby losing access to Eritrea by land. In an apparent attempt to redeem itself by hastening the overthrow of the Sudanese government, the Mengistu regime took a measure that it had never before resorted to. It sent its heavy artillery across the border in support of the SPLA, which enabled it to penetrate the Blue Nile Province like never before. This development had a number of repercussions.

First, the OLF was completely cut off from its northern allies particularly the EPLF, with which it was conducting joint operations in Wallagga province. Second, it seriously shook the newly installed government in Khartoum, which also had warmer relations with the EPLF than its predecessor. Third, the EPLF had by then finalized its plan to snatch Massawa from the Derg, thereby completing the besiegement of Ethiopian troops stationed in Eritrea. Under these circumstances, the EPLF could not sit back and watch the precarious situation of its allies, the Sudan government and the OLF. Hence, in the first few days of 1990, it sent an entire division through the Sudan and launched a joint operation with the OLF, successfully driving the troops of both the Derg and the SPLA out of Asosa province within a few days. The Derg had to move a division out of Eritrea's Assab province to regain Asosa. While Mengistu was busy dealing with the situation in the southwest, disaster struck in the north. The EPLF made its final bid to take Massawa, totally liberating it by 15 February 1990. From then until the Derg's defeat in May 1991, close to one hundred thousand Ethiopian troops in Eritrea had to be supplied by air alone. The capture of Massawa once again triggered a cascade of events that had far-reaching implications for the Ethiopian state and the region, as it had done a century earlier.

The SPLA's Internal Convulsion

The loss of its most committed regional supporter, the Derg regime, spelled disaster for the SPLA. SPLA troops and southern Sudanese refugees made a hasty evacuation into southern Sudan ahead of the advancing troops of the victorious Ethiopian liberation fronts. Trouble compounded when the Nuer overall commander of SPLA troops in the Upper Nile, Riek Machar, along with his fellow Nuer lieutenants and a Shilluk commander called Lam Akol, announced that they had unseated Garang. The result, however, was an impasse, as these persons failed in taking controlling of the entire SPLA and Garang was similarly unable to subdue the rebellion. From then on the SPLA continued to fragment along lines roughly coinciding with communal identities. The catastrophic result of this fragmentation for rural civilians of the Upper Nile has been sufficiently documented by Hutchinson (2001) to make repeating it here unnecessary.

The political developments of the 1990s, however, must be briefly summarized. One of the issues that Riek Machar introduced into his dispute with Garang concerned the SPLA's political agenda. Garang had always advocated the preservation of Sudan's unity through its transformation into a *new Sudan*. Most southern Sudanese, however, appeared to prefer separation. Garang seemed to appease these tendencies by also talking about the *nationalities question* in the Sudan. (The flexible ways in which Garang interprets SPLA aims are elaborated by Peter Woodward [1994] and thus will only be touched upon here.) The term "nationality" is very common in Ethiopian political circles and is used in reference to collectivities called tribes elsewhere in Africa. While often mentioning the right of Sudanese nationalities, Garang also repeatedly declares his movement's intention to eradicate "tribalism" (see Garang 1992: 27, for example). When his attempted bid to depose Garang proved unrealizable, Riek Machar declared that he had formed a new organization called South Sudan Independence Movement (SSIM), with the independence of southern Sudan as its agenda. Thereafter he made Garang's refusal to embrace the principle of self-determination as one of the causes of the dispute between the two. This issue was settled when Garang also declared his willingness to accept the self-determination of not only southerners but also marginalized groups in the north such as the people of Ingessana Hills and Nuba Mountains.

Demands for some kind of autonomy or self-determination had been spreading even to the north since independence. And movements tabling such demands tended to mushroom every time military regimes were overthrown. For example, the General Union of Nuba Mountains and the Beja Congress emerged after the Abboud regime was toppled. While these two demanded "a degree of autonomy for their respective regions ... the Sudan African National Union claimed federal status for the south"

(Kurita 1994: 209). When Numairy was overthrown in 1985, some of these movements resurfaced along with additional ones such as the Front for the Renaissance of Dar Fur, the Southern Sudan Political Association, and the Sudan African Congress. A group representing the people of the Nuba Mountains had joined the SPLA at an early date, thereby extending the armed struggle into its home area. After the military takeover of 1989, even the Beja Congress went over to the SPLA side. The SPLA continued to win more allies from the north, which ultimately coalesced into the National Democratic Alliance (NDA), embracing even some of its earlier enemies, such as the Umma Party, DUP, and others.

I will wrap up this section by briefly enumerating how the SPLA's prospects continued to see-saw during the 1990s. Its dismal prospects of the early 1990s improved when relations between Sudan and Eritrea started to sour soon after the latter's independence, leading to total rupture by late 1994. Thereafter Eritrea started to openly support the SPLA and other opponents of the Khartoum government. Things got even better after Ethiopia also openly joined the anti-Sudan camp after an unsuccessful attempt in Addis Ababa to assassinate the Egyptian president in which Sudanese authorities were reportedly implicated. With massive Eritrean and Ethiopian support, the SPLA started regaining some of the territory it had lost to the government during the time of internal turmoil. But things took a turn for the worse once again when Eritrea and Ethiopia quarrelled in 1998 and started scrambling to make peace with Khartoum.

INTRODUCTION

UNTIL THE DISINTEGRATION OF STATE and society in the 1990s indicated the opposite, Somalia's homogeneity appeared to render its nation-building prospects one of the least challenging in Africa. Why then did Africa's most homogeneous nation fail so tragically? Inferring that Somalia's so-called homogeneity was more apparent than real, some commentators are now suggesting that its nation-building challenges were comparable with those of other African states. Such writers cite language differences, differing myths of descent coupled with dissimilar lifestyles, and the existence of racially distinct subordinate groups to make their case. I will briefly discuss these social fault lines and how they remained troublesome despite the external projection of total homogeneity.

DIALECT, DESCENT, AND POWER

The biggest fault line concerns the division of Somali society into two grand coalitions of clan families, the Saab and Samaale. Speaking different versions of the Somali language and living differing lifestyles set these two groups apart. Members of the Saab branch are the more sedentary agro-pastoralists of the south, namely, the Digile and Mirifle, who speak the Mai version of Somali. Members of the Samaale branch are strictly pastoralists and speak the Maha (or Mahaatiri) version. And these are further divided into the Irrir (made up of Isaaq, Dir, and Hawiya subdivisions) and the Darood (comprising the Majerteen, Marehan, Dhulbahante, and other smaller groups). Assertions that members of both branches are united in tracing their descent to the Quraishy Arab tribe of the Prophet Mohammed used to be common in the literature (for example Laitin 1977: 50). However, some Somali scholars now dismiss this assertion by stating that "the Arabic factors ... were more influential among the nomadic groups of northern Somalia" who are "belligerent, less law abiding, arrogant, destructive and look down on any profession except herding" (Mukhtar 1995: 17).

The distribution of power and the elevation of Maha to the status of state language in due course came to widen the gulf separating these two branches. Let us first look at the issue of language. United Somalia faced the unique challenge of dealing with the complications resulting from inheriting two colonial languages, English and Italian. This by itself would have necessitated alphabetizing and using the Somali language for education and administration. Emulating neighbouring Ethiopia would have provided an additional motivation for adopting such policy. Successive civilian administrations, however, were unable to determine whether Arabic, Latin, or a home-grown alphabet called Osmaniya was most appropriate for the Somali language. This wrangling was still going on when Siad Barre came to power in October 1969 by staging a coup d'état. Hence, it was his regime that imposed the Maha version of Somali as the state's official language, with the Latin alphabet. This might not have perhaps mattered much had it not coincided with the growing political marginalization of the Maai speakers.

As commonly happened in the rest of Africa, the Maai speakers stood a better chance to inherit the post-colonial state due to their sustained contact (in this case) with the Italian colonialists. This prospect, however, started dimming first when the British Military Administration (BMA) favoured the mostly Darod and Hawiya-based Somali Youth League (SYL) by giving civilian and military posts to its members. When the Italians tried to revive their earlier close relations with the southerners and to support them after replacing the BMA in 1950, they were effectively deterred by SYL opposition (Maxted 2000: 163). Regardless, the Italians were able to fairly apportion National Assembly seats during the run-up to independence and unification with the former British Somaliland. Seats were "proportionately divided among the three major southern clans: thirty Reewin, thirty Hawiye, and thirty Darood, irrespective of party affiliation" (Mukhtar 1997: 52). This started to change after unification, however, for a couple of reasons. First, unification augmented the demographic proportion of the Hawiyya and Darood, thus enabling them to increase their share of power. Second, whatever was left over was reserved mostly for the northern Isaaqs to appease them away from the separatist tendency that had surfaced among them immediately after unification. Since they were highly under-represented in civilian and military posts, the southerners were completely absent from the junta that took power in 1969. Consequently, the combination of speaking a non-Maha version of Somali and being marginalized in politics signalled the demotion of southerners to the status of virtual second-class citizens.

Race and Enslavement

These marginalized sectors could perhaps take comfort in the fact that they were better off than another social sector. According to Besteman (1996), they actually look down on the descendants of the Oromos and Bantus that their ancestors used to enslave. Descendants of these former slaves, despite practising Islam, attaching themselves to some Somali clan, and speaking Somali, are despised by the rest of the Somalis (Maxted 2000: 160). Other Somalis commonly refer to these former slaves as Habash (Laitin 1977: 29). Assigning them this name has several implications. Since Habash means Abyssinian, the application of the same term to these groups signals their portrayal as the negativity of "genuine" Somalis. Somalis also used to refer to their Italian colonial masters as "the [H]abash of Europe" (Laitin 1977: 68) when they want to disparage them. The despised descendants of the former slaves are actually said to have "fearsome magical abilities" (Besteman 1995: 47). Hence, the term "Habash" seems to apply to peoples hated, feared, and despised by the rest of the Somalis at the same time.

The True Cause of Cohesion

Some members of the marginalized agro-pastoral sector now trace Somalia's inability to translate homogeneity into cohesion to the policy of inventing "Somali tradition, which glorified the nomadic tradition but also ignored and degraded other Somali traditions" (Mukhtar 1995: 21). Those "belligerent, less law abiding, arrogant, [and] destructive" nomads are thus blamed for the post-1991 tragedy in this discourse. Others go further to attribute the disintegration to the fact that the Somali people are "contrary to a nation" because they are "internally broken up into clans and traditionally lack the concept of state as a hierarchical power" (Mansur 1995: 107). The attributes that define ethnicity and those that generate this form of segmentation along clan lines are quite similar in the views of others (see Hashim 1997 for an interesting discussion). Each of the collectivities known as clan families resembles a nationality, according to Adam (1994: 159). Other scholars assert that maintaining "the fiction of a unified Somalia devoid of internal (or sub-ethnic) conflicts" was made possible by routinely decreeing "harmonious communal goals for the Somali people among whom no divisions could be acknowledged" (Geshekter 1997: 74). And the most important "harmonious communal goal" was regaining the "foreign controlled territories of the Somali nation." Thus, "the cohesion of the Somali Republic in the 1960s was built upon [the] common national purpose" of regaining these territories (Laitin 1977: 129). And there is no doubt that Somali cohesion and national consensus remained solid so far as achieving this harmonious national goal appeared to be on track.

Meanwhile, Somali politicians played the usual African game of mobilizing support on the basis of clan while roundly denouncing "tribalism." As Said Samatar puts it, "it is hard to find a Somali politician who would feel free enough to declare openly and without qualms that his loyalty is, first and foremost, to his clan; on the other hand it is equally hard to find one who would place the interests of the nation above those of the clan, or who would act politically in a way independent of clan affiliation" (qtd. in Markakis 1987: 86). The early nationalist parties thus naturally based themselves on the support of the major clan families such as the Darood, Isaaq, and Rahanweyn. However, by the time of the last 1969 elections "clan politics had fallen back to smaller lineage groups" with over "60 one-man lineage parties" competing for 123 seats (Mukhtar 1997: 53). Once this last election was over, however, all elected deputies save one crossed the floor to merge with the victorious SYL, thus virtually ushering in a single party civilian rule. Coinciding with "growing disillusion with the traditional campaign for the unification of the missing Somali territories" (Mukhtar 1997: 53), this crass manipulation of party politics paved the way for the 1969 coup. But the Somali political elite's proclivity of going from total fragmentation to absolute unity had pointed to a future in which the direct opposite process could happen.

The military regime thus came to power promising to stamp out "tribalism" and to work much more vigorously for the redemption of the lost territories. With a view to achieving the first objective, Siad Barre proclaimed his regime's determination "to replace archaic, divisive lineage loyalty, by productive revolutionary allegiance to the nation" (Lewis 1991: 90). When he presided over the public demonstration in 1971 during which effigies representing the various clans were ritually buried (Lewis 1991: 89), he evidently considered the job done. However, while engaging in this public posturing, "the head of state himself was covertly relying on older, time-honored ties of loyalty" (Lewis 1991: 90). In private conversations with his Marehan clansmen, he was at the same time cautioning them to remain wary of Majerteen thirst for power and Isaaq cunning (Hussein 1997: 171). He ultimately came to base his power on the support of his Marehan clansmen, the Ogadenis (his maternal uncle's clansmen) and the Dhulbahantes (his son-in-law's clansmen).

Meanwhile, he was scoring impressive diplomatic and military successes in preparation for Somali unification. Somalia's admission to the Arab League and the Islamic Conference Organization, both off limits to Ethiopia, more than compensated for its alienation in African forums. Considerable financial input was thus accessed from these quarters. In addition, increasing contact with the Socialist world finally culminated in the signing of the Treaty of Cooperation with the Soviet Union. This alliance made possible a spectacular growth in the size of the army and the quality of its armament. The period lasting up to the early successes in the 1977–78 Ethiopian-Somali war can now be seen as the zenith of Somali internal consensus and cohesion. Although repression of dissent did play a considerable part, the pervasive commitment to unification constituted its most profound foundation. Most members of the political elite were willing participants in the practice of denying the existence of any internal diversity, let alone division within Somali society.

Ogaden: The Strategic Prize

The three regions awaiting redemption and unification with the independent Somali Republic were: Kenya's Northern Frontier District (NFD), the Ogaden Province of the Ethiopian Empire, and the French colony of Djibouti. Success in acquiring the Ogaden could easily be seen as the decisive step that could make inevitable the recovery of the other two regions. A number of factors supported this assessment. The Ogaden is the most populous of the three regions. It juts deep into Somalia, threatening to cut it almost in half. This peculiar geographical penetration posed both as "a grave threat and a great opportunity" (Markakis 1987: 169). The Ethiopians could easily split the country into two and could thus isolate the north from the south. On the other hand, the Somalis could easily reach and overrun key Ethiopian positions. The pivotal impact of the Ogaden's retrieval on regaining the other regions thus made the conflict with Ethiopia much more pronounced.

Historical precedents might have been invented to project back into previous centuries the existence of historical discord with Ethiopia. However, the existence of an actual war between Moslems and Christians in the sixteenth century involving Somalis, rendered such an invention unnecessary. The history of Somali nationalism was thereby stretched back to that period. The true identity of the leader of the Moslem armies involved in those wars, the Imam Ahmed bin Ibrahim al Ghazi (a.k.a. Gagn), perhaps will never be definitively determined. While he was a Darod Somali (Touval 1963: 49) according to Somali tradition, he was the illegitimate offspring of a Somali woman and an Abyssinian priest (Touval 1963: 51) in Abyssinian sources. The Oromos also claim him by citing the names of his relatives and of his birthplace (Hubata), both of which happen to be Oromo. Still others trace him to "the Muslim Bejas of Eritrea" (Adam 1994: 141). David Laitin (1977: 27) speculates that the Somali Ahmed Gurey and the historical Ahmed Gragn who led the wars against the Christians could be two different persons. He goes further to conclude he was "not a Somali himself but the leader of Somali troops" (Laitin 1977: 53). His troops were not purely Somali either since members of other societies reportedly participated in the jihad led by him (Touval 1963: 50). Perhaps less controversial is the likelihood that he saw himself as a Moslem first and as a Somali second (if at all) (Laitin 1977: 53). The same was perhaps true regarding the self-identification of the diverse members of his armies.

Nevertheless, when that history was appropriated to portray Somali nationalism's existence since the sixteenth century, his memory was invoked "as a Somali national hero and leader in the wars against Ethiopia" (Touval 1977: 51). Somali scholars then took to inferring the prevalence of a more cohesive nationalism during the glory days of Ahmed Gragn in contrast to later centuries marked with perennial squabbles among Somalis (Samatar 1988: 24). References to him as "the first Somali 'nationalist'" (Laitin 1977: 27) or as one of "the two most revered Somali nationalist figures" (Laitin 1977: 53) started appearing in the literature. State propaganda was much more explicit in portraying the wars of the sixteenth century as being a Somali (Moslem) nationalist struggle against Ethiopian (Christian) imperialists as well as promoting Imam Ahmed Gurey as the precursor of all Somali nationalists. This interpretation of history, coupled with the widespread Somali conviction that being a Moslem and a Somali are identical, created a complication in entering into an alliance with other adjacent Moslem but non-Somali nationalists. This complication had much to do in frustrating the realization of the sacred mission of unification. How tension between the Oromo people's struggle and Somali aspirations inevitably resulted from this complication has been mentioned earlier. In fact, the Siad-backed WSLF killed more OLF leaders than did the Ethiopian regime, the Front's primary enemy.

As Geshekter (1977: 75) so aptly puts it, "The military debacle of 1978 shattered all hopes for achieving a Greater Somalia and signaled the demise of pan-Somalism." An unsuccessful coup attempt by Majerteen officers unleashed the regime's fury against members of this clan, permanently under suspicion for harbouring vengeful sentiments for the unseating of the civilian government dominated by them. What is more important is the decision by the survivors of the pogrom to seek asylum in Ethiopia, thus breaking the taboo of consorting with the traditional enemy. As the Isaaqs and Hawiyyas also jumped on the bandwagon of courting Ethiopia's hospitality, the outward projection of enmity started turning inwards. When Siad also decided to outwit his armed opponents by striking a deal with the similarly hard-pressed Mengistu, the decades-old definition of Somali nationalism as the antithesis of Ethiopian imperialism was completely dissipated. And the course was set for the ultimate implosion of the Somali state, nation, and society. Hence, the most promising nation-building aspiration ended up in generating the direct opposite.

INTRODUCTION

POLITICAL DEVELOPMENTS IN THE HORN OF AFRICA since the mid-1870s and their historical resonance were briefly sketched in the previous chapters. As we have seen, ideas broached in the past can trigger events much later in history. Similarly, actions taken decades earlier can influence developments or attitudes later on. This temporal resonance has its spatial counterpart. Events in one corner of the Horn can influence those in another quarter. This horizontal resonance also has its vertical counterpart, confrontations between states echo downwards to impact on the day-to-day lives of ordinary people. Scholars who have observed this phenomenon have tried to diagnose the problems facing the Horn states and their inhabitants and to suggest solutions to overcome them. To these issues we now turn.

REGIONAL SECURITY COMPLEX

An enduring synergy between conflicts within states and those between them has been identified by numerous scholars. Discussing relations between Ethiopia and the Sudan in particular, Lemmu Baissa catalogues alternating periods of friendship and hostility. He writes, "while friendship and cordiality characterized the periods, 1956-1964, 1971-1976, 1980-1982, hostility and confrontation have marred relations in 1965-1970, 1977-1979, 1983-1990" (1991: 1). This situation persisted even after the period covered in his study. The Sudanese and Ethiopian regimes enjoyed friendly relations from 1991 to mid-1995, and they have continued to do so since mid-1998. The years 1995-98, on the other hand, were marked by fierce confrontation between the two regimes. The souring of relations during these years was triggered by an attempt on 25 June 1995

163

to assassinate Egypt's President Mubarak in the Ethiopian capital allegedly by Moslem radicals supported by Sudan. The restoration of friendly relations did not result from the conclusive resolution of this controversy. Instead it was due to conflict erupting between the Eritrean and Ethiopian regimes in mid-1998 that prompted both sides to befriend Khartoum with the aim of covering their respective flanks, reminiscent of developments a century earlier as detailed in chapter 5.

Baissa's study shows how Ethiopia and Sudan were quite successful in addressing such conventional causes of interstate conflict as border disputes. He therefore attributes the periodic relapse of mutual suspicion and hostility to the policy of both countries to exploit the other's domestic conflicts instead of resolving them. He draws the following important conclusion from this observation: "The *simultaneous* solution of the persistent domestic conflicts—not through the failed policy of resorting to force and intimidation, but through the restructuring of power, the equitable sharing of national resources and the fair participation of the component elements without domination by any group—within Ethiopia and the Sudan is the key to greater opportunities" (1991: 21; italics added). As will be shown below, many other scholars concur with his conclusion that intrastate and interstate conflicts need to be resolved simultaneously if the region is to enjoy peace and stability. Recapitulating the developments of the 1990s will further underscore the intimate interplay between interstate and intrastate peace and partnership in the Horn region.

Pragmatic considerations impelled the incumbent Sudanese regime and the Eritrean, Oromo, and Tigrean liberation fronts to foster a fragile spirit of cooperation at the dawn of the 1990s. Despite its fragility, cooperation between the Eritrean, Oromo, and Tigrean guerrilla armies, partly induced by Sudanese pressure, was instrumental in averting total breakdown of order after the defeat of the Derg army. Hopes were raised in the early days of this coalition of fronts and governments that partnership at the intrastate and interstate level could endure. In fact, the resolution of a number of thorny issues was made possible by the prevalence of partnership at these two levels. Eritrea's relatively smooth ascension to the status of de facto independence in 1991 figures prominently among such issues. The other was the simultaneous restructuring of the rump Ethiopian state with a view to resolving other outstanding demands for self-determination. This emerging ad hoc alliance, while it lasted, was tacitly premised on de-emphasizing the conventional distinction between domestic and interstate interactions.

Diplomatic exchanges between the Sudanese and Ethiopian capitals during this period perhaps fit into the conventional interstate category of friendly relations. Although Sudan became the first country to recognize Eritrea's independence and to exchange ambassadors, the elevation of this relationship to a standard interstate level was tacitly presumed pending the consummation of Eritrea's de jure independence. The relationship between the OLF and the TPLF also had its own peculiarity. Formally, it resembled some sort of intrastate partnership. However, the fact that this partnership was based on a clear agreement to rearticulate Ethiopia's sovereignty as the composite of the sovereign rights of the country's diverse inhabitants puts it in a category of its own. Exchanges between the Eritrean capital, Asmara, and the Ethiopian capital, in practice, fell somewhere between these forms of relationships. Meanwhile, open bilateral contacts and cooperation between these diverse actors continued, signalling their willingness to eschew drawing rigid boundaries between intrastate and interstate relations.

The simultaneous cultivation of intrastate and interstate cooperation suffered its first setback in mid-1992, with the ejection of the Oromo Liberation Front from the Ethiopian Transitional Government (for details see Lata 1998 and 1999). This was immediately followed by the decision of the Eritrean and Sudanese governments to alienate the OLF with the intention of currying favour with the Tigrean-dominated Ethiopian regime. Meanwhile, the regime's determination to monopolize Ethiopia's politics and thus gain access to its economy and natural resources was partly due to its hope of enticing Eritrea back into the Ethiopian state in one form or another. As already mentioned, inducing or even forcing "the Eritrean leadership to re-enter into some form of political union with Ethiopia" by extending considerable economic privileges to Eritrea and Eritreans could not be implemented without such a monopolization of power. Using the resources particularly of southern Ethiopia to consolidate inter-Abyssinian (state-nation) solidarity was pioneered by Menelik, as was discussed in chapter 5. The intention of the present Tigrean rulers of Ethiopia to entice their Eritrean cousins back into the fold by a similar approach demonstrates the enduring nature of this policy.

What is germane to the issue under discussion is this policy's implication for promoting intrastate and interstate cooperation. Cooperation within Ethiopia had to be scuttled partly in order to achieve the reversal of the quasi-interstate nature of Ethiopian-Eritrean relations. Enticing Eritrea back into Ethiopia, however, was doomed because the Eritrean leadership was determined to turn the new state into a modern nation par excellence through traditional nation-building. Misreading each other's long-range intentions hence partly contributed to the eruption of the 1998–2000 war between the Ethiopian and Eritrean regimes. This war is peculiar in that it matches neither the conventional interstate nor intrastate variety, as elaborated in a separate writing (Lata 2003). Tekeste Negash and Kjetil Tronvoll (2000: 94) come closest to grasping its true nature when they describe it as a war that "has most of the characteristics of a civil war between one people spread out into two countries."

A new promising period of peace and cooperation, at least at the interstate level, appeared to have dawned at the beginning of the 1990s. For example, writing in mid-1993, the editor of the *Horn of Africa Bulletin* concluded that "For the first time for decades—maybe in history—all the countries of the Horn actually do live in peace with each other." Some optimists expected that the lingering domestic conflicts would be resolved to usher in a period of peace within and between the Horn states. But the decade ended with the resumption of hostile regimes supporting each other's armed opposition. The developments of the 1990s hence clearly demonstrate the endemic nature of the synergy prevailing between intrastate and interstate conflicts.

What I recapitulated for the 1990s holds true for the entire period of the existence of the Horn states as independent entities. The linkages between interstate and domestic conflicts in the region are now increasingly recognized by scholars. One such scholar, Terrence Lyons (1996: 85), writes that "The Horn of Africa region … has been the site of endemic inter- and intrastate conflict for decades." According to him, "The many conflicts are interlinked in a regional 'security complex,' a group of states whose primary security concerns link together sufficiently closely that their national securities cannot realistically be considered apart from one another." Lionel Cliffe concurs with this view by designating the Horn among those African regions whose internal conflicts are interwoven with interstate hostilities. He goes on to conclude that "such conflicts are intermeshed in such a way that 'solutions' to any one country's problems in isolation are extremely difficult" (1998: 1). He echoes Baissa's conclusion by asserting that the resolution of these interconnected conflicts requires "a two-tier process, and there has to be a simultaneity in settling two or more disputes" (Cliffe 1998: 2).

Lyons goes into more detail in envisioning the resolution of these conflicts. He recommends instituting new forms of governance at multiple levels and involving diverse actors as the antidote for the Horn's enduring predicaments. He believes that, while some authority and responsibility could continue to reside at the old level of the state, creating new structures or regimes at the local (provincial), sub-regional (Horn of Africa), continental, and global levels would be necessary. And such an overhaul of the exercise of authority would necessitate "redefining sovereignty, the basis of citizenship, the meaning of borders, and other legal abstractions that have been used by political leaders to control their territories" (Lyons 1996: 95-96).

Pausewang draws a similar conclusion by using Ethiopia's experience as a point of departure. Decentralization and responsible competition in a multi-tier government system, he believes, offer a way out of endemic conflicts. Neither the mere coalescence of existing entities into an East African or pan-African federation nor the replacement of existing states by their smaller replicas would suffice to achieve such an end, he concludes. He underscores the need to replace "the autonomous power of the state government with people's representation, not only in state organs, but at all levels of democratic government from the local to the supranational" (1994: 224). Such radical restructuring of power demands not only splitting sovereignty between different levels but the "discreet burial" of "the national sovereignty of state government," itself a remnant of the Napoleonic wars in Europe. What Baissa, Lyons, and Puasewang recommend from their diverse perspectives is in keeping with the state and self-determination as rearticulated chapters 3 and 4 of this work.

Regionalized Economy and Ecology

The scholars mentioned above drew their conclusions by focusing primarily on the political aspects of intrastate and interstate conflicts in the Horn of Africa. Their analyses demonstrate how the Horn fits into some sort of regional "security complex." Other scholars add an environmental dimension to draw an even more comprehensive picture of the Horn's interdependence. John Markakis (1998: 5) designates the Horn of Africa as "a region with a multitude of physical, social, cultural, economic and other integrating features that distinguish it from adjacent regions." Furthermore, it is "an eco-geographical region: one that is unified in an ecological sense, and is distinct in that sense from the regions contiguous to it." Abebe Zegeye's study (1994), which underscores the need for interstate cooperation if increasing environmental degradation is to be stemmed, reinforces Markakis's vision of the Horn of Africa as a cohesive eco-geographical region.

Markakis's detailed study of interstate and intrastate conflicts and conflicts over access to resources at various levels clearly shows how all these three resonate in the Horn of Africa. He believes that the nation-state model and the accompanying pursuit of cultural homogeneity through coercive assimilation and centralization of power further exacerbate these diverse forms of conflict. He goes on to recommend that serious consideration be given to the dissolution of the "wedlock of nation and state," and the abandonment of the "the nation-building exercise," thus giving way to the institution of multi-nationalism "reflecting the reality of ethnic pluralism" (1998: 187/188).

What Markakis calls the "wedlock of nation and state" Crawford Young refers to as "the steel grid of the nation-state" (1991: 345). Young finds Africa's invocation of decolonization a departure from the more widespread occurrences elsewhere in which "ethno-linguistic identity is asserted as prescriptive entitlement to self-determination" (1991: 341). He discusses how Africa's proscription of identity-based demands for self-determination and the entrenchment of the existing states' legitimacy due to the international endorsement of this proscription have contributed to the stability of African states. Only the states of the Horn of Africa have been unable to benefit from this norm. It is only in this region that the clash between the nation-state and aspirations for self-determination are generating catastrophic human suffering necessitating the search for imaginative solutions. He is clear on what needs to be abandoned. Hence, he recommends that "The steel grid of the nation-state and its excessively unitarian ideology must somehow yield to more flexible formulations" (Young 1991: 345). In another essay (1991a: 59), he stipulates that "far-reaching reconstruction of their institutional and power structures" may be indispensable to achieve the resolutions within the framework of existing states. The responsibility to determine the ultimate nature of such formulations or reconstruction lies with the protagonists, he states. But he envisages that these could assume the form of either "some loose-knit, broader Horn umbrella entity" or "confederal arrangements within existing state units" (1991: 345). Simultaneously shaping such an umbrella entity and restructuring existing states appears even more promising, as the studies cited in an earlier section point out.

Eritrea's post-independence experience supports Markakis's caution against the proliferation of smaller states imbued with the "exclusiveness and inflexible sovereignty of their predecessors" (1998: 187). How the proliferation of such entities could merely introduce additional actors in interstate conflicts without removing their intrastate dimension has been borne out by Eritrea's experience during the second half of 1990s. In addition, smaller entities are not likely to achieve much on their own.

Hence, they will inevitably be under pressure "to cooperate, coordinate and even integrate their activities" (Markakis 1998: 187). Others go a little further in envisaging the nature of such integration. The "geographical proximity, manageable size, historical and cultural links" of particularly between "Ethiopia, Eritrea, Somalia, Somaliland and Djibouti are best able to evolve an entity that possess [*sic*] not only economic but also loosely political links and coordination as well," writes Hussein M. Adam (1994: 156). He goes on to make a call for the creation of the Commonwealth of Independent Horn of Africa States.

Denouncing one form of the nation-state while advocating the realization of its replica has been a common feature of struggles for self-determination. Markakis's and Young's recommendations that the rigid bond between nation and state be loosened hence cannot be realized without rearticulating both the state and the principle of self-determination. A comprehensive elaboration of Strobe Talbott's (2000: 155) admonition that "the concept of self-determination" be defined and applied "in a way that is conducive to integration and not to disintegration" can perhaps serve as the basis of an alternative vision. The paradoxical reality of many contemporary states being too small and too large at the same time seems to apply to the entities of the Horn. Thus, the Horn of Africa seems well suited for multi-dimensional self-determination as an approach that would simultaneously institute empowerment at the grassroots level and integration at the regional level.

Theory and Practice in the Horn

According to Crawford Young (1991a: 44), the invocation of numerous demands for self-determination makes the Horn a unique sub-region in Africa. Indeed, nowhere else in Africa have struggles and debates over the nature of the state and the concept of self-determination raged as in the Horn. Volumes have been dedicated to variously depicting Ethiopia as a millennia-old nation-state or one form of empire or another. Divergent definitions of the nation and the accompanying varieties of self-determination also have been invoked. In fact, the majority of political forces that appeared on Ethiopia's political landscape starting in the early 1970s, including the so-called Ethiopia-wide ones, have embraced the principle of self-determination. Even recent regimes have found it potentially perilous not to at least pay lip service to the concept.

The Sudan has likewise been the scene of fierce confrontations over the articulation of the state since its independence. Much ink (and even more blood) has been spilled to resolve whether it should be shaped as an African or an Arab nation. Explicitly demanding separation was the preserve of the southerners in the 1950s and 1960s. The aspiration to some sort of decentralization was aired contemporaneously in some quarters of the north. Demands for various forms of self-determination continue to figure prominently in the ongoing struggles. In the Sudan, as in Ethiopia, few are the parties that openly question the relevance of self-determination.

Irredentism and counter-irredentism have surfaced between Eritrea and Ethiopia and between Ethiopia and Somalia. This indicates the extent to which these entities share the same identity communities and common ecological and economic resources as well as vital infrastructures such as ports. Unfortunately, the pursuit of the nation-state model has turned these potentials for partnership into causes of friction. Somalia is the most tragic casualty of the nation-state model. There, the failure to consummate the in-gathering of all Somali speakers into a single state helped pave the way to disintegration and attendant chaos. Lingering irredentism and the related aspiration to regain access to the Red Sea also partly account for the 1998–2000 war between Ethiopia and Eritrea. The societies of both entities are still reeling from the economic and emotional aftershocks of this war.

Eritrea, after becoming the first African country to achieve independence by breaking away from another, seems determined to realize an anachronistic aspiration. Often described "as much an ethnic mosaic as the rest of Ethiopia" (Clapham 1994: 33), Eritrea is pursuing the traditional policy of nation-building at a time when this project's futility is increasingly being recognized. The experience of not only the Horn but also other parts of the contemporary world indicates the futility of this agenda. Clapham speculates that Eritrea may be "the last adherent in the Horn of the ideology of the centralised multiethnic state" (1994: 37). Eritrea's current nation-building project, in fact, goes beyond targeting the identities of the so-called ethnic groups. According to Tronvoll (1998: 461–82), eroding the provincial identities of the Tigrinya-speakers of Akele-Guzai, Hamasein and Seraye, which go back centuries, is being entertained. However, while curtailing it at home, the Eritrean authorities support identity politics in neighbouring states. Hence, the support they extend to the Beja Congress in the Sudan and numerous national liberation fronts in Ethiopia indicates a presumption that Eritrea alone is immune to this type of politics. Eritrea's anachronistic pursuit of conventional nation-building has its counterpart in Ethiopia where the ruling EPRDF party continues to practise the failed USSR approach to federalism. Consequently, struggles for some form of self-determination continue in both states.

GRASSROOTS INNOVATIONS

Although they often tap into the existing grievances of grassroots communities, the current struggles for self-determination in the Horn of Africa are articulated and led by elite groups. This articulation is often tailored to fit into internationally established norms and paradigms. The concerned elite groups thus start with a universal model and, at best, try to adapt it to reflect the particular situation of their constituencies. Grassroots communities, however, approach the matter without any recourse to such borrowed abstractions. They start from the reality of their prevailing misfortune that is routinely exacerbated by the inability or unwillingness of the state or non-state elite to take appropriate action. Hence, when such communities are left with no alternative but to take their immediate and distant destiny into their own hands they often fall back on age-old coping strategies. It is under such circumstances that grassroots communities have articulated and implemented innovative solutions to real problems. As most of these unsung occurrences are, as often as not, undocumented, we can only mention a few examples.

The Quasi Parliament of the Nuba

The conceptualization of Sudan's conflict as being south versus north lends peculiarity to the challenges facing the Nuba branch of the SPLA. The Nuba Mountains, the home areas of the Nuba peoples, is geographically part of the north. However, the attitude of the British and successive post-independence Sudanese regimes towards the southerners and the Nuba people happened to be roughly the same. Hence, forging some sort of alliance between the Nuba peoples and the southern Sudanese was seen as natural going back to the era of parliamentary governments. Such an alliance was realized only in the 1980s when some Nuba leaders joined the SPLA and extended the armed struggle into the Nuba Mountains.

The operations of the SPLA in the Nuba Mountains suffered from numerous handicaps. Provisions were routinely inadequate due the area's distance from Ethiopia, the traditional and reliable source of supplies. In addition, these operations attracted only the marginal attention of the predominantly southern leadership of the SPLA. On the other hand, they attracted the Sudanese regime's disproportionately higher attention because they were conducted deep inside the north. Continuing resistance under these circumstances became even more hazardous after 1991 due to several reasons. First, the overthrow of Ethiopia's Derg regime by forces friendly with Khartoum resulted in the SPLA losing its most reliable regional backer. Second, the ensuing splintering of the SPLA in southern Sudan largely along lines of "ethnic" allegiance further exacerbated this already grave situation. The factional fighting that then started raging in large parts of the south effectively cut off the Nuba Mountains from the outside world by making travel to and from East Africa impossible. With it even the trickle of essential supplies completely dried up.

The Sudanese regime, not surprisingly, found this an opportune moment to deliver the death blow to the Nuba branch of the SPLA. Hence, starting in January 1992 it deployed upwards of forty thousand troops backed with aircraft and heavy artillery to do the job in as short a time as possible. The ensuing scorched-earth military operation coupled with the forcible relocation of the civilian population to hasten Islamization and Arabization posed the greatest threat ever to the very survival of the Nuba as a people. It was at this juncture that the commander of the SPLA units in the area took a measure uncommon among guerrilla movements. He convened the South Kordofan Advisory Council (SKAC), often referred to as the Nuba Parliament, to ask "for a vote of confidence from ordinary Nuba." He wanted the council to choose between surrendering and continuing the resistance despite the overwhelming odds stacked against them. More than two hundred mostly civilian delegates met for four days of frank and unfettered debates after which they "voted overwhelmingly to continue the war" (Flint 2001: 104).

At the conclusion of this first meeting of the Nuba Parliament, the SPLA commander took responsibility for all preceding events and went on to remind the delegates that "from here it is the responsibility of all of us" (Flint 2001: 104). The Parliament has met annually ever since, with a few exceptions. But the most remarkable development isn't the birth of a full-fledged Parliament and a truly democratic order. Rather, it is that the attempt to subordinate the guerrilla army to a predominantly civilian elected body is laying the foundation for a more promising future relationship between military and civilian officials. In directly soliciting popular consent for the continuation of the resistance, the first steps have been taken in the direction of meaningful self-determination. Perhaps this could enable the Nuba peoples to avoid the same disappointing fate as others whose "self-determination" reflected military effectiveness more than the political accountability of the champions of liberation to the society at large.

People-to-People Peace in Southern Sudan

While the Nuba were experimenting with popular representation as a response to impending catastrophe, the situation in southern Sudan was progressing from bad to worse. Fighting among SPLA splinter groups, often assuming an intercommunal form, allowed the Sudan army to regain areas that had been off limits for years. Hence, rising incidents of intracommunal and intercommunal strife joined the proliferating cases of interfactional fighting and natural calamities to put at risk the very survival of an increasing number of southern communities. This situation appeared unstoppable until 1997, when a peacemaking initiative was launched by the New Sudan Council of Churches.

The initiative, called the People to People Peace (PPP)—for details see Juma 2002—emanated from the southern church group's consultation with the SPLA leading to a consensus that the churches have a role in grassroots peacemaking. Protracted discussions with the chiefs and elders of West Bank Nuers and Dinkas as well as ordinary people ultimately led to the March 1999 general meeting between the notables of the two communities. The peace and reconciliation subsequently concluded by three hundred Dinka and Nuer chiefs ushered in the period of relative calm that is holding to this day. Encouraged by this outcome, the church group made another attempt to reconcile the Dinka and the Didinga, again with relative success. After achieving these encouraging breakthroughs, those involved were emboldened to address the most murderous Nuer-Dinka hostility around Bor on the East Bank. Here too the effort was capped with success, resulting in an agreement of peace and reconciliation in May of 2000. "This meeting ended with a public covenant between all ethnic groups and the signing of a comprehensive document pledging peace and reconciliation" (Juma 2002). A multi-dimensional self-determination, enacting the terms for peace within and between different groups, is hence explored in south Sudan as a response to a multi-faceted conflict.

The Somaliland Guurti

The Somali state's disintegration and descent into chaos appeared irreversible after the murderous 1988 attack by Siad Barre's army on the Isaaqs of the north. And, as elsewhere in Somalia, Siad tried to shore up the position of his army by fanning conflict among the various clans living in this area as well. Grassroots attempts to reverse the ensuing state of violence between and within clans was started in 1991. During the following two years, numerous local inter-clan reconciliation conferences were convened, involving elders, religious leaders, and other notables. And in early 1993, representatives of all the clans inhabiting the north assembled in Borama to deliberate on comprehensive terms for peace and the formation of an independent northern Somali state that would oversee it. The Borama Conference, which dragged on for five months until May 1993, came to a conclusion with the declaration of an independent Somaliland Republic, signalling the rebirth of the former British Somaliland as a new state.

How the declaration of Somaliland's independence materialized is peculiar in a number of respects. Unlike similar movements, the main anti-Siad armed opposition, the Somali National Movement (SNM), was not successful in installing itself as the new government, although it did try. Fighting among the various subclan groups of the Isaaqs and between the Isaaqs and other clans made the ambition unsustainable. Hence, the SNM had to go along with the initiatives of societal leaders to build peace and consensus up from the grassroots. This demonstrates a clear departure from the usual result of armed struggles for self-determination. The inevitably protracted process of promoting consensus stage by stage also constitutes a departure from the usual post-decolonization perception of self-determination as a single-day event. In this perception, the midnight ceremony of hoisting the flag of independence heralds the precipitous replacement of domination by liberation.

The novelty of the division of power articulated at the Borama Conference reveals an even more significant peculiarity of Somaliland's experience. The system of government as conceived at the conference embraces three autonomous bodies: the government (executive), the Parliament, and the Guurti, or council of elders (Heinrich 1997: 97–100). Mediating between the other two branches is the primary task of the Guurti. In this sense, its role approximates that of a constitutional court. These highest bodies of the new state preside over elected district and village councils, which are sensitive to clan representation. The revenue needed to perform duties at every level is raised by levying taxes in a similarly decentralized manner.

Treaty-Making by Borana Oromo

The above cases of grassroots responses to conflicts and other predicaments were implemented, as often as not, with some input from elite elements. In fact, we owe their better documentation primarily to the involvement of elites. And successful grassroots initiatives, conducted without elite participation, might possibly remain undocumented. How imaginative and sophisticated such purely grassroots initiatives could be is demonstrated by the one documented case we have at our disposal.

The Borana Oromos are one of numerous pastoralist societies whose settlement straddles Ethiopia's borders with Kenya. They all eke out a precarious existence in a region that is very arid. When drought recurred with unusual frequency after the mid-1980s, even this frugal existence was seriously threatened. Whatever livestock survived did so by congregating in the last remaining area of available water and pasture, which happened to be located mostly in the Borana-Oromo homeland. The trespassing of the livestock of other communities into this area was traditionally tolerated as a temporary affair pending the return of the rains. But the protracted nature of this presence, itself the result of drawn-out drought, inevitably led to war.

The eastern neighbours of the Borana, the Arbore and Hamar, were two out of some fifteen such groups that clashed with the Borana as a result. However, "After years of violence around water holes and grazing lands, and after all appeals to the government failed to solicit any positive response, the elders of the Arbore and the Hammer decided it was time to meet with the Borana to settle the conflict in a fair and equitable way" (Suliman 1999: 288). When the first contact of 13 January 1993 started laying the basis for an understanding, it was decided to involve all other stakeholders. As a result, the representatives of "fourteen ethnic groups" started deliberations on a comprehensive peace on 8 March 1993. The agreement concluded at this meeting had all the elements commonly associated with interstate treaties. Two fundamental principles were embraced: "The Arbore and all other ethnic groups agree that the Borana have all traditional rights over their land. Traditional right over land is understood as right of use, not absolute ownership"; and "The Borana accept that all rival groups and their animals have an inalienable right to survival" (Suliman 1999: 288). A council of forty representatives of all the parties was created to enforce adherence to the agreement. The practical implication of the agreement was very simple. A limited number of non-Borana animals were afforded access to Borana lands for a limited period of time, and were expected to depart at the start of the rainy season. The other measures agreed to included opening and running a boarding school, establishing a veterinary centre, and supporting water management schemes. A similar conflict among the Fur of western Sudan and their neighbours over pasture and water holes, unfortunately, assumed an intractable nature primarily due to the meddling by town dwellers and government agents.

If the agreement between the Borana and their neighbours does not constitute the essence of self-determination, one wonders what does. After all, enacting a compact that binds together all the residents of a contiguous territory constitutes the essence of this concept. In addition, the above agreement indicates a sophisticated understanding of the principle of collective security. Recognizing that one's security and survival cannot be guaranteed at the expense of those of others demonstrates a wisdom borne out of practical experience as well as the prevalence of a democratic mentality.

Much more importantly, how the above agreement was concluded and is expected to function underlines the need for democracy to prevail both within and between the contracting parties. The delegates could engage in the deliberation out of confidence that they have the backing of their constituencies. The concerned constituencies would similarly honour the agreement because they are convinced that their delegates negotiated the best terms possible under the prevailing circumstance. It is the absence of this mutual confidence between regimes and the societies they dominate that often undermines both the legitimacy of states and the conventions they hypocritically enter into.

Rethinking the State

The Borana were able to conclude the above agreement perhaps for two reasons. First, state officials were unconcerned and hence did not try to impose their own solution. Second, in the absence of an imposed solution, the Borana were able to fall back on their traditional democratic way of handling issues. That the Oromo people's relatively sophisticated democratic system, the Gada, survived more among the Borana than anywhere else is documented by many scholars. This perhaps better enabled the Borana to approach treaty-making with their neighbours in a democratic way. State elite groups, however, have pursued the policy of eradicating this exemplary remnant of homegrown democratic culture instead of acknowledging and building on it. At the same time, paying lip service to democracy has become fashionable. Democracy as currently understood by elite groups is reduced to, at best, parties battling each other over seats and offices in the capital. Their capital-centred democracy, even where it appears to function, has rarely improved the lot of the rural masses. Consequently, various types of regimes have often exchanged places without changing state-to-society relations at the grassroots.

The Oromo academic Mohammed Ali (1996) concluded an interesting study of the conflicts raging in the Horn of Africa by emphasizing the need to institute self-determination as a means to empower grassroots communities. He articulates a principle that could maintain a balance between unity and diversity. In addition, he identifies popular support as the key factor legitimating a regime's task of mobilizing and allocating resources. And gaining popular support would not be possible without grass-roots democratization. He thus ends by stating "That is why democracy should go where it rightly belongs: the grassroots level" (1996: 216).

Mohammed Ali sees the realization of self-determination as part of this overhaul of political systems. He interprets various peoples' (ethnic groups') sovereign rights as the right to associate with others and vice versa. He enumerates five possible outcomes that might result from exercising this right.

1. Several ethnic groups can establish an association founded on cultural and linguistic similarities.
2. A number of ethnic groups can form a larger community because of complimentary production systems.
3. A set of ethnic groups can join together to exploit a given natural resource or share the benefits of a transportation network.
4. A few ethnic groups can agree to build a multi-purpose community because they have a history of cooperation and an absence of any bitter memories of conflicts among themselves.
5. A combination of any of these factors may enable the ethnic groups in the Horn of Africa (or Northeast Africa, as he calls it) to establish a community of their choice. (1996: 188–89)

These five ways of exercising self-determination reflect Mohammed Ali's independent articulation of what others call multi-dimensional self-determination. Employing this principle to shape a Horn-wide edifice of consensus and cooperation clearly cannot be accomplished overnight. However, the application of much energy, determination, and willingness through a sustained step-by-step process might conceivably bring it about. Hussein Adam mentions another essential ingredient for advancing this regional convergence: "the politics of mutual and reciprocal recognition" among "nationalities, religious groups, clan-families and clans" (1994: 156). He too simply echoes the principle of *just recognition* that we cited in chapter 4. The Abyssinian, inter-riverine Sudanese, and Darod Somali elite elements, in descending order, are likely to find most unpalatable according others this recognition due to the mentality of supremacy entrenched in their traditions. These elements must, and should be persuaded preferably through dialogue, to forego this attitude and start recognizing that the identity of other communities is just as legitimate and innately worthwhile as their own. The alternative would be only the continuation of violent conflict amid rising poverty and environmental degradation.

Mohammed Ali's admonition that democratization initiatives should be grassroots-oriented inevitably brings to the fore what is commonly referred to as ethnicity. This is due to the grassroots communities' inevitable resort to their own languages in conducting deliberations on issues of common concern. We will return to the role of language in promoting democratization and social and economic development later on in this section. Here we will briefly touch on the need to reassess the very essence of the state as a body that oversees the maintenance of peace from the local to the regional level.

Abdi Samatar rearticulates self-determination as a concept to reconcile "contradictions within and between three different, but related moments: local, national and regional" (1991: 68). Samatar addresses the relevance to the Horn of two divergent European conceptualizations of the function of the state. Liberal democratic thought conceives the state as a class-neutral force. Marxism, however, perceives the state as the ultimate upholder of the privileges of the dominant class or classes. These conflicting visions of the state have generated equally divergent beliefs about democracy. Multi-party elections and the notion of equality before the law are seen as the sufficient basis for social order, according to the former. The latter, pointing to the failure of liberal democracy to promote the equitable distribution of wealth, enunciates democracy as rule by a single party that upholds the interests of the toiling majority.

This divergence notwithstanding, both systems are united in their relevance to industrialized societies. And these societies were characterized by their class differentiation into the politically and economically dominant bourgeoisie and the demographically dominant working class. The revolutions of the eighteenth century, particularly the French Revolution, played a pivotal role in directing attention to interclass conflict as the determinant factor in social and political change. These manifestations of fierce interclass conflicts played an influential role in the Marxist conceptualization of the nature of the state.

The state has been conceived in theocratic terms at various times in the history of the Horn of Africa, as discussed in previous sections. It is conceivable that vestiges of this conception continue to linger in some quarters. At the same time, the region has witnessed attempts to experiment with other contemporary conceptualizations of the state. Hence, those defending "national" states as well as those invoking self-determination have, tacitly or explicitly, drawn on one or the other contemporary state type. They have adopted (as some continue to do) the liberal democratic state, despite the absence of the bourgeois and proletarian classes and the improbability of their emergence in the near future. Invoking the Marxist state, which was in vogue a few decades ago, has now become at the very least problematic due to the collapse of the USSR, which is widely perceived as testimony to this state variant's implausibility. Consequently, liberal democracy is being tacitly adopted as the only remaining framework for envisioning the state and the concept of self-determination. (Those falling back on Islamic thinking are the only exception to this rule.) However, the failure of the liberal-democratic state to serve the political and security interests of Africans has been sufficiently documented to detain us here.

The Marxist state's success in Africa looked no more promising in past decades, despite its feasibility appearing more credible then than it does today. According to Amilcar Cabral (1979: 136), such success could be realized only if the group capturing power after a revolutionary armed struggle is willing to commit "suicide as a class." This already highly implausible proposition has proven even more unthinkable in the period after the end of the Cold War. As a result, we are indisputably facing a serious ideological void under the prevailing circumstances. Samatar's resort to the Gramscian state type might offer us a way out of the current intellectual bankruptcy and thus deserves widespread and sustained debate. Samatar's realism is anchored in his articulation of the state as the sum of public institutions, which much more closely reflects the Horn's cultural and economic reality at the local, national (state), and regional spheres.

The local level, populated predominantly by peasants and pastoralists, is the site of primary material production (reproduction) as well as of cultural definition. The traditional (pre-capitalist) and contemporary systems of production and the social elements and cultures representing them face each other at this level. Traditional communal solidarity (the established coping strategy) is being eroded by the rising individualistic mentality of the "modern" sector. This duality is simplistic for contradictions manifest themselves in three different forms. Samatar summarizes these as: "(1) within the traditional (pre-capitalist) society, (2) between the traditional and modern (capitalist) social relationships and (3) within the capitalist sector" (1991: 70). The local sphere is the ultimate locus where "two competing historic logics: subsistence, reciprocal social system and peripheral capitalism" are engaged in a fierce struggle exacerbated by the synergy of the contradictions within each category. The Horn-wide synergy between intrastate and interstate conflicts very likely impacts on, and is in turn impacted by, this reality at the grassroots.

Samatar explores the feasibility of the Gramscian state, advancing it as one better tailored to handle these interlocking multiplicities of conflicting interests. He goes along with Gramsci's more realistic conceptualization of the state as the inevitable upholder of the dominance and privilege of the elite. Gramsci, however, envisaged that such a state's legitimacy would increasingly become unsustainable unless the ruling elite judiciously exercised "expansive hegemony." To put it simplistically, expansive hegemony operates when the rulers demonstrate sensitivity to the needs and interest of subordinate social sectors, not necessarily out of altruism, but in order to sustain their own interests. Enforcing the exaction of resources, services, and loyalty as a one-way operation would inevitably render the state and its managers illegitimate. If the state and its managers behaved in this manner they would resemble the foolish peasant who, intent on maximizing the supply of milk, leaves none for the calf, with the clearly predictable end result. This analogy is one that the Horn's majority rural dwellers could relate to, and they might, if only begrudgingly, obey the state that eschews this kind of self-defeating selfishness.

Hence, the state, if it is to attain some semblance of legitimacy, must create an "unstable equilibrium" between its proclivity to act as a receiver of services, resources, and allegiance and its duty to at least partially reciprocate these forms of societal acquiescence. One can extend the same to the articulation of identity. The official projection of collective identity should at least partially embrace the identities of component elements. Samatar's definition of self-determination corresponds to the above as "the capacitation of individuals and collective groups to, minimally, have an authentic say or, maximally, have full control over their economic, political and cultural environment" (Samatar 1991: 81). In the context of "expansive hegemony," a gradual advancement from the realistic minimal exercise of power to the more ideal maximal position should be perceptible over time. This appears to be the only way to replace the prevailing rising sense of utter pessimism with growing hope and confidence, the essential basis of stability. Samatar, citing global pressures, "regional and common identity," and "a common regional fate" as imperative factors, concludes his essay by calling for regional integration in the Horn of Africa. The need to restructure power from the local to the state and regional (supra-state) levels has been underlined in this context too.

Rethinking Democracy

Mohammed Ali advocates the direction of democratization efforts to the grassroots level. Samatar links the articulation of an appropriate state and supra-state structure of consensus with the reality prevailing at the local (grassroots) level. They both underline the need to establish a more fitting democratic order on a foundation linking interdependent grassroots communities together. This spatial redirection of democracy will not likely succeed if our understanding of democracy remains restricted to what predominates in the Western countries. Two issues come to the fore when we try to imitate the Western democratic system. First, it achieved its present status through a gradual process of the expansion of participation to involve more and more sectors of society. Second and more importantly, there are ongoing attempts to address and remove lingering practices and structures of exclusion, even in the Western system. The currently unfolding redefinition of democracy, championed primarily by such subordinate elements as women and "ethnic" and racial minorities, is very informative. And it matches much more closely traditional African approaches to democracy than does the mainstream liberal form that African elite groups often try to import wholesale.

Electoral democracy, the nation-state, and the popular sovereignty rationale of self-determination all appeared at the same time in the history of Western Europe. We have discussed in some detail how this process erupted during the French Revolution. As that discussion demonstrated, vesting power in an elected body coincided with the scramble by the various social sectors to exclude their protagonists. Hence, we do not need to recapitulate how new rationales for exclusion were devised to achieve such an aim. The gradual reduction of barriers to participation by all sectors of society has also been discussed elsewhere. And how the proscription of gender, class, racial, and religious attributes as rationales for political exclusion was promulgated as a universal norm in the period after the Second World War is also widely known.

Despite the formal adoption of universal adult suffrage as a global norm in the post-war era, even democratic states are far from functioning as fully representative polities. A couple of factors attest to this mismatch between reality and the officially projected images of democratic states. For example, the representation of women in elected bodies continues to fall far short of their population ratio. The same could be said about racial and ethnic minorities. The disproportionate under-representation of such social sectors does not result from formally enacted impediments to representation. Uncovering and dealing with the factors that contribute to this unfairness is what motivates current efforts at improving democratic representation. Hence, recent important advances in theorizing democracy derive from this endeavour. But before we delve into that topic, a few remarks about the suitability of liberal democracy for the promotion of peace and stability in Africa seem to be in order.

Maximizing the interests of individuals and groups is the hallmark of democracy as currently practised in Western countries. It is referred to as the *interest-based model* of democracy by its critics. This model presumes that the interest of society as a whole is the aggregate of the concerned individuals' private expression of preference in a rational process of vote-casting. It functions best within and corresponds closely with the free-market economy, according to which the private determination of individual consumers serves as the best guiding principle for the production and distribution of goods and services. Each individual's right to try to maximize his or her interests presumably adds up to constitute the concerned society's collective maximum well-being at a particular time. What in reality happens is the determination of which leaders, rules, and policies will best serve the *greatest number of people*. And this number is arrived at by registering the electorate's privately expressed selection of the factors that best advance his or her interests. Consequently, the minority has to accept the platform having the approval of the majority even when it wins by a narrow margin. This win-lose contest maintains social peace in Western countries due to a number of factors. The apathy of their largely contented, wealthy middle class is assured because its sense of comfort normally is only marginally affected by the outcome of the polling process. And the apathy of the poor is bought by keeping their material comfort at a relatively tolerable level through the extension of social security safety nets. On the other hand, this model's plausibility looks questionable under two very contrasting situations. First, in situations of extreme material paucity and high insecurity, the losing minority may find going along with the majority insufferable. And second, in severely divided societies, the resulting permanent subordination of minority groups may foster enduring disaffection. And when poverty, pervasive mutual suspicion, hostility, and severe social division coincide, as they do in large parts of Africa, the ability of this model to prop up social peace and stability becomes even more questionable.

The interest-based model of democracy is faulted even by its Western critics on a number of grounds. Iris Marion Young (1997) is one such critic. According to Young, the model's focus on maximizing private utility can produce irrational outcomes. This is due to its neglect of the citizenry's potentials to transform privately perceived preferences during the process of seeking public-minded goals through open-minded public discussion. It thus fails to promote willingness by the citizens to leave their own private and parochial pursuits in order to recognize their fellows in a public setting where they address one another about their collective needs and goals. Also, the advertising used to influence the statistical end results of interest-based democracy's polling exercise favours the economically and numerically dominant sectors of society. The proponents of these criticisms of the interest-based model of democracy advocate its replacement with a more egalitarian version called deliberative democracy.

Deliberative democracy contrasts with the interest-based model in a number of ways. Deliberative democracy encourages the meeting of people to decide public ends and policies through rational discussion, as often witnessed in the functioning of voluntary associations even in the Western countries. Consensus is the preferred outcome of such discussions. The "force of the better argument" is the only factor impelling free and equal participants in deliberations towards consensus. Even when consensus eludes the participants, all possible care is taken to bring the ultimate decision closer to the collective judgment rather than simply presuming it as the aggregate of private preferences.

Young believes that deliberative democracy has potentials to reduce the exclusionary implications of money and political power in the interest-based model. However, she believes exclusion could continue to linger even in deliberative democracy for two reasons. First, because "Its tendency to restrict democratic discussion to argument carries implicit cultural biases that can lead to exclusions in practice" (1997: 62). In addition, the win-lose contest prevailing in the interest-based model persists here too because "Parties to a dispute aim to win the argument, not to achieve mutual understanding" (1997: 63). Young enumerates several ways in which this emphasis on argument leads to exclusion. For instance, people who like contests and know the rules of debate are more privileged than those who do not. Thus men, who tend to be more adept at assertive and confrontational speech, are more favoured than women, whose speech tends to be more tentative, exploratory, or conciliatory. Furthermore, knowledge of the formality and rules of parliamentary procedure favours better-educated, white middle-class people, who are most exposed to these norms through education. Insisting on well-structured arguments that proceed from premise to conclusion also disfavours those who did not learn this style in classrooms. Finally, the identification of objectivity with calm and the absence of emotional expression disfavour racial minorities and women whose speech culture tends to be more excited and embodied, allowing for the expression of emotion and the use of figurative language.

Young's second criticism of deliberative democracy is that "Its assumption that unity is either a starting point or goal of democratic discussion, moreover, may also have exclusionary consequences." Her discussion of the relationship between unity and diversity is even more important for those dealing with severely divided societies. She acknowledges deliberative democracy's relative effectiveness in transforming the individual's self-regarding and often subjective preferences into a more objective conceptualization of the collective good. The need of the individual to vocalize his or her preferences with the aim of persuading others already starts this process. In addition, listening to and learning from others could effect changes in the original position of the individual. Young, however, takes issue with the inference of the advocates of deliberative democracy that the unity of participants is either discovered or constructed in this process. She rejects the presumption of prior unity or its achievement as an end in all situations. "First, in contemporary pluralist societies we cannot assume that there are sufficient shared understandings to appeal to in many situations of conflict and solving collective problems. Second, the assumption of prior unity obviates the need for self-transcendence ... [meaning] none need to revise their opinions or viewpoints in order to take account of perspectives and experiences beyond them" (1997: 66).

Young then enunciates the minimum condition needed to construct the common polity serving its diversified inhabitants. According to her, trying to live together in a polity is the only motivation for engaging in democratic discussion. "The unity that motivates politics is the facticity of people being thrown together, finding themselves in geographical proximity and economic interdependence such that activities and pursuits of some affect the ability of others to conduct their activities" (1997: 67). She identifies three elements that would render this common existence as fair and democratic as possible:

1. a certain degree of interdependence must exist and be recognized;
2. the stakeholders must have a commitment to equal respect for one another and a willingness to listen to each other's perspectives; and
3. they must adopt commonly acceptable procedural rules of fair discussion and decision-making.

"Within the context of this minimal unity, a richer understanding of processes of democratic discussion results if we assume that differences of social position and identity perspective function as a resource for public reason than as divisions that public reason transcends" (1997: 67).

Difference and unity should not be conceived of in absolute terms, she advises. Hence, although "difference is not total otherness," the existence of "differences of meaning, social position, or need" that one does not share should be kept in mind. Thus, individuals should be aware that they do not fully comprehend the perspective of others in different circumstances, in the sense that the experience of others cannot be fully assimilated into one's own. The essence of democracy should be the ability to speak across differences of culture, social position, and need without necessarily erasing them. The conclusion Young draws is so important that I must quote it at length:

> Preserving and listening across such differences of position and perspective causes the transformation in preference that deliberative theorists recommend. This occurs in three ways. 1) Confrontation with different perspectives, interests, and cultural meanings teaches me the partiality of my own, reveals to me my own experience as perspectival. 2) Knowledge that I am in a situation of collective problem solving with others who have different perspectives on the problems and different cultures and values from my own, and that they have the right to challenge my claims and arguments, forces me to transform my expressions of self-interest and desire into appeals to justice .... 3) Expressing, questioning, and challenging differently situated knowledge, finally, adds to the social knowledge of all the participants. (1997: 68)

She believes that with the following refinements deliberative democracy can attain these ideals. Deliberations should provide for the exchange of greetings, expressions of deference, and even flattery to stem the rising anger and disagreement often witnessed in such circumstances. Since making assertions and merely giving reasons may not suffice in enabling people with different aims, values, and interests to uncover just solutions to collective problems, humour, wordplay, and figurative speech should be encouraged. Also, storytelling may enhance the deliberation of common problems.

The progressive sectors of wealthy countries are pioneering these developments in democratic theory. Ironically, what is being discovered by them is in the process of being stamped out in various parts of Africa under pressure from the so-called modernization process. Regardless, there are still pockets of surviving African democratic systems. However, these instances not only remain undocumented but are also dismissed as irrelevant because they are associated with supposedly backward tribal societies. Hence, the Somali Xeer (Heer), sporadically mentioned in the literature, has yet to be studied comprehensively as a separate subject. Practically, however, it was resort to the traditional Guurti institution that contributed to Somaliland's relative calm in contrast to the chaos prevailing in the rest of former Somalia. The Oromo Gada democratic system until recently was also discussed in a similar haphazard manner. We are lucky to now have a more comprehensive elaboration of how it functions. In his latest book on the Oromo Gada democratic system, Legesse details how deliberation is conducted in the following way:

> The nature of conduct and the pattern of discourse in the national assembly are well elaborated. To begin with, there is no concept of a "quorum." All members must be present at all important meetings and failure to do so is heavily penalized. Nor is there a concept of a "majority" that can impose its will on a "minority." Debate must be continued until the councilors come to agreement. That does not mean, however, that their debates are endless or extremely protracted. There are effective methods of pressuring the participants to refrain from adversarial talk for its own sake. Indeed the participants in Gumi Gayo (National Assembly) are reminded that clever disputation or clever thinking has no place in the meetings. Nor should people attempt to pull rank or resort to self-praise. (2000: 213)

The meeting actually opens by the chair exhorting the participants to adhere to established principles for productive deliberation and to avoid vituperative or cantankerous oration. The underlying guiding principle for productive deliberation is put as follows by Legesse. *"Do not look for the worst in what others have said in order to undermine their position and win an argument; look for the best they have to offer, so as to find the common ground"* (2000: 214; italics in the original). After sufficient discussion, the presiding officer asks for closure by saying "Would there be anything but peace if we came to such and such a decision?" The motion is declared passed if the assembly responds by chanting "Peace!" "Peace!" "Peace!" Instead, if such consensus proves difficult the dissenters can be brought around by the process of blessing.

Language, State, and Self-determination

Removing the exclusionary implications of differing styles of speech within even a unilingual community is the aim of some who wish to reconceptualize democracy to enhance fair representation and egalitarianism. Hence, addressing the language issue becomes unavoidable if the process of promoting democracy in multilingual settings is to succeed. The central role of language in democratization initiatives should become self-evident in these cases. The relationship between language and self-determination should likewise be unquestionable if the latter is intended to serve democratic purposes. Unfortunately, the experience of large parts of Africa has been to the contrary.

As Crawford Young states, assertions of entitlement to self-determination by speech communities have been missing only in Africa. As the history of the French Revolution demonstrates, the emergence of the notion of popular sovereignty (one feature of self-determination) coincided with and triggered the blossoming of French literature and a spectacular growth in publishing. The use of standardized French as the means of public communication enhanced the participation of its speakers in politics. However, the elevation of French to the national status became the cause of two enduring problems. First, the notion of nation-building necessitated the imposition of French on non-French speaking inhabitants of France. Naturally, the participation of non-French speakers in politics was much more constrained as a result. In addition, they became subjects of racist slurs. Hence, as Feigenbaum puts it, the "dominant cultures in nation-building states often took their white subordinates to be of a different and inferior race," as has already been cited. Parisians could thus openly refer to some of these non-speakers of French, for example, as the savage Redskins of Europe as late as the 1840s. A nineteenth-century English scholar could similarly liken the Irish to chimpanzees and blacks. The negative implications of this dominant/subordinate division of French and British society survive to this day.

Second, the appropriation of French as one of the defining features of France's nationhood triggered a process with long-lasting implications. This association between the French language and French nationalism eroded the role of French as the language of high culture throughout Europe, ultimately ending it. The resulting popularization of the *one nation, one language* concept resulted in the aspiration to render the state and linguistic boundaries coterminous. There arose then the ambition of forging one state out of numerous smaller states inhabited by the speakers of a single language, as witnessed in Germany and Italy. The completion of German unification went on to figure among the causes of the Second World War.

At the same time, the notion of *one nation, one language* put the Russian, Austro-Hungarian, and Ottoman Empires on the course that ultimately led to their disintegration. Rising confrontation between two opposing aspirations made this end inevitable. The dominant groups of these empires pursued the agenda of realizing a single language-community by imposing their own languages on their diverse subjects. The concerned subordinate groups responded by increasingly demanding a state of their own. Making the state and language coterminous was imperfectly applied at the end of the First World War. And these imperfections have come back to haunt Europe, as the wars of the 1990s in the Balkans demonstrate.

The *one state, one language* policy ultimately evolved into a global norm despite its disruptive role in European history. However, the policy has not succeeded, even in states that have pursued it for the longest time, as was discussed in an earlier section. Kembo-Sure (1998) draws a similar conclusion when he writes, the "homogenization or assimilationist theory has not succeeded" in shaping monolingual entities out of Spain, France, Britain and the United States, the states that have pursued the aim for the longest time. Should African states then continue to emulate this problematic and ultimately unsuccessful policy? Kembo-Sure (1998: 185) argues that "the role of the state in the 20th century has changed so drastically that an outmoded linguistic assimilationist policy does not seem to stand a chance of succeeding without enormous social and cultural cost." He articulates the peoples' right "to use the language they know best to educate their children and to receive government services and participate in their development affairs in local languages." In addition, citing studies showing that "those who start with mother tongue for a considerable period transfer the skills easily to the second language ... and perform better than those who are taught all the way in the second language," he proposes that the mother tongues of pupils be used at least for most of primary education.

Kembo-Sure's articles focus mostly on African countries' continued resort to the language of their former colonial rulers as official or co-official languages. He cogently argues that these languages will ultimately damage African languages unless corrective measures are taken. He enumerates three such measures in another article: first, offering primary education in the child's mother tongue; second, using indigenous African languages in the extension of government services; and finally, increased use of indigenous languages in the mass media, higher education, and the courts (1999). A Ghanaian academic's writings include similar recommendation for that country's indigenous languages (Prah 2001).

Hence, most African scholars dealing with language policy are addressing the alienating consequences of the continued use of English, French, and Portuguese as the languages of government business, education, and mass communication. The imposition of an indigenous language predominates in the Horn of Africa and has also generated most of the controversy there. But there is another case in which an African language was elevated to the status of an official language. Malawi is one of very few African countries that chose this language policy. Kamuzu Banda, wishing to complete his *one nation, one leader* vision by adding the *one language* dimension, in 1968 proclaimed Chichewa (formerly Chinyanja) as Malawi's official language (Kishindo 1994). All broadcasting and publishing in the other fourteen languages were legally banned. His propagandists then proceeded to laud this policy's effectiveness in furthering "the cultivation of national identity" and in reducing inter-ethnic antagonism. A Malawian writer, however, contends that this "cultivation of a national identity has failed" and has in fact contributed to the heightening of inter-ethnic antagonism. The bitterness of non-Chichew-speakers was made "worse by Chichewa-speakers' triumphal assertions that other people of the country were cultureless because they had no language" (Kishindo 1994: 141). The tendency of privileged groups to dismiss the others as inferior and uncultured inevitably arises in these situations imbuing state-society conflicts with an intercommunal dimension. From this he goes on to draw the following important conclusion:

> Yet African politicians as well as scholars who advocated the use of indigenous African languages often decried what they called the "brutalizing and programmed humiliation" of African languages by the colonial masters. The mirror image of this argument can be seen in a state where only one language has been given the status of national language. Those whose language has not been so elevated experience the same sense of brutalization and humiliation of their language as shown above." (Kishindo 1994: 141)

This corresponds closely with the experience of the Horn of Africa. Amharic automatically qualified as the national language due to the creation of the state through military conquest by the Amhara feudalists. Arabic was similarly adopted as the national language in the Sudan because the independence movement there was spearheaded by the Arabic-speaking elite. One variety of Somali was adopted as the national language in Somalia. Rhetoric aside, Tigrinya is functioning as the national language in Eritrea. All those who do not speak these languages are expected to do so in due course as modernization proceeds.

Let me conclude this section by extensively quoting Oommen's views on why language should be accepted as an important factor in enhancing democratic participation, justice, and speedy development.

> First, experience the world over clearly demonstrates that in order to bring about participatory development communication is imperative. Second, adequate and appropriate communication is possible through the languages of the people, that is, their mother tongues. Third, if they are going to be viable and effective at different levels, administrative units ought to be coterminous with communication units, that is, linguistic areas. Fourth, generally speaking, when language is directly linked to a specific territory it provides the basis for a common lifestyle and communication pattern. Fifth, most languages, irrespective of their graphemic status, are capable of effective communication in the context of everyday life. Sixth, while it may not be possible, or even desirable, to establish separate administrative units for all the linguistic areas it is viable and feasible (based on population size, financial viability, territorial spread) it is preferable to establish such units. Finally, if compulsory primary education is imparted through the mother tongue, this single step will substantially contribute to the eradication of illiteracy and should lead to more efficient communication, thereby accelerating the process of development and democratization. (1997: 198)

The Ethiopian state, in response to decades of diverse pressures, has arrived at experimenting with this vision. This experiment remains precarious due to numerous internal and regional factors. Ethiopia cannot successfully and wholly implement this vision without it having repercussions for neighbouring states. Sudan, despite still sticking to a centralist nation-state model, has been forced to address the issue of regional diversity and self-determination. Even this regional vision will not work until the process of enhancing grassroots communities' participation is enhanced. Eritrea stands alone in still entertaining the vision of a centralized multi-ethnic state. But its contradictory approach to ethnicity does not promise sustainability.

GLOBAL AND LOCAL SELF-DETERMINATION

THE FIRST PART OF THIS WORK tracked the evolution of the concept of self-determination by looking at its role in articulating a match between the notions of *people, nation, state, territory,* and *sovereignty.* The ultimate aim of struggles for self-determination is, of course, to exercise *sovereignty* over the *state* defined by clearly demarcated *territory* and inhabited by the *people* who have coalesced into a homogeneous cultural and speech community called the *nation.* Hence, there is great value in examining how the sources of sovereignty and legitimacy have been conceived at various historical junctures and to what extent reality has corresponded with these conceptions. Focusing on how Western European states and their overseas offshoots conceptualized the sources of sovereignty is also informative because of the dominant role these states have played in shaping the political and economic order of the contemporary world, as they indeed continue to do. We have seen how some of them have finally concluded that concentrating sovereignty in a single location is no longer tenable and are thus experimenting with sharing this feature of political order both upwards and downwards. They are thus forced to increasingly seek "effective political units" that would serve as the building blocks of regional economic and political associations to achieve such an aim.

Let me briefly summarize the conceptual foundations of self-determination and their implications for the sources of sovereignty and legitimacy. First, the conviction that humans have the ability to determine their destiny constitutes the fundamental thinking on which self-determination is based. This novel thinking emanated from the growing rejection of the previous belief that power and legitimacy descend from Heaven. The contrary belief that humans individually and collectively determine their destiny necessitated the articulation of earthly principles that guide this process of self-determination.

Second, the fundamental reason why humans were called upon to take control of their destiny was to create conditions that promote and sustain peace within states and between them. This was the prominent role that self-determination was tasked with at the end of the First World War when the concept entered the popular vocabulary. This is evidenced by Wilson's anticipation that world peace would ultimately result from the convergence of the general wills of individual states to establish humanity's General Will, which would thus reconcile *humanity* and *nationality*. For Lenin, on the other hand, the recognition of self-determination constituted a tactical step in the direction of humanity's ultimate fusion into one cohesive conflict-free whole. These two avenues to global peace stood in competition during the many decades when the world was divided between adherents of one vision or the other. This was particularly the case during the Cold War period marked by the neat bipolarization of world politics. During this time, peace between the two antagonistic camps was maintained mostly because they were armed with nuclear weapons and the "mutual assured destruction" (MAD) that the existence of these weapons made possible. Nuclear weapons were in effect the Leviathans of the time, under whose sovereignty the two camps lived in an uneasy peace while engaging each other through proxies in the other parts of the world. The Horn of Africa was one of the regions where these camps supported surrogates, thus fanning conflicts within and between states. With the end of the Cold War a new threshold appeared, one that afforded humans unprecedented control over world affairs and opportunities to thus realize peace within and between states to a degree never before thought possible.

Tragically, what actually happened instead was the tacit acceptance of "the real world order," in which some areas are "zones of peace, wealth, and democracy" and others "zones of turmoil, war, and development [read poverty]" (Singer and Wildavsky 1993: 3). The coincidence of wealth and democracy in one set of zones renders war among the concerned states imponderable, in the immediate, since democracies presumably do not fight each other. And the states of the "zones of turmoil" do not pose any direct military threat to these wealthy democracies because of the latter's overwhelming military capability. So the wealthy states can afford to sit and watch as the vicious cycle of poverty and conflict wreaks havoc with the lives of those who live in the zones of turmoil. Meanwhile, the wealthy states can continue to get even wealthier as they are able to tap a disproportionate share of world resources. The following data attest to this prospect: "Between 1960 and 1990 the countries where the richest 20 percent of the world's people live, increased their share of gross world product from 70.2 percent to 82.7 percent. By 1991-1992 these countries were 60 times better off than those with the poorest 20 percent of the global population—a gap which had doubled over thirty years. The disparity between the world's richest billion people and its poorest billion was estimated, at the start of the 1990s, at 150: 1" (Gelber 1997: 32).

The issue of the appropriate share of world resources brings to the fore another dimension of the search for peace within and between political units. And that is the role of self-sufficiency in conceptualizing the perfect society. The relation between self-sufficiency and a perfect society has engaged the minds of thinkers from Aristotle to Thomas Aquinas, asserts Jacques Maritain (1951: 197), and he summarizes the issue as follows: "self-sufficiency is the essential property of *perfect society*, which is the goal to which the evolution of political forms in mankind tends; and the primary good ensured by a perfect society ... is its own internal and external peace." He describes how the search for a match between self-sufficiency and a perfect society tends to continuously widen human aggregation in the following words: "when neither peace nor self-sufficiency can be achieved by particular kingdoms, nations, or states, they are no longer perfect societies, and it is a broader society, defined by its capacity to achieve self-sufficiency and peace—therefore, in actual fact, with reference to our historical age, the international community politically organized—which is to become perfect society" (1951: 198). Jacques Maritain wrote these words in the aftermath of the Second World War, when seeking a more meaningful basis of world peace was still occupying the minds of thinkers.

Such an effort should have intensified after the Cold War had the presumption of the world as divided into zones of turmoil and peace not resulted in the complacency of powerful states. Even the emergence of "the international community politically organized" by itself alone appears inadequate under the contemporary reality due to a couple of indisputable facts. First, there is hardly any self-sufficient zone in the contemporary world. Second, world-wide consumption at a minuscule percentage of the level currently enjoyed by wealthy states would definitely expose the lack of global self-sufficiency. Third, lack of global self-sufficiency for now is not manifesting itself in the absence of peace among wealthy states primarily due to their ability to tap world resources at a disproportionate rate. This reality constitutes one of the factors that is dividing the world into zones of peace and turmoil. Once again, partial global peace prevails because powerful states have abdicated responsibility to an even more intangible source. The new sovereign Leviathan maintaining peace in one part of the world is called the market, where the almighty US dollar and the associated currencies of the other wealthy states interact to allow their citizens permanent wealth and security while condemning the rest of humanity to the opposite. These states are able to enjoy relative peace because of the special relationship that exists between their leaders and this immoral god, thus allowing the latter to share its sovereignty to a greater degree than others can expect. For these others, however, even the slightest ripples in the economy of the wealthy states resulting from the capricious mood of this new Leviathan can trigger destructive tidal waves that spell utter disaster. If wealthy states have abdicated considerable control over their affairs to the so-called market forces, thus conceding elements of their self-determination, the fate of weaker and poorer states is determined much more powerfully by this capricious force. Hence, unless humans pool their will to regain control at the global stage, self-determination at the local level will remain highly deficient. In this situation meaningful self-determination by Africans both collectively and individually seems futile.

There is no denying the fact that Africans need to exert energy to determine their destiny, but they cannot be expected to do so in a wholly autarkic manner in today's highly integrated world. Meanwhile, the sovereign almighty dollar could continue to lull the population of the world's wealthy states into complacency by channelling a disproportionate share of world resources to satisfy their ever increasing level of consumption. And societies in these parts of the world may take comfort in the impression that they have left behind the kind of poverty and turmoil reigning in the rest of the world. The finite nature of world resources, however, should alert them to the fact the predicaments of the world's poor zones may actually be their future as well. Unless all states work together to regain power over the new Leviathan, we could foresee one very worrying possibility. As the world becomes depleted even of fresh air, we can foresee our only remaining descendant inhaling the last remaining breath of fresh air and thus bringing human existence to an end. Because of the global nature of this pessimistic scenario it can be averted only by self-determination at the global stage.

Interim Changes

Regaining global self-determination from the immoral god (i.e., the market, the almighty us dollar, and associated currencies) demands global effort. How to achieve such an ambition by rearranging international economic relations falls outside the scope of this work. We can, however, indicate changes in international political relations that would contribute to the implementation of the vision articulated in this work. The changes in international relations required to realize this vision of the state and self-determination articulated in this work are succinctly put by the African-Canadian scholar, Obiora Chinedu Okafor (2000: 183) as follows:

> it is important that the emerging tendencies of international law and institutions toward the encouragement of de-centralisation (as opposed to the over-centralisation of the state), diversity and multicultural nationhood (as opposed to homogenisation and coercive nation-building), access to the international sphere (as opposed to the strict domestication of sub-state groups), deference to norm-based legitimacy (as opposed to the strict application of the doctrine of effectiveness), and infra-review (as opposed to the strict application of the doctrine of peer-review), ought to be encouraged and consolidated.

Since the other concepts appear relatively well known, we only need to elaborate what is meant by *peer-review* and *infra-review*. The *peer-review* process of according legitimacy to a state is conducted by the club of pre-existing ones without taking into consideration how the candidate state is treating its entire population or subsets thereof. The *infra-review* process, on the other hand, takes into account the acceptability or otherwise of the state to the concerned populace or portions of it. If the system of international relations adheres to these principles, there should result an environment in which self-determination can serve as the principle for legitimating political units at the sub-state, state, and supra-state levels. The International Commission on Intervention and State Sovereignty has rearticulated sovereignty as "the responsibility to protect." This is a refreshing contribution to the evolving nature of international relations. However, it needs to go further to embrace Okafor's recommendations and to suggest how to make them operational. This is the minimum contribution that global forces can put at the disposal of those trying to shape effective political units that underpin a modicum of physical and economic security for grassroots communities.

The Future Lies in the Past

This work began as an attempt to look to the past in order to anticipate a future when structures enhancing grassroots political participation can be made possible. With this intention I tracked the history of self-determination from the time it was initially mooted to the present. The same was done concerning the major features and functions of the state underpinned by the principle of self-determination at different stages of history. This journey into the past in order to look forward ironically led me to look backwards to structures that were supposedly rendered obsolete by modernity. Ernest Gellner's (1997: 107) "reasonable" anticipation that even "the advanced industrial world will once again, *like the agrarian world of the past*, be one in which *effective political units* will be either *larger* or *smaller* than 'national' units based on similarity of culture" (italics added) demonstrates this ironic finding. "Effective political units" would hence be global, continental, regional, state, and sub-state in character depending on the tasks they are meant to accomplish. Furthermore, since the industrialized world's *agrarian past* is the Horn of Africa's present reality, creating effective political units at the level of the village, district, state, and the region appears more imperative.

My search for progressive theories of democracy articulated for the purpose of diminishing the exclusion of underprivileged social sectors resulted in a similar irony of finding out that the future is actually the past. The theory of communicative democracy, developed by Iris Marion Young, happens to be almost identical to the kind of democracy practised by many Africa societies, in particular the Gada democratic system of the Oromo people. And it is these kinds of grassroots democratic practices that modernizing "nation-builders" work hard to eradicate. We cannot, of course, resurrect the past intact, but can only anchor new institutions and practices in its positive aspects. Such solidly anchored structures can be more effective in promoting the respect of human rights and other liberties than rootless administrative systems or regimes. Hence, it would be advisable to eschew the either/or approach when considering tradition versus abstractions arrived at through intellectual analysis. What is being offered for discussion here is the need to open dialogue between such abstractions and the lived experiences of traditional societies. Arriving at "effective political units" and at the appropriate kind of democratic practice should be highly contextual and dependent on available intellectual and material resources.

The tacit dominance of liberal democracy in the post-Cold War era renders such an undertaking quite difficult. I personally have never been

a fan of liberal democracy and its war-like, winner-take-all competitive-
ness in which harsh words and money substitute for lethal weapons.
This kind of competition, if introduced wholesale into resource-strapped
societies, could easily instigate conflicts involving lethal weapons. This is
what led me to seeking critics of liberal democracy and the alternatives
they are offering and finding them in the writings of feminist intellectuals. But even these abstractions cannot be copied intact. Neither is it
advisable to totally reject all the values of liberal democracy. What I am
suggesting is an encounter between traditions reflecting the lived experiences of grassroots communities and abstractions arrived at by studying theories with the hope that a common ground be found to mark the
starting point for a new journey into a more promising future. Neither the
ideas of a gravely deracinated elite nor the highly parochial traditions of
local folk are sufficient in and of themselves. This work instead calls for
the adoption and the adaptation of theories and lived experiences.

Common Sense

As the reader may have noticed, I have tried to sidestep that endless
debate concerning the taxonomy of human collectivities: tribes, ethnic
groups, nations, nationalities. Most of the positions I have come across
are judgmental, value-laden, and focused on isolating the good from the
bad, the civil from the barbarous from the very outset. In this scramble
to pass judgment I find that some fundamental questions are easily
overlooked. This is exemplified, for example, by the writings of Jocelyne
Couture, Kai Nielsen, and Michel Seymour (1998). In the introduction
(pp. 1-61) and the afterword (pp. 579-662) to their jointly edited collection, they go to great lengths to argue that some nationalisms are reconcilable with liberalism. Their main objective is to argue that the
nationalisms of the Catalans, Faeroesians, Scots, Quebeckers, and Welsh
are liberal and should hence not be lumped together with the "barbarous
nationalisms" of the Third World. However, they nowhere stop to ask
why nationalism is rearing its head up in societies that have lived for
many generations under some of world's most successful liberal democracies. Perhaps liberal democracy's foundational principle of according
supremacy to individual rights should itself be re-examined. (For liberal
democracy's incompatibility with the African grassroots reality, see
Osabu-Kle 2000.)

First, I am of the conviction that group and collective rights can blos-
som only when they are respected and enjoyed in a reciprocal manner.
Promoting group rights at the expense of individual rights and vice versa

can only lead to an all-round loss of freedom. Similarly, the injunction that an individual's legitimate rights should not encroach on those of another equally applies to group rights. Furthermore, I believe that the right to collective self-identification is the foundation of humanity's fruitful social existence, meaningful religious fellowship, and democratic political life. Individuals aggregate into collectivities to satisfy some clearly desired needs or appetites, such as religious fellowship and social and political activities. And how individuals congregate to shape political order also shapes the environment that determines whether other forms of aggregation are constructive or not. Hence, the most effective and least exclusive collective self-identification at the grassroots level should provide the building block for sub-state, state, regional, continental, and global political structures. And collective self-identification on the basis of culture and language appears highly necessary for enhancing the political participation of grassroots communities. Language is what binds together political and cultural life. Language, culture, and political order share the common nature of requiring aggregation into collectivities. There is no individual culture, language, or political order. Communication is imperative for social and political life, and for individuals their "mother tongue" is the most effective and comfortable medium of communication. It should be underscored, however, that political opinion and privately owned property fall into the realm of individual rights.

Some collectivities are associated with territory as evidenced by, for example, Scotland, Deutschland, Ireland, and England. In such countries, it is the inhabitants that define the *territory* and not the reverse. Where such relatively well-known homelands coincide with the settlement patterns of speech communities, we have at least a potential *nation*. This is what leads me to concur with Oommen's definition of *nation*. A glance at the Horn of Africa reveals that the region comprises Dinkaland, Nuerland, Oromoland, Amharaland, Affarland, and the homelands of many other communities. Having said this, however, two issues should be clarified immediately. First, the inhabitants of zones where two or more homelands meet know the general area where one homeland ends and the other starts. This has been the case in large parts of Africa since time immemorial. Second, the area inhabited by all the people speaking the same language may not and should not necessarily be incorporated into one state territory. This has never been the case and may never be realized. Difficulties often arise when members of nations partitioned by state territories are mistreated by the authorities of one of these states. The only way to overcome these difficulties is by harmonizing political order at the regional level, which leads me to believe that democratic decentralization cannot proceed in one state alone.

Most African societies have all along welcomed and hosted members of other societies in their midst without infringing on their individual rights. And as the treaty enacted by the Borana Oromos demonstrates, many African societies make a clear distinction between ownership and the right to use land either temporarily or permanently. Traditionally, newcomers do not try to dispossess their hosts or try to humiliate them in any manner. And the appellation "ethnic" applies more appropriately to these "individuals of different national backgrounds who still in some way identify themselves in terms of language, culture, and tradition of their country of origin" (Couture, Nielsen, and Seymour 1998: 48). When clarified in this manner, Amhara, Gurage, Somali, and other individuals living dispersed among Oromos, and Oromo individuals living in the homelands of these nations, are ethnic. As well, Dinka, Nuer, and Shilluk residents of Wad Medani in Sudan are ethnic, while "Arabs," Fallatas, and Nubas living in Dinkaland, Nuerland, and Shillukland are similarly ethnic. The security of the person and property of such ethnic individuals should be respected as much as that of members of the society among whom they reside. The newcomers cannot, however, legitimately ask their hosts to become like them by adopting their manners, customs, cultures, and languages.

Ongoing Conflict Resolution

As I write these pages, two exercises in conflict resolution are taking place concurrently in the Horn of Africa. Efforts to resolve Sudan's decades-long violent conflict and the conflicts raging in Somalia since chaos started to reign in the early 1990s are underway in Kenya under the auspices of the Inter-Governmental Authority on Development (IGAD). That two such efforts are actually taking place simultaneously is quite encouraging. A more deliberate orchestration of efforts to resolve these conflicts and others is the fundamental conclusion of this study. And the resolution of conflicts within Sudan and Ethiopia appears pivotal for addressing and finding sustainable settlements for all other conflicts. Ethiopia is, after all, the region's most populous state, and borders on all the other entities of the Horn, while the Sudan is similarly the Horn's largest state territorially.

A democratic Ethiopia that enjoys internal stability and peace could hence play a decisive role in working towards such an order in the region. It would in fact find this to be in its best interests. On the other hand, an undemocratic and internally challenged Ethiopia would naturally be averse to democracy taking root in neighbouring states. Satisfying the quest for self-determination by its largest nation, the Oromos, constitutes Ethiopia's pivotal move in the direction of democracy. Oromo contributions to Ethiopia's healthy political life would definitely have regional repercussions. As the history related previously shows, the Oromo struggle has impacted on and been impacted by developments in both Somalia and the Sudan.

Abbay, Alemseged (1998). *Identity Jilted or Re-imagining Identity: the Divergent Paths of the Eritrean and Tigrayan Nationalist Struggles.* Lawrenceville, NJ: Red Sea Press.

AbdelSalam, Elfatih, A. (1989). "Ethnic Politics in the Sudan." In Sayyid H. Hurriez and Elfatih A. AbdelSalam (eds.), *Ethnicity, Conflict and National Integration in the Sudan.* Khartoum: University of Khartoum, pp. 29-68.

Abraham, Emmanuel (1995). *Reminiscences of My Life.* Oslo: Lunde forlag.

Adam, Hussein M. (1994). "Eritrea, Somalia, Somaliland and the Horn of Africa." In Amare Tekle (ed.), *Eritrea and Ethiopia: From Conflict to Cooperation.* Lawrenceville, NJ: Red Sea Press, pp. 139-68.

Adhana, Adhana Haile (1994). "Mutation of Statehood and Contemporary Politics." In Abebe Zegeye and Siegfried Pausewang (eds.), *Ethiopia in Change: Peasantry, Nationalism and Democracy.* London: British Academy Press, pp. 12-29.

Agnew, J.A. (2000). "The Geopolitical Contest of Contemporary Ethnopolitical Conflict." In S. Byrne, and C.L. Irvin (eds.), *Reconcilable Differences: Turning Points in Ethnopolitical Conflict.* West Hartford, CT: Kumarian Press, pp. 3-22.

Ali, Mohammed (1996). *Ethnicity, Politics, and Society in Northeast Africa: Conflict and Social Change.* Lanham, MD: University Press of America.

Ammar, Wolde-Yesus (1997). "The Role of Asmara Students in the Eritrean Nationalist Movement, 1958-68." *Eritrean Studies Review* 2,1: 59-84.

Anderson, J., and J. Goodman, (1999). "Transnationalism, 'Postmodern' Territorialities and Democracy in the European Union." In K.J. Brehony and N. Rassool (eds.), *Nationalisms Old and New.* London: Macmillan Press, pp. 17-34.

Arou, Mom, K.N. (1989). "Ethnic Conflicts in the Southern Schools After the Establishment of Regional Government." In Sayyid H. Hurriez and Elfatih A. AbdelSalam (eds.), *Ethnicity, Conflict and National Integration in the Sudan.* Khartoum: University of Khartoum, pp. 300-18.

Ayoade, John A.A. (1988). "States without Citizens: An Emerging African Phenomenon." In Donald Rothchild and Naomi Chazan (eds.), *The Precarious Balance: State and Society in Africa.* Boulder, CO: Westview Press, pp. 100-17.

Baissa, Lemmu (1991). "Ethiopian-Sudanese Relations, 1956-1991: Mutual Deterrence through Mutual Blackmail?" *Horn of Africa Journal* 13, 3/4: 11-25.

—— (1998). "Contending Nationalisms in the Ethiopian Empire and the Oromo Struggle for Self-Determination." In Asafa Jalata (ed.), *Oromo Nationalism and the Ethiopian Discourse: The Search for Freedom and Democracy.* Lawrenceville, NJ: Red Sea Press, pp. 79-108.

Balsvik, Rand Ronning (1994). "An Important Root of the Ethiopian Revolution: The Student Movement." In Abebe Zegeye and Siegfried Pausewang (eds.), *Ethiopia in Change: Peasantry, Nationalism and Democracy.* London: British Academy Press, pp. 77-94.

Barker, A.J. (1968). *The Civilizing Mission: The Italo-Ethiopian War 1935-36.* London: Cassell.

Baycroft, Timothy (1998). *Nationalism in Europe, 1789-1945.* Cambridge: Cambridge University Press.

Becker, Carl (1953). *The Declaration of Independence.* New York: Knopf.

Beiner, R.S. (1998). "National Self-Determination: Some Cautionary Remarks Concerning the Rhetoric of Rights." In M. Moore (ed.), *National Self-Determination and Secession.* Oxford: Oxford University Press, pp. 158-80.

Benedict, Anderson (1983). *Imagined Communities: Reflections on the Origin and Spread of Nationalism.* London: Verso.

Besteman, Catherine (1995). "The Invention of Gosha: Slavery, Colonialism, and Stigma in Somali History." In Ali Jimale Ahmed (ed.), *The Invention of Somalia.* Lawrenceville, NJ: Red Sea Press, pp. 43-62.

—— (1996). "Representing Violence and 'Othering' in Somalia," *Cultural Anthropology* 11, 1: 120-33.

Boutros-Ghali, Boutros (1992). *An Agenda for Peace: Preventive Diplomacy, Peacemaking and Peace-keeping.* New York: United Nations.

Bull, H. (1977). *The Anarchical Society: A Study of Order in World Politics.* London: Macmillan Press.

Cabral, Amilcar (1979). *Unity and Struggle: Speeches and Writings.* London: Monthly Review Press.

Cassese, A. (1995). *Self-Determination of Peoples: A Legal Reappraisal.* Cambridge: Cambridge University Press.

Castles, S. (1998). "Globalization and the Ambiguities of National Citizenship." In R. Baubock and J. Rundell (eds.), *Blurred Boundaries: Migration, Ethnicity, Citizenship.* Aldershot: Ashgate, pp. 223-44.

Cervenka, Zdenek (1969). *The Organization of African Unity and Its Charter.* New York: Praeger.

Chapman, Tim (1998). *The Congress of Vienna: Origins, Processes and Results.* London: Routledge.

Clapham, Christopher (1988). *Transformation and Continuity in Revolutionary Ethiopia.* Cambridge: Cambridge University Press.

—— (1994). "Ethnicity and the National Question in Ethiopia." In Peter Woodward and Murray Forsyth (eds.), *Conflict and Peace in the Horn of Africa: Federalism and Its Alternatives.* Dartmouth, UK: Aldershot, pp. 27–40.

—— (2002). "Controlling Space in Ethiopia." In Wendy James, Donald L. Donham, Eisei Kurimoto, and Alessadro Triulzi (eds.), *Remapping Ethiopia: Socialism and After.* Oxford: James Currey.

Clarence-Smith, W.G. (1999). "The Modern Colonial State and Global Economic Integration, 1815–1945." In D.A. Smith, D.J. Solinger, and S.C. Topik, (eds.), *States and Sovereignty in the Global Economy.* London: Routledge, pp. 120–37.

Clark, Patrick (1998). "The Battle of Omdurman in the Contest of Sudanese History." In Edward M. Spiers (ed.), *Sudan: The Reconquest Reappraised.* London: Frank Cass, pp. 202–22.

Cliffe, Lionel (1998). *The Regional Dimensions of Conflicts: The Horn of Africa and Southern Africa Compared.* Occasional Papers Series on Environment and Development in an Age of Transition (Paper NO. 5), Centre for Development Studies. Leeds: University of Leeds.

Cobban, Alfred (1969). *The Nation State and National Self-Determination.* New York: Thomas Y. Crowell.

Colley, L. (1992). *Britons: Forging the Nation, 1707–1837.* New Haven, CT: Yale University Press.

Collins, Robert O. (1997). "The Blood of Experience: The Conflict in the Southern Sudan: A Search for Common Ground." Paper presented at the Conference on "The Conflict in the Southern Sudan: A Search for Common Ground," Cedar Glen Conference Centre, Ontario, 14 February 1997.

Connell, Dan (1997). *Against All Odds: A Chronicle of the Eritrean Revolution.* Lawrenceville, NJ: Red Sea Press.

Couture, J., K. Nielsen, and M. Seymour (1998). "Introduction: Questioning the Ethnic/Civic Divide" and "Afterword: Liberal Nationalism Both Cosmopolitan and Rooted." In J. Couture, K. Nielsen, and M. Seymour (eds.), *Rethinking Nationalism.* Calgary: University of Calgary Press, pp. 1–61 and pp. 579–662.

Cusimano, Maryann K. (2000). "Beyond Sovereignty: The Rise of Transsovereign Problems." In Maryann K. Cusimano (ed.), *Beyond Sovereignty: Issues for a Global Agenda.* Boston: Bedford/St. Martin's, pp. 1–43.

—— (2000a). "The Challenge to Institutions." In Maryann K. Cusimano (ed.), *Beyond Sovereignty: Issues for a Global Agenda*. Boston: Bedford/St. Martin's, pp. 284–331.

Daly, M. S. (1988). "Transfer of Power in the Sudan." In Prosser Gifford and Wm. Roger Louis (eds.), *Decolonization and African Independence*. New Haven: Yale University Press, pp. 185–98.

Danspeckgruber, W. (1997a). "Self-Determination, Subsidiarity, and Regionalization in Contemporary Western Europe." In W. Danspeckgruber, and A. Watts (eds.), *Self-Determination and Self-Administration: A Sourcebook*. Boulder: Lynne Rienner, pp. 221–54.

—— (2002). "A Final Assessment." In W. Danspeckgruber (ed.), *The Self-Determination of Peoples: Community, Nation, and State in an Interdependent World*. Boulder: Lynne Rienner, pp. 335–57.

Danspeckgruber, W., and A. Watts (1997). "Introduction." In W. Danspeckgruber and A. Watts (eds.), *Self-Determination and Self-Administration: A Sourcebook*. Boulder: Lynne Rienner, pp. 1–19.

Davidson, Basil (1992). *The Black Man's Burden: Africa and the Curse of the Nation-State*. London: James Currey.

Deng, Francis M. (1995). *War of Visions: Conflict of Identities in the Sudan*. Washington, DC: Brookings Institution.

—— (1997). "Sudan: The Challenge of Nationhood." In W. Danspeckgruber and A. Watts (eds.), *Self-Determination and Self-Administration: A Sourcebook*. Boulder: Lynne Rienner, pp. 337–69.

Donham, Donald (1999). *Marxist Modern: An Ethnographic History of Ethiopian Revolution*. London: James Currey.

Duvenhage, A. (1998). "The Crisis of the Nation-State: A Global Phenomenon with an African Accent." *Africa Quarterly* 38,4: 1–36.

El-Affendi, Abdelwahab (1991). *Turabi's Revolution: Islam and Power in the Sudan*. London: Grey Seal.

Elazar, D.J. (1997). "Commentary" on Herbst's essay "Global Change and the Future of Existing States." In W. Danspeckgruber, and A. Watts (eds.), *Self-Determination and Self-Administration: A Sourcebook*. Boulder: Lynne Rienner, pp. 91–94.

Ellingson, Lloyd (1977). "The Emergence of Political Parties in Eritrea, 1941-1950." *Journal of African History* 18,2: 261–81.

Emerson, R. (1964). *Self-Determination Revisited in the Era of Decolonization*. Cambridge, MA: Harvard University, Center for International Affairs.

Erlich, Haggai (1978). *The Struggle over Eritrea, 1962-1978: War and Revolution in the Horn of Africa*. Stanford University: Hoover Institution Press.

—— (1986). *Ethiopia and the Challenge of Independence*. Boulder: Lynne Rienner.

—— (1980). "The Horn of Africa and the Middle East: Politicization of Islam in the Horn and Depoliticization of Ethiopian Christianity." In Joseph Tubiana (ed.), *Modern Ethiopia: From the Accession of Menelik II to the Present.* Rotterdam: Balkema, pp. 399–408.

Esposito, John L. and John O. Voll (1996). *Islam and Democracy.* Oxford: Oxford University Press.

Feigenbaum, Harvey B. (1997). "Centralization and National Integration in France." *Mediterranean Quarterly* 8,1: 60–76.

Feldblum, M. (1998). "Reconfiguring Citizenship in Western Europe." In C. Joppke (ed.), *Challenge to the Nation-State: Immigration in Western Europe and the United States.* Oxford: Oxford University Press, pp. 231–70.

Flint, Julie (2001). "Democracy in a War Zone: The Nuba Parliament." In Suleiman Rahhal (ed.), *The Right to Be Nuba: The Story of a Sudanese People's Struggle for Survival.* Lawrenceville, NJ: Red Sea Press, pp. 103–12.

Freeman, Michael (1999). "The Right to National Self-Determination: Ethical Problems and Practical Solutions." In Desmond M. Clarke and Charles Jones (eds.), *The Right of Nations: Nations and Nationalism in a Changing World.* Cork: Cork University Press, pp. 45–64.

Garang, John (1992). *The Call for Democracy in Sudan.* London: Kegan Paul International.

Garang, John de Mabior (1996). "The Shaping of a New Sudan." *Mediterranean Quarterly* 7,4: 6–16.

Gashaw, Solomon (1993). "Nationalism and Ethnic Conflict in Ethiopia." In Crawford Young (ed.), *The Rising Tide of Cultural Pluralism: The Nation-State at Bay?* Madison, WI: University of Wisconsin Press, pp. 138–57.

Gelber, H.G. (1997). *Sovereignty through Interdependence.* London: Kluwer Law International.

Gellner, E. (1997). *Nationalism.* London: Weidenfeld and Nicholson.

Geshekter, Charles (1997). "The Death of Somali in Historical Perspective." In Hussein M. Adam and Richard Ford (eds.), *Mending Rips in the Sky: Options for Somali Communities in the 21st Century.* Lawrenceville, NJ: Red Sea Press, pp. 65–98.

Ghebre-Ab Habtu (1993). *Ethiopia and Eritrea: A Documentary Study.* Trenton, NJ: Red Sea Press.

Gilkes, Patrick (1999). *Ethiopia—Perspectives of Conflict 1991-1999.* Bern: Swiss Peace Foundation.

Ginther, K., and H. Isak (eds.) (1991). *Self-determination in Europe: Proceedings of an International Workshop Held at the Akademie Graz, July 5-6, 1989.* Vienna: Bohlau Verlag.

Gooch, John (1998). "Italy, Abyssinia and the Sudan, 1885–98." In Edward M. Spiers (ed.), *Sudan: The Reconquest Reappraised*. London: Frank Cass, pp. 128–45.

Greenfield, Richard (1965). *Ethiopia: A New Political History*. London: Pall Mall Press.

Grovogui, Siba N'Zatioula (1996). *Sovereigns, Quasi Sovereigns, and Africans: Race and Self-Determination in International Law*. Minneapolis: University of Minnesota Press.

Guibernau, Montserrat (1996). *Nationalisms: The Nation-State and Nationalism in the Twentieth Century*. Cambridge: Polity Press.

—— (2001). "Globalization and the Nation-state." In Montserrat Guibernau and John Hutchinson (eds.), *Understanding Nationalism*. Cambridge: Polity Press, pp. 242–68.

Habte Selassie, Bereket (1988). "The OAU and Regional Conflicts: Focus on the Eritrean War." *Africa Today* 3/4: 61–67.

Habte-Wold, Aklilu (1963). OAU mimeographed text CIAS/GEN/INF/43, p. 34.

Halperin, M.H., D.J. Scheffer, and P.L. Small (1992). *Self-Determination in the New World Order*. Washington, DC: Carnegie Endowment for International Peace.

Hashim, Alice Bettis (1997). *The Fallen State: Dissonance, Dictatorship and Death in Somalia*. Lanham, MD: University Press of America.

Hassen, Mohammed (2000). "A Short History of Oromo Colonial Experience: Part Two, Colonial Consolidation and Resistance 1935–2000." *Journal of Oromo Studies* 7,1/2: 109–98.

Hastings, A. (1997). *The Construction of Nationhood: Ethnicity, Religion and Nationalism*. Cambridge: Cambridge University Press.

Heater, Derek (1994). *National Self-Determination: Woodrow Wilson and His Legacy*. New York: St. Martin's Press.

Heinrich, Wolfgang (1997). *Building the Peace: Experiences of Collaborative Peacebuilding in Somalia 1993–1996*. Uppsala: Life and Peace Institute.

Herb, G.H. (1999). "National Identity and Territory." In G.H. Herb and D.H. Kaplan (eds.), *Nested Identities: Nationalism, Territory, and Scale*. Lanham, MD: Rowman and Littlefield, pp. 9–30.

Herbst, J. (1997). "Global Change and the Future of Existing States." In W. Danspeckgruber and A. Watts (eds.), *Self-Determination and Self-Administration: A Sourcebook*. Boulder: Lynne Rienner, pp. 79–91.

Herbst, Jeffrey (2000). *States and Power in Africa: Comparative Lessons in Authority and Control*. Princeton, NJ: Princeton University Press.

Hess, Robert L. (1966). *Italian Colonialism in Somalia*. Chicago: University of Chicago Press.

Holcomb, Bonnie, and Sisay Ibssa (1990). *The Invention of Ethiopia: The Making of a Dependent Colonial State in Northeast Africa.* Trenton, NJ: Red Sea Press.

Holt, P.M. (1970). *The Mahdist State in the Sudan 1881-1898: A Study of Its Origins, Development and Overthrow.* Oxford: Clarendon Press.

Holt, P.M., and M.W. Daly (1979). *The History of the Sudan: From the Coming of Islam to the Present Day.* London: Weidenfeld and Nicolson.

Horowitz, D.L. (1998). "Self-Determination: Politics, Philosophy, and Law." In M. Moore (ed.), *National Self-Determination and Secession.* Oxford: Oxford University Press, pp. 181-214.

Horsman, M., and A. Marshall (1994). *After the Nation State: Citizens, Tribalism and the New World Disorder.* London: HarperCollins.

Hurriez, Sayyid H. (1989). "Ethnic, Cultural and National Identity in the Sudan: An Overview." In Sayyid H. Hurriez and Elfatih A. AbdelSalam (eds.), *Ethnicity, Conflict and National Integration in the Sudan.* Khartoum: University of Khartoum, pp. 69-101.

Hussein, Shamis (1997). "Somalia: A Destroyed Country and a Defeated Nation." In Hussein M. Adam and Richard Ford (eds.), *Mending Rips in the Sky: Options for Somali Communities in the 21st Century.* Lawrenceville, NJ: Red Sea Press, pp. 165-92.

Hutchinson, Sharon E. (2001). "A Curse from God? Religious and Political Dimensions of the Post-1991 Rise of Ethnic Violence in South Sudan." *Journal of Modern African Studies* 39,2: 307-31.

James, C.L.R. (1973). *The Black Jacobins: Toussaint L'Ouverture and the San Domingo Revolution—1791,* 2nd edition. New York: Vintage Press.

Juma, Monica (2002). Forthcoming.

Kaufeler, Heinz (1988). *Modernization, Legitimacy and Social Movement: A Study of Socio-Cultural Dynamics and Revolution in Iran and Ethiopia.* Zurich: Ethnologische Schriften Zurich.

Keating, M. (1998). "Minority Nationalism or Tribal Sentiments? The Case of Scotland, Quebec and Catalonia." In K. Christie (ed.), *Ethnic Conflict, Tribal Politics: A Global Perspective.* Surrey: Curzon Press, pp. 35-59.

Keating, Michael (2001). *Nations against the State: The New Politics of Nationalism in Quebec, Catalonia and Scotland.* London: Palgrave.

Kebede, Massay (1999). *Survival and Modernization—Ethiopia's Enigmatic Present: A Philosophical Discourse.* Lawrenceville, NJ: Red Sea Press.

Keller, E.J. (1995) "The Ethnogenesis of the Oromo Nation and Its Implications for Politics in Ethiopia." *The Journal of Modern African Studies* 33,4: 621-34.

Kembo-Sure (1998). "Linguistic Standardization and State Rationalization in Kenya: A Move towards Nation-Building." *Journal of Third World Studies* 15,1: 185-203.

—— (1999). "Bilingual Education on an Uneven Playfield: The Kenyan Case." *Journal of Third World Studies* 16,1: 147-63.

Kishindo, Pascal (1994). "The Impact of a National Language on Minority Languages: The Case of Malawi." *Journal of Contemporary African Studies* 12,2: 127-50.

Krasner, Stephen D. (1999). *Sovereignty: Organized Hypocrisy.* Princeton, NJ: Princeton University Press.

Kurita, Yoshiko (1994) "The Social Bases of Regional Movements in Sudan 1960s-1980s." In Katsuyoshi Fukui and John Markakis (eds.), *Ethnicity and Conflict in the Horn of Africa.* London: James Currey, pp. 202-16.

Laitin, David D. (1977). *Politics, Language and Thought: The Somali Experience.* Chicago: University of Chicago Press.

Lata, Leenco (1998), "The Making and Unmaking of Ethiopia's Transitional Charter." In Asafa Jalata (ed.), *Oromo Nationalism and the Ethiopian Discourse: The Search for Freedom and Democracy.* Lawrenceville, NJ: Red Sea Press, pp. 51-77.

—— (1999). *The Ethiopian State at the Crossroads: Decolonization and Democratization or Disintegration?* Lawrenceville, NJ: Red Sea Press.

—— (2003). "The Ethiopia-Eritrea War." *Review of African Political Economy,* 97: 369-88.

Lefort, Rene (1981). *Ethiopia: An Heretical Revolution?* London: Zed Press.

Legesse, Asmarom (2000). *Oromo Democracy: An Indigenous African Political System.* Lawrenceville, NJ: Red Sea Press.

Lenin V.I. (n.d.). *Questions of National Policy and Proletarian Internationalism.* Moscow: Progress Publishers.

Levine, Donald (1974). *Greater Ethiopia: The Evolution of a Multiethnic Society.* Chicago: University of Chicago Press.

Lewis, David L. (1988). *Race to Fashoda: European Colonialism and African Resistance in the Scramble for Africa.* London: Bloomsbury.

Lewis, Gwynne (1993). *The French Revolution: Rethinking the Debate.* London: Routledge.

Lewis, I.M. (1991). "The Ogaden and the Fragility of Somali Segmentary Nationalism." In Georges Nzongola-Ntalaja (ed.), *Conflict in the Horn of Africa.* Atlanta, GA: African Studies Association Press, pp. 89-96.

Lyons, Terrence (1996). "The International Context of Internal War: Ethiopia/Eritrea." In Edmond J. Keller and Donald Rothchild (eds.), *Africa in the New International Order: Rethinking State Sovereignty and Regional Security.* Boulder: Lynne Rienner, pp. 85-99.

Malwal, Bona (1981). *People and Power in Sudan: The Struggle for National Stability.* London: Ithaca Press.

Mansur, Abdalla Omar (1995). "Contrary to a Nation: The Cancer of Somali State." In Ali Jimale Ahmed (ed.), *The Invention of Somalia.* Lawrenceville, NJ: Red Sea Press, pp. 107-16.

Marcus, Harold G. (1975). *The Life and Times of Menelik II: Ethiopia 1844-1913.* Oxford: Clarendon Press.

—— (1964). "A Preliminary History of the Tripartite Treaty of December 13, 1906." *Journal of Ethiopian Studies* 2,2. Addis Ababa: Institute of Ethiopian Studies, pp. 21-40.

Maritain, Jacques, (1951). *Man and the State.* Chicago: University of Chicago Press.

Markakis, John (1987). *National and Class Conflict in the Horn of Africa.* Cambridge: Cambridge University Press.

—— (1998). *Resource Conflict in the Horn of Africa.* London: Sage.

—— (1994), "Ethnic Conflict and the State in the Horn of Africa." In Katsuyushi Fukui and John Markakis (eds.), *Ethnicity and Conflict in the Horn of Africa.* London: James Currey, pp. 217-37.

Maxted, Julia (2000). "The Impact of Conflict on Minority Groups in Somalia." In Pietro Toggia, Pat Lauderdale, and Abebe Zegeye (eds.), *Crisis and Terror in the Horn of Africa: Autopsy of Democracy, Human Rights and Freedom.* Dartmouth, UK: Ashgate, pp. 151-79.

McPhee, Peter (1993). "Counter-Revolution in the Pyrenees: Spirituality, Class and Ethnicity in the Haut-Vallespir, 1793-94." *French History* 7,3: 313-43.

Mukhtar, Mohamed Haji (1995). "Islam in Somali History: Fact and Fiction." In Ali Jimale Ahmed (ed.), *The Invention of Somalia.* Lawrenceville, NJ: Red Sea Press, pp. 1-28.

—— (1997). "Somalia: Between Self-Determination and Chaos." In Hussein M. Adam and Richard Ford (eds.), *Mending Rips in the Sky: Options for Somali Communities in the 21st Century.* Lawrenceville, NJ: Red Sea Press, pp. 49-64.

Murphy, A. B. (1999). "Rethinking the Concept of European Identity." In G.H. Herb and D.H. Kaplan (eds.), *Nested Identities: Nationalism, Territory and Scale.* Oxford: Rowman and Littlefield, pp. 53-73.

Musgrave, T.D. (1997). *Self-Determination and National Minorities.* Oxford: Clarendon Press.

Negash, Tekeste, and Kjetil Tronvoll (2000). *Brothers at War: Making Sense of the Eritrean-Ethiopian War.* Oxford: James Currey.

O'Leary, Brendan (2001). "An Iron Law of Nationalism and Federation? A (Neo-Diceyian) Theory of the Necessity of a Federal Staatsvolk, and of Consociational Rescue." *Nations and Nationalism* 7,3: 273-96.

O'Leary, Damian (1999). "Cultural Identity and Constitutional Reform: The Challenge of Northern Ireland." In P.J. Hanafin and M.S. Williams (eds.),

Identity, Rights and Constitutional Transformation. Aldershot: Ashgate pp. 89-110.

Okafor, Obiora Chinedu (2000). *Re-Defining Legitimate Statehood: International Law and State Fragmentation in Africa.* The Hague: Martinus Nijhoff.

Oommen, T.K. (1997). *Citizenship, Nationality and Ethnicity: Reconciling Competing Identities.* Cambridge, UK: Polity Press.

Osabu-Kle, Daniel T. (2000). *Compatible Cultural Democracy: The Key to Development in Africa.* Peterborough, ON: Broadview Press.

Pankhurst, Richard (1967). *An Introduction to the History of the Ethiopian Army.* Imperial Ethiopian Air Force 101st Training Centre.

Pausewang, Siegfried (1994). "Local Democracy and Central Control." In Abebe Zegeye and Seigfried Pausewang (eds.), *Ethiopia in Change: Peasantry, Nationalism and Democracy.* London: British Academy Press, pp. 209-30.

Pomeranz, Kenneth (1999). "Two Worlds of Trade, Two Worlds of Empire: European State-Making and Industrialization in a Chinese Mirror." In A.D. Smith, D.J. Solinger, and S.C. Topik, (eds.), *States and Sovereignty in the Global Economy.* London: Routledge, pp. 74-98.

Prah, Kwesi Kwaa (2001). "National Languages: Conditions for a National Book Industry." Keynote Address at Symposium: Education and Book Industry, Contribution to Poverty Alleviation, Educfair, Trade Fair, Accra, 9 October 2001.

Rosenfeld, Chris Prouty (1976). *A Chronology of Menelik II of Ethiopia 1844-1913: Emperor of Ethiopia 1889-1913.* East Lansing, MI: Michigan State University.

Rubenson, Sven (1976). *The Survival of Ethiopian Independence.* London: Heinemann.

——— (1989). "'The Last Unsolved Problem of Africa' In Fifty Years' Perspective," *Proceedings of 8th International Conference of Ethiopian Studies.* Addis Ababa: Institute of Ethiopian Studies, pp. 401-12.

Rupesinghe, K. (1996). "Conflict Resolution: Current Options and New Mechanisms." In D. Clark and R. Williamson (eds.), *Self-Determination: International Perspectives.* London: Macmillan Press, pp. 337-55.

Ryan, Stephen (1998). "Preventive Diplomacy, Conflict Resolution, and Ethnic Conflict." In D. Carment and P. James (eds.), *Peace in the Midst of Wars: Preventing and Managing International Ethnic Conflict.* Columbia, SC: University of South Carolina Press, pp. 63-92.

Salwen, Michael B. (2001). *Evelyn Waugh in Ethiopia: The Story behind Scoop.* Lewiston, NY: Edwin Mellen Press.

Samatar, A.I. (1991). "Horn of Africa: The Exigencies of Self-Determination, Territorial Integrity and Collective Self-Reliance." In Georges Nzongola-

Ntalaja (ed.), *Conflict in the Horn of Africa*. Atlanta GA: African Studies Association Press, pp. 67–88.

Samatar, Abdi I. (1999). A*n African Miracle: State and Class Leadership and Colonial Legacy in Botswana Development*. Portsmouth, NH: Heinemann.

Samatar, Ahmed I. (1988). *Socialist Somalia: Rhetoric and Reality*. London: Zed Books.

Sbacchi, Alberto (1985). *Ethiopia under Mussolini: Fascism and the Colonial Experience*. London: Zed Books.

Scholte, Jan Aart (1999). "Globalisation and Governance." In P.J. Hanafin, and M.S. Williams (eds.), *Identity, Rights and Constitutional Transformation*. Aldershot: Ashgate, pp. 132–53.

Sewell, William H., Jr. (1994). *A Rhetoric of Bourgeois Revolution: The Abbe Sieyes and What Is the Third Estate?* Durham: Duke University Press.

—— (1996). "Ideologies and Social Revolutions: Reflections on the French Case." In T.C.W. Blanning (ed.), *The Rise and Fall of the French Revolution*. Chicago: University of Chicago Press, pp. 285–313.

Sklar Richard L. (1985). "The Colonial Imprint on African Political Thought." In G.M. Carter and P. O'Meara, (eds.), *African Independence: The First Twenty-Five Years*. Bloomington: Indiana University Press, pp. 1–30.

Smith, Anthony D. (1999). "Social and Religious Origins of Nations." In Desmond M. Clarke and Charles Jones (eds.), *The Rights of Nations: Nations and Nationalism in a Changing World*. Cork: Cork University Press, pp. 26–44.

Smith, M.D. (1969). *Garibaldi*. Englewood Cliffs, NJ: Prentice-Hill.

Stalin, Joseph (1947). *Marxism and the National and Colonial Question*. London: Lawrence and Wishart.

Stavenhagen, R. (1996). "Self-Determination: Right or Demon?" In D. Clark and R. Williamson (eds.), *Self-Determination: International Perspectives*. London: Macmillan Press, pp. 1–11.

Strange, S. (1994). "The Power Gap: Member States and the World Economy." In F. Brouwer, V. Lintner, and M. Newman (eds.), *Economic Policy Making and the European Union*. Conference proceedings, London European Research Centre, University of North London, 14 April, Federal Trust.

Suliman, Mohamed (1999). "Conflict Resolution among the Borana and the Fur: Similar Features, Different Outcomes." In Mohamed Suliman (ed.), *Ecology, Politics and Violent Conflict*. London: Zed Books, pp. 289–90.

Sureda, A. Rigo (1973). *The Evolution of the Right of Self-Determination: A Study of the United Nations Practice*. Leiden: A.W. Sijthoff.

Talbott, Strobe (2000). "Self-Determination in an Interdependent World." *Foreign Policy* 118 (Spring): 152–64.

Tareke, Gebru (1991). *Ethiopia: Power and Protest: Peasant Revolts in the Twentieth Century.* Cambridge: Cambridge University Press.

Tibebu, Teshale (1995). *The Making of Modern Ethiopia, 1896-1974.* Lawrenceville, NJ: Red Sea Press

Touval, Saadia (1963). *Somali Nationalism: International Politics and the Drive for Unity in the Horn of Africa.* Cambridge, MA: Harvard University Press.

Triulzi, Alessandro (1981). S*alt, Gold and Legitimacy: Prelude to the History of a No-man's Land Bela Shangul, Wallagga, Ethiopia (ca. 1800-1898).* Napoli: Istituto Universitario Orientale.

Trivelli, Richard (1999). "Background Notes on the Ethiopian-Eritrean War." *Afrika Spektrum,* Fall Edition, Hamburg.

Tronvoll, Kjetil (1998). "The Process of Nation-Building in Post-War Eritrea: Created from Below or Directed from Above?" *Journal of Modern African Studies* 26,3: 461-82.

Ullendorff, Edward (1965). *The Ethiopians.* Oxford: Oxford University Press.

Umozurike, U.O. (1972). *Self-Determination in International Law.* Hamden, CT: Shoe String Press.

van den Berghe, P.L. (1992). "The Modern State: Nation-Builder or Nation-Killer?" In *International Journal of Group Tensions* 22,3: 191-208.

Vlist, Leo van der (ed.) (1994). V*oices of the Earth: Indigenous peoples, New Partners and the Right to Self-Determination in Practice.* Utrecht: International Book NCIP.

Watson, A. (1997). *The Limits of Independence.* London: Routledge.

Woodward, Peter (1990). *Sudan, 1898-1989: The Unstable State.* Boulder: Lynne Rienner.

——(1986). "Islam and politics." In Mudathir Abd al-Rahman, et al. (eds.), *Sudan since Independence: Studies of the Political Development since 1956.* Gower: Aldershot, pp. 1-6.

——(1994). "Sudan: State Building and the Seeds of Conflict." In Peter Woodward and Murray Forsyth (eds.), *Conflict and Peace in the Horn of Africa: Federalism and Its Alternatives.* Dartmouth, UK: Aldershot, pp. 78-85.

——(1994a). "Conflict and Federalism in Sudan." In Peter Woodward and Murray Forsyth (eds.), *Conflict and Peace in the Horn of Africa: Federalism and Its Alternatives.* Dartmouth, UK: Aldershot, pp. 86-102.

Yohannes, Okbagzi (1991). *Eritrea, a Pawn in World Politics.* Gainesville, FL: University of Florida Press.

Young, Crawford (1994). *The African Colonial State in Comparative Perspective.* New Haven: Yale University Press.

——(1991). "Self-Determination, Territorial Integrity, and the African State System." In Francis M. Deng and I. William Zartman (eds.), *Conflict Resolution in Africa.* Washington, DC: Brookings Institution, pp. 320-46.

——— (1991a). "Self-Determination Revisited: Has Decolonization Closed the Question?" In Georges Nzongola-Ntalaja (ed.), *Conflict in the Horn of Africa*. Atlanta, GA: African Studies Association Press, pp. 41–66.

Young, Iris Marion (1997). *Intersecting Voices: Dilemmas of Gender, Political Philosophy, and Policy*. Princeton, NJ: Princeton University Press.

Young, John (1996). "The Tigray and Eritrean Peoples Liberation Fronts: A History of Tensions and Pragmatism." *The Journal of Modern African Studies* 34,1: 105–20.

Zegeye, Abebe (1994). "Environmental Degradation, Population Movement and War." In Abebe Zegeye and Siegfried Pausewang (eds.), *Ethiopia in Change: Peasantry, Nationalism and Democracy*. London: British Academy Press, pp. 172–91.

Zewde, Bahru (1991). *A History of Modern Ethiopia 1885–1974*. London: James Currey.

——— (1994). "Hayla-Sellase: From Progressive to Reactionary." In Abebe Zegeye and Siegfried Pausewang (eds.), *Ethiopia in Change: Peasantry, Nationalism and Democracy*. London: British Academy Press, pp. 30–44.

www.ingramcontent.com/pod-product-compliance
Lightning Source LLC
Chambersburg PA
CBHW072119020426
42334CB00018B/1654